CONFESS

CONFESS

THE AUTOBIOGRAPHY

ROB HALFORD

WITH IAN GITTINS

hachette
BOOKS
New York

Hachette Books
Hachette Book Group
1290 Avenue of the Americas
New York, NY 10104
HachetteBooks.com
Twitter.com/HachetteBooks
Instagram.com/HachetteBooks

First Edition: September 2020

Published by Hachette Books, an imprint of Perseus Books, LLC, a subsidiary of Hachette Book Group, Inc. The Hachette Books name and logo is a trademark of the Hachette Book Group.

The Hachette Speakers Bureau provides a wide range of authors for speaking events. To find out more, go to www.hachettespeakersbureau.com or call (866) 376-6591.

The publisher is not responsible for websites (or their content) that are not owned by the publisher.

Print book interior by EM&EN

Library of Congress Control Number: 2020942867

ISBNs: 978-0-306-87494-9 (hardcover); 978-0-306-92539-9 (signed edition); 978-0-306-92540-5 (BN signed edition); 978-0-306-87495-6 (e-book)

Printed in the United States of America

WAL

10 9 8 7 6 5 4 3 2

Disclaimer

I have been totally candid in this memoir.
This is my gospel truth, but it is not for me to insist
that other people bare their souls quite so freely.
A few names and other identifying details in
Confess have been changed—to protect
the innocent *and* the guilty.

Contents

Introduction

I'm suffocating!

It's half past eight on a weekday morning in the early sixties. Time for school. Say "ta-ra" to my mom and slip out of the front door. Left out of the gate, walk to the end of our street, turn left onto Darwin Road. Go along for a bit, do a right, take a deep breath...and cross the canal.

At the side of the canal—or the "cut," as we say in Walsall—stood a huge smelting metalworks called G. & R. Thomas Ltd. It was the kind of infernal factory that gave the Black Country its name during the Industrial Revolution: the sort of crashing, heaving, stinking hellhole that most Walsall blokes spent their working days in.

During my childhood it would be crashing and heaving and stinking 24/7. It would take far too long, and cost too much, to close its vast furnaces down and fire them up again, so the factory never stopped. And the filth and the poison that would belch out of there was unbelievable.

Metalworks like G. & R. Thomas Ltd. shaped and dominated where I lived—and *how* I lived. At home, my mom would hang our white bedsheets out on the line on washing day, and bring them in streaked with gray and black soot. At school, I would sit and try to write at a desk that was vibrating to the rhythm of the giant steam press in the factory over the road:

THUNK! THUNK! THUNK!

Sometimes, on my way to school, I would see the silhouettes of the G. & R. Thomas workers tipping up the giant furnace's cauldron over the sandpit. The molten metal would flow down like lava and instantly solidify into huge slabs of pig iron.

Pig iron. The name seemed to sum up the ugliness.

Passing it on my daily walk to school was an endurance test that I was not always sure I would survive. The choking fumes that swirled out of that factory and over the cut were incredibly toxic. If the wind was in the wrong direction, which it always seemed to be, fine pieces of grit caught in the smoke would blow hard into your eyes and stay there for days. They hurt like fuck.

I've always said that I could smell and taste heavy metal before the music was even invented…

So, I would take a deep breath, clutch my school bag close to me, and run across the bridge as fast as I could. On the worst days, when the smog and the pollution were so thick that you felt as if you could cut them, my brain would panic and rebel against the ordeal:

I'm suffocating!

I never *did* suffocate, somehow, and I always got to the other side, even if I was coughing and spluttering. Then I would do the whole thing again when I came home that afternoon. I was used to it. That was life in the Black Country.

There have been plenty of other times in my life when I have thought *I'm suffocating.* There were the claustrophobic, desperate years—so many of them!—when I felt trapped: the lead singer of one of the biggest heavy metal bands on the planet, and yet too frightened to tell the world that I was a gay man. I used to lie awake at night, worrying and wondering:

What would happen if I came out?

Would we lose all our fans?

Would it kill Judas Priest?

That fear and angst took me to some very dark places. It was hard to breathe when I was deep in the shitpit of alcoholism and addiction. It was hard to breathe when I was pinballing between doomed relationships with men who did not even share my sexuality. And it was hardest of all the day that a troubled lover hugged me goodbye…minutes before he put a gun to his head. And pulled the trigger.

When you are suffocating, *that* is how you are going to end up if you're not careful, and I almost did: my self-destructive lifestyle nearly killed me. I even tried to do it myself. Yet, I survived. I came out the other side. I took a deep breath, and I got over the bridge and across the cut.

Today, I am clean, sober, in love, happy…and fearless. I am living an honest life and that means that nothing, and nobody, can hurt me anymore. I am a rock version of an early, very secret, hero of mine: Quentin Crisp (who appears later in this tale). *I am the stately homo of heavy metal.*

I thought of the perfect title for this memoir: *Confess.* It could not be more appropriate. Because, believe me, this venal priest has sinned, sinned, and sinned again, but now it is time to confess those sins…and maybe even to get your blessing.

So, let us pray.

Confess is the story of how I learned to breathe again.

1

Speed, bonnie boat...

In the beginning was the Beechdale Estate.

And it was good.

After the end of the Second World War, the British people thanked Winston Churchill for his efforts by dumping him out on his arse and electing a Labor government. This administration quickly set about a major socialist program of building hundreds of thousands of publicly owned new homes to offset the post-war housing shortage.

Under the prime minister, Clement Attlee, and the housing minister, Aneurin Bevan, new council estates sprang up all over the country to replace the homes that had been bombed to bits during the war, and to give Britain's working-class families somewhere to live. And typical of these developments was the Gypsy Lane Estate in Walsall, which soon got renamed the Beechdale.

A fifteen-minute walk from Walsall town center, and ten miles north of Birmingham, the Beechdale was built, gleaming new, on industrial wasteland at the start of the fifties. For the first two decades of my life, it was my crucible. It was the center of my world, my hopes, my dreams, my fears, my triumphs, my setbacks. Yet, funnily enough, I wasn't born there.

After my mom and dad, Joan and Barry Halford, married in March 1950, they lived with Mom's parents in Birchills, Walsall. It was a tiny house, so when Mom got pregnant with me, she and my dad moved in with Mom's sister Gladys and her husband, Jack, in Sutton Coldfield, on the way to Brum (as we Black Country folk call Birmingham).

I was born on August 25, 1951, and christened Robert John Arthur Halford. Arthur was a name that ran in the family: it was my dad's middle name and my grandad's first name. (Grandad's middle name was Flavel; I'm pleased I didn't inherit that!)

My sister, Sue, arrived a year later, and my parents were given a council house in Lichfield Road, Walsall. Then, in 1953, my family settled at 38 Kelvin Road on the Beechdale estate.

The Beechdale's sturdy redbrick terraced and semi-detached houses were basic, as British council houses tend to be, but, like a lot of the Bevan-era dwellings, there was a kind of idealism behind them. They were bigger than the minimum size that was stipulated in government legislation, and even had their own front and back gardens.

Walsall Council doubtless envisaged these houses having pretty lawns and flower gardens…but it didn't work out like that. In the post-war years, rationing was still going on, so Beechdale families used their outside spaces to grow spuds and veg. Basically, you walked out of your front door onto an allotment.

I can still picture the exact layout of 38 Kelvin Road. It had a living room, kitchen, and little den downstairs, and upstairs was the loo, a tiny bathroom, my parents' room, a box room, and the bedroom Sue and I shared. I had the bed by the window.

The Beechdale was neighborly and had a real community spirit. People were always popping into each other's houses. Some folk thought the estate was rough, but I didn't. Mom* told me to

---

* Most British people write "Mum," but Sue and I always used "Mom" because that was how we said it. Every Mother's Day, we'd have a devil of a job finding cards spelled like that in Walsall.

steer clear of a handful of streets—"Whatever you do, don't go down there!"—but I never saw anything worse than a few rusty old fridges in gardens. It was hardly the Gorbals.

Like all working-class Black Country men, my dad worked in the steel factories. He started out as an engineer at a firm called Helliwells, who made airplane parts and were based at Walsall Aerodrome—now long gone.

The job suited my dad as he had always had a passion for planes. He used to be in the RAF reserves, and when his National Service came around, he longed to be called up to the Air Force. Instead, he got put in the Army and spent the Second World War on Salisbury Plain.

Dad's passion for planes rubbed off on me and we'd make Airfix models together—Flying Fortresses, Spitfires, Hurricanes. He'd take me to Walsall Aerodrome to see gliders taking off, and once or twice we went down to London to watch planes at Heathrow Airport. *That* was exciting.

After Helliwells, my dad moved on to a steel-tubing factory. When a colleague left to form a new company, Tube Fabs, Dad joined him. He left the shop floor to become a buyer, and we stopped growing spuds in our garden and got a dinky little lawn with a path down the middle. We also got a car. It felt really special. It was only a Ford Prefect, nothing flash, but somehow it felt as if our status had improved. I loved being driven around instead of getting the bus everywhere.

Mom stayed at home when Sue and I were kids, as women did back then, cleaned every day and kept the house spotless. She was a devout believer that "Cleanliness is next to Godliness." At any time of the day or night, our house looked like a show home.

We had coal fires, and Mom would pester one of our distant relatives, Jack, when he delivered a big sack of coal. I'd watch from the window as he lifted the bag off his lorry and, covered in soot, walked down our entry, past my dad's motorbike, to drop it in our coal shed.

"Dow mek too much dust, Jack!" Mom would scold him.

"It's coal, bab!" Jack would laugh. "What do yow expect?"

The future arrived at our house in the form of an immersion heater. To save money, Mom would only let us put it on for fifteen minutes before a bath, so we'd be sitting in a few inches of tepid water. Or all the lights would go off, because we'd forgotten to feed the meter.

Mom and Dad put pennies in the meter in its box in the living room. The box was so cold that Mom put jellies in there to set. When the meter man came to empty it, there would be five or six pennies left over. If we were lucky, Mom would give Sue and me one or two.

On winter nights, 38 Kelvin Road was like Siberia. I would lie buried under blankets in bed, watching ice form on the insides of the windows. Our bedroom floor was lino. To use the loo in the night, I had to sprint across the freezing floor.

The loo room was tiny, with just enough space to sit on the bog, as we called it, with your knees touching both walls. Dad was a heavy smoker and would take the newspaper in and sit on the toilet for an hour, puffing away.

Mom would warn him as he went in: "Oi! Make sure you open the window!" In winter, he never did. After he came out, we'd have to wait five minutes for his fag smoke to clear. *And the rest.*

Dad put his pay packet on the table every Friday night and Mom handled all of the finances. Meals were basic: meat and two veg; fish and chips from the chippy, or from the chip van that toured the estate every Friday; and a tasty local delicacy, faggots and peas.*

* To all of my American gay mates: yes, there really *is* a meatball-based meal in England called faggots and peas!

Speed, bonnie boat…

The time came to start school. I was so scared walking to Beechdale Infant School on my first day, holding Mom's hand as we trudged through mud, as some of the estate was still being built. The school was only two streets from our house, but it felt like a hundred miles.

The horror, the horror! When we got there and Mom hugged me in the playground, bade me that curious Black Country farewell— "Ta-ra a bit, Rob!"—and walked away…I freaked out. *I am abandoned!* I howled and I blarted (that's what kids in Walsall call crying).

My first few days in school were traumatic, but then I bonded with a very glamorous female teacher who, to my five-year-old eyes, looked like a film star. I clung to her skirt every morning. *If this lady is here, school is OK!*

That teacher was a vision, a lifesaver, and an angel for me. If only I could remember her name! In fact, I can't recall too much about my infant school apart from that initial terror—and the agony of being in the nativity play.

Christmas rolled around, as it does, and I got cast as one of the Three Kings. I can still remember my line: "We have seen his star in the East!" The problem I had was that, like all good kings, I had to wear a crown.

My crown was made of cardboard and held together at the back with a bulldog clip that jagged into my head. As soon as the teacher put the crown on my head, I felt like that clip was drilling a hole in my cranium. I kept trying to move it, and the teacher kept losing her rag with me:

"Robert Halford, stop moving your crown!"

"But, Miss, it really hurts! Ow!"

"It will stop hurting in a minute!"

It didn't. All through our kiddie take on the miracle of Christ our Lord being born, that bloody bulldog clip buried itself in my skull until my head was pounding.

I never knew Mom's parents, as they died when I was young, but I worshipped my dad's, Arthur and Cissy, and spent a lot of my weekends at their house, two miles away. Dad would drop me off on a Friday night and pick me up again on Sunday afternoon.

Their loo was outside, so going at night at their house was even worse than at ours. I'd psyche myself up to open the kitchen door and scurry into the darkness to their little brick hut in the back garden. In winter, the seat would be so icy cold, I'd think I was stuck to it.

Nor did my grandad believe in loo roll. "No need to waste money on that!" he'd say. "Newspaper is just as good! That was what we used in the war!" There I'd sit, seven years old, in the garden, my teeth chattering in the pitch-black, wiping my arse on the *Walsall Express & Star*.

Nan and Grandad had brilliant stories. They told me how they ran to the air-raid shelter during the war, looking up to see Nazi bombers in the night sky on their way to destroy Coventry. I can still picture their ration books for milk and sugar, in little orangey-brown, manila covers, like raffle books.

Grandad had fought at the Somme in the First World War but, like most men who had survived that hell, he never talked about it. Yet one day while I was poking around their house, I made an amazing discovery.

My nan used to make me a little bed in their room by pulling two chairs together and sticking a couple of pillows on them. It was the comfiest bed in the world. Next to it was a little closet with a curtain across it, and one day I pulled open the curtain and found a trunk.

Curious, I opened up the trunk…and found it was full of First World War memorabilia. There was a Luger gun, a gas mask, and a whole load of German uniform insignias. The most amazing find was a proper old General Kitchener helmet, with a spike on the top.

I put the helmet on and went to find Nan and Grandad, my little head wobbling under the weight. "What's this, Grandad?" I asked. He was annoyed when he first saw me, and shouted at me to take it off… but my grandparents never stayed angry with me for long.

In any case, I was getting more and more keen to spend weekends with them—because, at home, Mom and Dad were getting into horrible fights.

They never argued in front of us, but when Sue and I had gone up to bed, their rows would start. They would yell, and go at it hammer and tongs. Sue and I never really knew what the arguments were about, but we'd wince in our beds as we lay and listened.

It would kick off, their voices would get louder—and sometimes, Dad would hit Mom. It wasn't often, but we'd hear shouts, the SMACK! of a hand on flesh, and Mom howling. It's the worst sound in the world for a kid to hear.

Now and then they would scream at each other that they were going to leave. Once, Dad did it. Sue and I were in the living room, it kicked off in the kitchen, and we heard him yell, "That's it—I'm off!"

Dad ran upstairs, packed a suitcase, and slammed the front door. I gawped from the window as he vanished down our street into the twilight, and I thought my heart was breaking: *He's gone! Dad's gone! I'll never see him again!*

He got to the end of the road, turned around, and came back. But those few seconds felt like the end of my world…and having to hear those brutal arguments affected me in a way that I didn't fully realize until far later in life.

But *Confess* is no misery memoir—far from it! The rows affected me a lot at the time, but they fell away as Sue and I grew older. Mom and Dad were loving, protective parents, and never in a million years would I describe my childhood as abusive or unhappy.

CONFESS

My mom was a very calm, steady person, just the sort of rock any kid needs. When we were together as a family, I hardly ever saw her lose her rag…except on The Day We Went to the Wrestling.

I was still very young but I remember it like it was yesterday. We went to Walsall Town Hall and had good seats, near to the ring. We sat down, the first bout started—and my mom absolutely lost it.

One of the wrestlers pulled a sneaky move and Mom was out of her seat, on her feet, and yelling abuse at him: "You can't do that, you dirty cheat! Ref! Ref! Disqualify him!" She looked crazed. I had never seen her like this before!

I was dumbfounded, and my dad was mortified. "Sit down, woman!" he hissed at Mom. "You're showing us up!"

Mom took her seat again but was still fuming: "He should be chucked out of the ring for that!"

She wasn't done. The next dirty move the wrestling villain tried, Mom leapt out of her seat and ran like greased lightning to the side of the ring, where she started taking swings at him through the ropes with her handbag. *Wallop!*

I can still picture Dad's face. The Halford family never Went to the Wrestling again.

I liked making the short trip from the Beechdale into town. I loved the hustle and bustle of Walsall. Mom, Sue, and I would catch the trolleybus from outside the Three Men in a Boat* pub to go to the food market that ran up the hill to St. Matthew's Church.

Sue and I used to beg to go into Woolworth on Walsall's main drag, Park Street, to get a few sweets. Once, I had a panic attack in there. They announced over the loudspeaker that the shop was about to close, and I lost it.

"Mom!" I was yelling. "We've got to get out! Quick! They're shutting!" I was terrified by nightmare visions of a night shut in

---

* Named after a famous son of Walsall, Jerome K. Jerome, who wrote the comic novel *Three Men in a Boat*.

Woolies. Then I had a rethink: "Oh, hang on, we'll be locked in with the pick 'n' mix! *That'll* be OK…"

Mom would drop me and Sue off at the local cinema, the Savoy, for children's movie mornings some weekends. We'd watch films and episodes of *The Cisco Kid*. We couldn't *hear* them—the screenings were bedlam, with kids running about yelling, high on fizzy pop.

The Queen came to Walsall in 1957. I went to see her at the local civic park and beauty spot, the Arboretum. I was *so* excited: *It's the Queen! Off the telly!* She wore a very brightly colored coat. When she waved at the crowd, I imagined she was waving just to me.

Afterward I learned that the Queen got her saddles made in Walsall, and that made me even more proud. Walsall is famous for its leather industry; I once went on a school trip to a leather factory and saw how they made the leather chains, whips, and studs. I clearly took it to heart, as I'm still wearing them sixty years later. Come to think of it, *Leather Chains, Whips, and Studs*—that could have been a good title for this memoir!

Walsall felt magical at Christmas, its packed streets covered in snow. A bloke who looked like a tramp would be flogging hot potatoes and roast chestnuts. His hands were black from his brazier, but that never put me off: "Mom, can I please have a spud? Please?"

The guy would hand me the potato in a piece of newspaper with a little twist of salt. It seemed so exotic and it tasted like caviar to me—not that I had any idea what caviar tasted like then! In fact, come to think of it, I still don't.

Boyhood Christmas Days were all the same. I'd lie awake all night, sick with the anticipation of opening my presents, and it would all be over by eight in the morning. I'd get a selection box of sweets—KitKats, Rowntree's Fruit Pastilles, Smarties—and it would dominate the day:

"Mom, can I have a KitKat?"

"No, I'm cooking the turkey! It'll spoil your Christmas dinner!"

"Oh, *Mom*! Can I have a Smartie, then?"

"Yes, go on, but only one!"

"Thanks, Mom!"

Ten minutes later:

"Mom, can I have a KitKat?"

On and on it went, to the Queen's Speech and beyond…

One year, my dad got me a really cool present. It was a little steam engine with a burner that you put methylated spirits in and lit. You pushed the purple flame into a little boiler, poured water in, and it turned a wheel around. It was a beautiful piece of engineering.

In 1958 I changed schools to Beechdale Juniors, right next door to the infants. The lessons went up a notch, and I had to learn to write… with a fountain pen! It's amazing to think that we used to do that.

As I learned to read, I got heavily into comics. I had the *Beano* and the *Dandy* delivered each week. They'd come through our door just before I left for school, and I'd spend all morning in class aching to go home at lunch and start reading them.

I used to love the story strips—Dennis the Menace, Korky the Cat, Minnie the Minx—but I'm not sure they sent out the best messages. I remember a *Beano* character, Little Plum, who used to say, "Me um smokum um pipum of peacum!" British kids grew up thinking that Native Americans talked like that!

Well, the 1950s in Britain were not politically correct times. At my grandparents', I had a money box for pocket money. It was a metal torso of a black man with exaggerated lips. You put a big old penny in his cupped hand, pressed his shoulder, and his hand would rise and drop the coin between his lips. The manufacturer's delightful name for this toy? *Black Sambo.*

I can't see it making a comeback…

I loved TV and would race home from school at lunchtime to watch the kids' shows. I got into Gerry and Sylvia Anderson's black-and-white animation series. *The Adventures of Twizzle* was about a boy

14

whose arms and legs extended. *Torchy the Battery Boy* had a lamp on his bonce. *Four Feather Falls* was about a sheriff with magic guns and a talking horse.

As the Andersons got more sophisticated, they made *Fireball XL5, Stingray,* and *Thunderbirds.* I loved them all, as well as shows like *Muffin the Mule*—a posh lady at a piano serenading a dancing toy donkey—and *The Woodentops*, a jerky puppet family.

So, I was just an ordinary kid doing ordinary things at the end of the 1950s…and then I had an extraordinary moment. They call them epiphanies, right? Those moments when you feel your life—your destiny—falling into place?

It happened like this.

I was at Beechdale Junior in a music lesson and the teacher was selecting who she should put into the school choir. She was sitting at the front, playing an upright piano, and my class had to take turns to get up and sing.

The teacher was playing a Scottish lullaby lament about Bonnie Prince Charlie called "The Skye Boat Song." I knew the song because we had done it in class before, so when it came to my turn, I went to the front and sang:

> Speed, bonnie boat, like a bird on the wing
> Onward the sailors cry
> Carry the lad that's born to be king
> Over the sea to Skye.

I liked the song, so I belted it out. When I finished, the teacher sat at the piano and stared at me. She didn't say anything at first, then she told me:

"Do that again for us."

"Yes, Miss."

She turned to the rest of the class. "All of you, now, stop what you're doing, be quiet, and listen to Robert," she told them. "Listen!"

I wasn't quite sure what was going on, but she played "The Skye

Boat Song" on the piano again and I gave it some welly—some power—again. And this time, at the end, something strange happened: the class spontaneously started clapping.

"Come with me," the teacher told me, and led me to the classroom next door. We went in and she spoke to the teacher, who nodded.

"Class, I want you to listen to Robert Halford sing this song," he said.

This was getting VERY strange now.

I sang "The Skye Boat Song" yet again, this time *a cappella*, without the piano. I finished, and the class started clapping, just as mine had done. I stood there, looked at them, and soaked up the applause.

I bloody loved it!

I know every kid loves to be loved, and craves attention, but for me, it was more than that. In that moment, for the first time, I thought, *OK, this is what I want to do!* It felt wonderful, and I am only half joking when I say I think of that day as the start of my career in show business. Because, in many ways, it was.

As my time at Beechdale Juniors came to an end, I had my eleven-plus exam, which was what every kid in Britain took to tell if you were brainy and could go to the local grammar school, or if you'd get shoveled into the secondary modern. I passed, but I didn't want to be parted from my mates, so I turned down going to the grammar.

In any case, I had other things on my mind by then.

Because, as I neared puberty, I had started to realize that I really wasn't like the other boys.

2

Giving your mates a hand

I knew that I was gay by the time I was ten years old.

Well, that's probably not exactly right. I didn't know what "being gay" was, at that age. But I certainly knew that I liked being around boys more than being around girls, and I found them more attractive.

The first clue came at Beechdale Juniors, when I developed a major crush on a lad called Steven. I was really drawn to him and wanted to be near him all the time. I'd follow him around the playground at break times, trying to play with him.

I doubt that Steven even noticed, or if he did, he just thought I was a slightly clingy, irritating mate. He probably had no more idea what was going on than I did—but he definitely caused hormonal stirrings in my raw young heart.

Luckily, my thing for Steven soon passed, as prepubescent infatuations always do, and it was time to go to Big School. I transferred from the Beechdale Juniors to Richard C. Thomas, a big old secondary modern school in a neighboring small town called Bloxwich.

Each morning, I would put on my gray trousers, blazer, and blue tie with a gold stripe, grab my satchel, and do the twenty-minute walk to school. After the hold-your-nose dash past G. & R. Thomas

Ltd., I'd do a small detour to a bakery, where I'd buy a cob* hot from the oven for a ha'penny. I'd eat the middle and save the rest for later.

I'd do that walk every school day, even if it was pouring down with rain and there were gale-force winds. On those days, the class would all turn up drenched and there would be steam over our heads in morning assembly as our clothes dried out from the downpour. At least we all got a free little bottle of milk.

I settled into secondary modern quickly. Despite my early glimmers of sexual confusion, I was growing into myself and I was a confident boy. I had a good gang of mates and wasn't particularly timid, or loud. I was just a normal Walsall lad.

I was a decent student. My favorite subject was English literature, and I got into poets like W. B. Yeats. I liked music lessons and was good at geography. I'm a big believer in destiny so, to me, that all makes sense: I've spent my life writing lyrics, playing music, and touring the world!

I was also good at technical drawing, yet the subject didn't interest me at all. If anything, it scared me a little. Anything engineering-based smacked of the dreaded steel factories—and, with all respect to Dad, who spent his life in them, I didn't want to end up there. I had no idea what I wanted to do with my life yet. But I knew it wasn't *that*.

I also went abroad for the first time. When I was about thirteen, the school took us to Belgium for the weekend. We went to Ostend and all stayed in dormitory rooms in a hostel not far from the beach.

Going abroad felt like such an adventure and so important. I remember being overwhelmed at how *different* everything was: the food, the cars, the clothes, the people, and, of course, the language. All of it, down to the linen tablecloths in the hotel restaurant, felt more *sophisticated* than Walsall.

My best mate at school was a lad from the Beechdale called

* Black Country–speak for a bread roll.

Tony. We shared the same sense of humor. We'd walk home reciting Peter Cook and Dudley Moore's *Derek and Clive* sketches, or make up our own. They were very rude, which, of course, always appeals to adolescent boys.

The *other* thing that adolescent boys find endlessly fascinating, of course, is sex—and this began playing an increasingly central role in my life. It all began when I got taught how to wank.

My instructor was a kid a year or two older than me who lived just up the road on the Beechdale. I was hanging out on the estate one weekend with a couple of mates from school when this lad came up to us.

"Do you want to learn how to do something cool?" he asked us.

"Yeah, OK! Sound!"

"Right. Follow me!"

We went to his house and he took us to a downstairs room, closed the door…and got his cock out. "This is how you do it," he said. "You hold it like *this*." He started rubbing himself, up and down, harder and harder. "If you do it faster, it makes you feel great!" he added, going a bit red.

I didn't know *what* to make of this, but my two mates had dropped their pants and were copying him, so I thought I'd better join in. I was self-conscious at first—*I mean, you would be, wouldn't you?*—but then I got into it and, you know what? He was right: if you did it faster, it *did* make you feel great!

The lad was probably a budding pervert, but he didn't touch us or say, "Let me hold yours"; he had just taken it upon himself to teach us the ancient, not-all-that-noble art of masturbation. And he opened up a whole new world of pleasure for me.

From then on, I was at it all the time. At home, I had been turfed out of the bedroom I was sharing with Sue. It was Sue's idea, because she wanted more space and privacy, but I didn't mind moving into the little box room. For one thing, it made it a lot easier to have a wank.

I'd knock one out any chance I got, and it was the same at school. I'd meet up with the mates I'd had the Beechdale masturbation tuition with, or a couple of others…and we'd wank each other off.

We had the perfect hidey-hole for it. I was still doing well at school and had been rewarded by being made school librarian. I liked that, and enjoyed going to the newsagent every day to pick up the papers to put them in the library.

The best thing about it, though, was that I got to use a little plywood annex to the library, to work on the Dewey decimal system. Nobody could see in—or so we thought—and so it was easy to nip in for a quick spurt of pleasuring each other when the mood took us. Which was…*always*.

One afternoon, I was in the little room with a good mate called Pete Higgs. Everything developed in the usual way—one minute we were working diligently on our English language class project; the next, we were tossing each other off.

Pete and I were rolling around on a table, our clothes askew, and our trousers around our ankles, when I glanced over at the closed door. Above it was a thin strip of glass I had never noticed before— and in that window appeared the shocked face of the English teacher.

Shit!

"Get down!" I hissed at Pete, and the two of us dropped beneath the table. We crouched there, hearts pounding like the steam hammers in the factory over the road.

The teacher didn't come in, but my heart was in my mouth.

Oh, fuck!

This was bad. There had to be consequences. Nothing happened for the next couple of days, but I was dreading our next English language class. It all went as normal, but when the bell went at the end and we were filing out, the teacher called us over.

"Halford! Higgs! Stay behind!"

He beckoned us to him, and we trudged over.

"Hands out!"

We both put our hands out in front of us.

"You *know* what this is for, don't you?"

Pete looked at me. I looked at him. We looked up at the teacher.

"Yes, sir," I said, nodding.

He whacked us both, hard, with his cane. Three swift strokes on each hand. Six of the best.

"You will *never* do that again in this school!" he admonished us.

"No, sir!"

"Now get out!"

My blood rose into throbbing welts on both of my palms and I was blinking back tears from the excruciating pain. But, obviously, it didn't stop us from doing it again…*and again*…

This may sound funny to you, but me and my friends wanking each other off wasn't a gay thing. We were just mates having a laugh and, well, *giving each other a hand*. My friends were straight: they went on to become dads, and I'm sure they are grandads by now.

But that was them. *I* was a very different story.

If I had suspected it at ten, by my early teens I knew for a fact that I was gay. I fancied boys more than girls: it was that simple. I wasn't even horrified by the realization: it felt natural and normal to me. But I instinctively knew to keep it quiet.

In any case, what did I know about gay sexuality? Walsall in the early sixties was not a hotbed of sexual information! I was a confused lad who knew nothing of this forbidden world I was drawn toward. But, occasionally, I would be given a clue.

Our family holidays were cheap and cheerful—we would no more have gone abroad than to the Moon—but they were great. Blackpool was a favorite. It would be freezing on the beach, and the sea looked like it was a mile away. I'd run over the sand, splash about in the waves, then sprint back up the beach and Mom would wrap me in a towel to ward off hypothermia. One year, we rented a battered old caravan by a railway track in Rhyl in North Wales. Every time a train went by, the whole caravan shook.

I would have been thirteen when we went to Westward Ho! in Devon. We were staying on a beachside caravan site, and one afternoon I wandered into the campsite shop just for something to do.

I saw a novel that had two men together on the cover, picked it up, and flicked through a few pages. It piqued my curiosity straight away. The story had some gay erotic scenes in it, so I bought it, hid it under my shirt, and took it back to our caravan.

For the rest of the holiday, I read the book every chance I got. I kept smuggling it into the campsite loo. It didn't stimulate me sexually but it explained a few things I hadn't previously understood: *Ah, OK, so that's what gay men do!* It was like a textbook, filling in some of the gaping holes in my knowledge.

When it came time to go home, I waited until my dad was putting all of our stuff in the boot of the car and, when his back was turned, I shoved it right at the back. I didn't want anybody to find it— least of all Dad! The bizarre thing was that, having been so careful about hiding it, I forgot all about the book when we got home. It's a long drive from Devon to Walsall, so my parents left it until the next day to unpack the car. When I saw them, the realization hit my horrified mind like a thunderbolt: *Fucking hell! That book!*

Maybe they won't find it? I tried to convince myself. Fat chance… I was sitting in the front room watching TV when Dad came storming in. He threw the book at me.

"What's *this* all about?"

"What?"

"You know what! This book!"

"It's just a book."

"Oh, yeah? Well, do you know what this book is about?"

"Yes," I said.

Dad fixed me with a glare: "And do you deny it?"

I suppose there were a few things I could have said. I could have said, "I was curious, Dad! It was just a laugh!" It would even have been true, sort of. But I didn't say that.

"No," I said. "I don't deny it."

And that was me coming out to my dad, aged thirteen. He stared at me, turned around, went out, and slammed the door.

He never mentioned it again—to me, anyway. But the book caused a bit of a family hoo-hah. I know Dad talked about it to Mom, and a while later the news found its way to my nan, Cissy. When I saw her, she seemed blissfully unperturbed by the whole thing.

"Dow yow worry about it, bab!" she reassured me. "I remember your dad going through a phase like that!"

What? I knew my dad had been a very handsome young man, and it turned out that, way before he met Mom, some bloke had had a big crush on him and kept buying him things. Or so Nan told me. Did they ever get it on? Who knows?

I wasn't even all that shocked by what Nan said. It just added to the general sense of befuddlement that was fast enveloping me.

In any case, Dad had his own secret literature. At home on my own one day, I was mooching around Mom and Dad's bedroom, for no particular reason. I looked in their wardrobe, moved a few pairs of shoes…and underneath them were three or four magazines.

They were *Health and Efficiency*, a publication for naturists, which my parents *definitely* weren't. "What are *these* doing here?" I wondered. "They can't be Mom's—they must be Dad's!" They weren't dirty mags, or pornography, as such. If anything, they were quite, well, *natural*, but I found the photos of naked blokes in normal situations very arousing.

I found another highly instructive publication in a youth club in Bloxwich. One day I went to the bog and found a book of black-and-white erotic pictures by a guy named Bob Mizer, who I now know was a groundbreaking, homoerotic American photographer.

At fourteen or fifteen, I didn't have a bloody clue who Bob Mizer was, but I was transfixed by his photographs. The book was full of shots of hunky blokes in little thongs, lying on rocks, or standing next to posts. As I flicked through it in the bog cubicle, it blew my bloody head off.

I had a quick wrestle with my conscience: Should I nick it, or not? *Fuck it!* My conscience was never going to win *that* one! I stuffed the book down the back of my trousers, made some lame excuse to my mates that I had homework to do, and scurried home as fast as I could.

That book was a treasure trove! It was full of staged photographic stories. There would be a guy in a vest saying to another guy in a vest, "My motorcycle has broken down, can you fix it?" Then, when the second guy leaned over the bike, the first guy would tell him, "Hey, that's a nice ass!" and start feeling his bum.

Those Mizer photos were gold dust to me. I went wank-mad over them. It's amazing how many wanks an adolescent boy can get out of one picture before he gets bored of it. I hid the book in my room. Given that Mom cleaned every day, it's amazing she never found it.

In that same Bloxwich youth club toilet, I found a dildo lying on a shelf. I gave it a wash in the sink and smuggled it home in my parka. It gave me many hours of unbridled pleasure. When not in use, it lay hidden under clothes in my wardrobe. My parents never suspected a thing.

Or so I thought. One evening, I was sitting watching TV in the front room. Dad was reading the *Express & Star*. Without even looking up from his paper, he addressed a comment toward me.

"You might want to get rid of *that object*, Rob."

My blood ran cold. *How did he know? How long had he known?* Yet, back in my bedroom, I couldn't bring myself to throw it away. It would have been like cutting off an arm! The dildo stayed hidden in the closet (as it were), and Dad never mentioned it again.

I was a discombobulated teenage lad whose hormones were all over the shop. I was scrabbling around for information, and getting nowhere. It was all a mystery to me. And what happened at my latest after-school activity didn't help.

A small local metalworks began an informal scheme where kids could go down one day a week after school and learn to use equipment like lathes, vices, and drills. I suppose the thinking was that they would get 'em young and we might be interested enough to take up apprenticeships with them a year or two later.

Even though I had no interest in working in the factories—as I've said, the idea horrified me—I still went along with a couple of my schoolmates. It was only for an hour after school and, well, *it was something to do*. It beat being bored at home.

Unfortunately, we quickly found that the bloke giving the mini-workshops had a very different take on the idea of "get 'em young." He wasn't interested in teaching us the finer points of engineering. He just wanted to cop a feel.

The mustachioed, middle-aged bloke would show us how to make garden trowels or pokers for the fire, then hover over us. He'd give me a piece of metal marked with a pen line, tell me to file down to the line, and, as I filed away, he'd put his hand on my bum or down the front of my trousers.

The guy would walk round the workshop, from boy to boy, feeling us all up, and nobody said a thing. He never said a single word to us while he was doing it. It happened every week…and yet me and my mates never even discussed it. It was like it never happened.

I was struggling to come to terms with being gay, and while what he was doing didn't arouse me—it seemed dirty, and sordid, and nasty—I just thought, *Well, OK, is this what gay guys do? Is this how it works?* It even made me wonder: *Does this stuff go on in all the factories, then?*

The weird thing was that we kept going, for six weeks at least. *Fuck knows why.* I just didn't know what else to do. Then one week, after a particularly intrusive fondling, I mentioned to one of my mates on the way home that I was a bit bored of the sessions.

"Me too!" he said, with what sounded a lot like relief. "Shall we stop going, then?"

"Ar," I said.

And that was it. We never mentioned it again.

I fancied boys, but I still went out with girls. A regular event was a fortnightly dance—this was in the days before discos—at Bloxwich Swimming Baths.

I've always liked dancing and had even done an old-time dancing after-school class, where I'd learned the lancer and the Gay Gordons. The Gay Gordons! Now *there's* a name to conjure with! I had progressed from the old-time by now, and when I took one girl, Angela, to Bloxwich Baths, I won their twist competition. I was disappointed by my prize—a diary from the *Eagle* comic, in a red plastic cover.

Mind you, I wasn't nearly as disappointed as Angela was with what I did next. The DJ had scraps of paper by his decks to request songs and give him messages to read out. For reasons known only to my dumb, adolescent self, I wrote this:

> Please will you play "These Boots Are Made for Walking"
> by Nancy Sinatra, and say: "This is to Angela, from Rob.
> These boots are made for walking, but what I'VE got is
> made for something else."

What the hell was I thinking of? I sounded a right dirty old perv! I'm pretty sure that was my last date with Angela…

Taking girls to Bloxwich Baths didn't come cheap and I decided to get a Saturday job. My grandad was working at Reginald Tildesley, a car sales garage. They had twenty cars on the forecourt, and for months, me and a schoolmate, Paul, went down at weekends and washed every single one.

It was hard work but I didn't mind it—I quite looked forward to it sometimes, because it felt grown-up. The owner would give us a couple of quid for doing it, a lot of money in the midsixties. But one day, after we'd slogged our guts out for four hours, he handed us 50p.

"What's *this*?" I asked him, horrified.

"It's yer money."

"50p? We always get two quid!"

"Well, that's all yow'm getting. Tek it or leave it."

We took it, but we didn't go back.

Language teaching wasn't big in secondary moderns at that time, but mine chose a few pupils to learn French and I was one of them. I loved it. I liked the teacher, Mrs. Battersby, and quickly became her keenest pupil.

I liked French because it seemed exotic. I worked hard to speak "non-accented" French, that is to say, not in a Walsall accent. I wanted to say, "*Ouvrez la fenêtre*" not "*Oo-vray lah fennetr-ah!*" Because *nobody* wants to hear the beautiful language of French mangled into yam-yam.

What is yam-yam? It's a derogatory term used by Brummies to ridicule the Black Country accent: "*Am yow from Walsall?*" "*I yam!*" To outsiders, Brummie and Black Country accents may sound similar— but they are very, very different.

With my liking for the perceived sophistication of French came a developing interest in music, the theater…and clothes. The school was quite liberal and let its older pupils drop school uniform and wear their own clothes. I became a dedicated follower of fashion.

Like any teenager, I just wanted to be cool and trendy. I took to swanning around the Beechdale in suede loafers that got marked so easily that I was scared each time I wore them in case they got scuffed or it rained.

I had a green corduroy coat that I wore so much Mom had to put patches on the elbows. I accessorized it with a cravat, and baggy

wide trousers. Thanks to Henry's, Walsall's one half-decent bou-
tique, I was quite the fashion plate.

You can't wear that kind of clobber around the Beechdale
without exciting comment, and I remember walking home from a
Bloxwich Baths dance one night when I was about fifteen. I fancied
some chips and stopped off at the hot dog van by the estate. I had
also taken to combing my hair bouffant and forward, like the Small
Faces, and my ensemble grabbed the attention of a couple of yobbos
chomping down hot dogs.

"Oi, mate, look how yow'm dressed, yer poof!" one of them
greeted me, in broadest yam-yam. "What am yow, a bloke or a girl?"

I didn't answer them, but the question stayed with me and, in a
way, haunted me. I knew by then that I was gay, but the yobs saying
that I looked like a woman made me worry: *Is that what everybody
thinks I look like? Is that part of who, and what, I am?*

When I was just turning sixteen, and gearing up for my exams,
the Halford family received a shock. It certainly surprised me and
Sue, and it was just as dumbfounding for Mom and Dad. We got a
new baby brother: Nigel.

Nigel certainly wasn't planned but it was great when he came
along. It was lovely to have a bab around the house, Mom and Dad
were delighted, and me and Sue doted on him. His arrival seemed
magical.

Despite this, after having Nigel my mom grew depressed. She
would have mood swings and go very quiet and withdrawn, until
her doctor put her on happy pills, as I have always called antidepres-
sants. I was to meet that black dog in my own, later, years.

But like any teenager, I was caught up in my own selfish life…
which led me to a distinctly odd supernatural encounter. *In Belgium.*
It was a rum do all round.

For some reason, me and my best mate, Tony, decided to
re-create the school weekend trip to Ostend. We got cheap coach-
and-ferry tickets and booked into a boarding house in the town. It

was a five- or six-story place, and the landlady gave us a room on the top floor.

Tony and I had beds on opposite sides of the room. On the first night, just after we had turned in, my bed began…shaking.

"Rob, what am yow *doing?*" asked Tony, suspiciously, through the darkness.

"Nothing!" I said, my heart thudding. "My bed's shaking!"

I got out of bed and put the light on. My bed was now still and looked totally normal. When I switched the light off and got back into bed, it started again. It didn't go on for that long, but I didn't get much sleep that night.

Tony and I mooched around Ostend the next day, and I was nervous going to bed that night. I was right to be. As soon as the light went out, my bed vibrated violently again. It shook so hard that I thought I might fall out.

It was like a full-on fucking scene from *The Exorcist*. My bed was shaking like crazy and even the pictures on the wall were rattling. It went on for a lot longer than it had the night before, and it was terrifying.

The next morning, as the landlady was serving us breakfast, I tried to tell her, in my pidgin French, with the help of my pocket dictionary, what had happened:

"Er, *excusez-moi, Madame! Hier soir, mon lit,* er, *tremblait!*"

She stared at me and shook her head. "We don't talk about that!" she barked, and walked off. So, that was that…but I think the very strong belief I have in the supernatural was born that weekend in Belgium.

Back in Walsall, I had been developing a very strong new interest—and it was one that I began to hope I could maybe turn into a career.

I used to watch a lot of TV drama series, such as *Z Cars, Dixon of Dock Green, The Saint,* and *The Avengers,* as well as the BBC's *Play of the Month.* Television, cinema, and theater fascinated me, and I was getting well into the idea of becoming an actor.

Could this be my future? The time was coming to leave school. I revised hard for my O levels and did OK, but I had no interest in staying on for the sixth form. Working-class kids didn't, in those days, and I wanted to get out into the world.

My parents were fine with that. Their attitude was basically that they would help me with whatever I wanted to do in life. Mom used to regularly ask me, "Rob, are you happy?" When I said "Yes," she'd say, "Well, if *you're* happy, *I'm* happy." It was a great thing to say to a kid.

So, my parents and I spent evenings poring over glossy brochures from the Birmingham School of Acting, wondering if that might be a good next step for me after I left school.

The brochures were full of photos of blokes in tights with big bulges, which was no disincentive for me! However, I thought it might be a problem that I had no acting experience. I doubted they would count an infant nativity, with a bulldog clip burrowing into my skull.

My dad had a friend who was into amateur dramatics, so he had a word with him. The friend said that he acted in productions at a local theater called the Grange Playhouse, and they were always looking for new talent: "Tell Rob to come down! He'll like it!"

"OK, I'll go and check it out," I said, donning my suede shoes, green corduroy coat, and cravat.

I checked it out…and I really liked it. They cast me in a kitchen-sink drama in which I played a young lad trapped in a dysfunctional family. The other actors were mostly older than me but were very welcoming. Dad's mate was particularly helpful and encouraging.

I enjoyed going to the rehearsals one evening a week and I learned my lines well. I was the only person onstage when the curtain went up at the start of the play, sitting at the front and cleaning my shoes. The director said he wanted me to sing a jingle from a TV commercial as I polished them.

"Which TV commercial?" I asked him.

"I don't mind," he said. "Anything. You choose one."

The only TV ad I could think of was for Pepsodent toothpaste. It had a jaunty little ditty that was hard to get out of your head, so I sang that:

> You'll wonder where the yellow went
> When you brush with Pepsodent!

The play ran for a week and the *Express & Star* sent a critic down. His review singled me out for praise: "Robert Halford gives a very cute, observant performance...watch this kid!" I was very pleased by this and resolved to stop wiping my arse on the local rag in Nan's toilet.

I wanted to do more acting, so I was delighted when Dad's mate got in touch again. He knew people who worked at the Grand Theatre in Wolverhampton, a prestigious Midlands playhouse. They were going for a drink in Walsall—would I like to come along, and he'd introduce me to them?

You bet! Yes, please! He told me where they were all meeting up... and it was a pub near my nan and grandad's house. So, I arranged with them that I'd crash out at their house at the end of the night, to save the trouble of getting all the way home.

Two nights later, Dad's mate picked me up from Kelvin Road after tea. First, he drove me to a theatrical costume warehouse that he somehow had access to. It was a real Aladdin's cave, and I boggled at all the fantastic medieval stuff and period clothing. I've always loved a good costume.

Then we went on to the pub. The theater people were nice, if a bit posh, and they were knocking back the drinks. Dad's mate bought me some rum and blackcurrants. Quite a lot of them.

I had hardly ever drunk before. Nan might give me a little glass of shandy, or a sip of her Snowball at Christmas. But this was proper drinking—*Rum! With theater people!*—and I was out of my depth. I wanted to join in, so I kept going. But soon I was completely pissed.

By the end of the night, the room was spinning. "I know—let's go to my place!" Dad's friend suggested. I was going along with anything by now and, before I knew it, the two of us were in his flat.

He might have given me another drink. I can't remember. He was talking about the theater, and the TV was on in the background. I was just trying to hold it all together and keep some sort of focus. Then, suddenly, the light was off and he was right next to me.

Dad's mate wasn't talking about the theater anymore. His hands were doing the talking. He was running them all over me—my arms, my chest, down to my crotch. He worked in silence: nothing was said. It was the factory metalwork class all over again—except, this time, it went further.

I was helpless. The guy knew what he wanted and he went for it. He undid my zip, pulled my cock out of my pants, bent down, and put it in his mouth. As I sat there, frozen, drunk, inert, and mute, he gave me my first-ever blow job.

What's this?

What's happening?

What do I do?

Can I make it stop?

I did…nothing. I have no idea how long it went on, but when it was done, Dad's mate got up without a word and walked out of the room. I remembered I was near my nan's house, found my coat, let myself out, and stumbled, panicky and disoriented, into the night.

I didn't know what to make of what had happened. I wasn't even sure what *had* happened. I lay in Nan's spare room feeling weird, then passed out. Next morning, my head throbbing with my first-ever hangover, my thoughts were all over the place: *Is THAT what gay men do? Is that what being gay is? Is that what theater people do? Had I been on a casting couch?*

Now, of course, I know that the guy was a total sexual predator—a pedophile. He saw my youth, he sensed my vulnerability, and he exploited it, and me. Then, I didn't know what to feel. I thought it must be my fault.

When I got back to Kelvin Road later that day, Dad asked me how the evening had gone.

"Great," I mumbled.

"Did my mate look after you?"

"Yeah," I told him. "Yeah, he did."

I never told my dad what his friend had done to me. It would have destroyed him. Nor would I have put it in this memoir, were my dad still alive.

Every cloud has a silver lining. It's hard to find an upside to sexual abuse, but that dark evening yielded one. A few days later, one of the other theater guys from the pub got in touch. There was a stage assistant job going at the Wolverhampton Grand—was I interested in it?

I was. I went along for an interview with the theater manager and he hired me, starting straight away. My immediate future was assured…and it was exactly what I wanted.

I was going into the theater.

3

Six barley wines and a Mogadon

Your first proper job is a big deal, a rite of passage, and starting at the Wolverhampton Grand at sixteen felt that way to me. Although I was mad about acting and the theater, I didn't know all that much about it, and I wasn't sure what to expect.

Well, it was bostin', as we say in Walsall. I loved the job.

They took me on as a stage assistant–cum-trainee-electrician-cum-all-round-drudge, working for the stage manager. I spent the first few weeks making tea, sweeping the stage, running errands, and getting used to the total change in my daily lifestyle.

There were no more early-morning dashes past G. & R. Thomas Ltd. Now I would catch the bus to Wolverhampton to get to the Grand by midday, work all day and on the evening shows, get a late bus back to Walsall, and let myself into the dark house about midnight.

It suited me (and turned me into the night owl that I still am to this day). The stage manager's son was the lighting technician and the two of them took me under their wings. I picked up the job quickly, and within months I was operating all of the lights for the shows.

In almost every theater, the lighting rig is in front of the stage, but in the Grand it was in the wings. It made it harder to operate, but I soon got the hang of it, and for months I watched, captivated, as amazing shows unfolded just feet away from me. I worked the lights for everything: variety shows, repertory shows, ballet, D'Oyly Carte opera, *Orpheus in the Underworld*. Performers were running on and off stage around me, or awaiting their cues to enter, and I was right in the middle of everything.

I loved getting close to big stars from the telly. Tommy Trinder, the famous comedian, visited the Grand. I'd watched him so many times on *Sunday Night at the London Palladium*, and it was a thrill when he rolled out his catchphrase: "You lucky people!"

Woodbine sponsored the variety shows and gave everybody a mini-pack of five free cigarettes as they came in. Every night, two thousand people puffed away as they awaited the show. When I pressed a button, and the curtain rose, a fog of fag smoke rolled from the auditorium across the stage.

Unsurprisingly, I started smoking myself—but, being a bit of a snob, I rejected Woodbines or Player's No. 6 for Benson & Hedges. For some reason, I thought they were more sophisticated. What a berk!

I learned all about how to work theater lights at the Wolverhampton Grand. The other skill I quickly picked up was how to *drink*.

The theater had a work-hard-play-hard ethos. The ritual was that ten minutes after the show finished, all the staff would congregate in the theater bar. We'd knock back as many drinks as we could, as fast as we could, then I'd stagger off to get the last bus to Walsall.

I got bored of the buses, saved up from my wages, and got a Honda 50 moped, which I paid off on the never-never (otherwise known as the installment plan). It didn't interfere with my after-show drinking, and I'd be weaving unsteadily down the A41 after midnight. I'm amazed I made it home some nights.

Drinking was great, I loved it, and once I'd turned eighteen, I could do it legally. I threw myself happily into the great British tradition of young blokes getting hammered. On nights off from work, I'd go down to a lively local boozer named the Dirty Duck.

Drinking became my social life…yet, right from the start, I was never a social drinker. It had a purpose. *I drank to get drunk.* I found the best route to oblivion was barley wine, so I'd down a couple of them, then seek out my chaser of choice—a Mogadon.

Mogadons are strong sleeping tablets and anxiety-relief pills. If I took one of them after a drink or two, it gave me the warm, spacey feeling I wanted. There was always a dodgy-looking character or two in the Duck with a few to flog:

"Ay, mate, 'ave yow got a Mogadon?"

"Arr. Get us a barley wine and I'll give yer one!"

I would get blindingly drunk. I'd wake up the next morning feeling like death, but by lunchtime I'd have shaken off the hangover and be set to go again. Like any teenager, I had superhuman powers of recovery.

Sue had left school, was training as a hairdresser, and bought herself a green Austin 100. It was her pride and joy. She'd give me a lift to the Duck as she was seeing one of the drinkers there, a lovely bloke who everyone called Brian the Lion due to his luxuriant mane of hair.

Inspired by Sue, I had my own short-lived attempt to learn to drive. Brian had a Mini, and one Sunday afternoon he said he'd let me have a go in it. He drove me to a quiet residential street not far from my nan's and sat me behind the wheel.

"Put it in gear and *very slowly* put your foot on the accelerator and let the clutch out," he told me.

I clumsily floored the accelerator, let the clutch out way too fast, and took off like a fucking rocket. We sped down the road, totally out of control, for fifty yards, smashed into a car parked on the left, and, just for good measure, smashed into one parked on the right.

"STOP! STOP! STOP!" roared Brian the Lion. I slammed the brakes on and jumped out of the car. We quickly swapped seats and tore off up the road. Looking back over my shoulder, I could see people coming out of their houses to see what the hell was going on.

"I'm so sorry, mate!" I told Brian, when we had got a safe distance away from the carnage and pulled over. The front of his car was all bashed up and I begged him to let me pay to repair the damage, but he wouldn't hear of it. I didn't drive a car again for fifteen years.

The Wolverhampton Grand had opened my eyes to all manner of great dramas and theatrical productions, but as I neared the end of my teens, another art form was taking over my affections. I was falling heavily in love with music.

I loved *Juke Box Jury* on TV, with the ridiculously posh David Jacobs spinning records to a panel of judges who would award them a mark. One judge was a teenage girl from Wednesbury, just down the road from us, called Janice Nicholls. If she liked a song, she'd always say, "Oi'll give it foive!" It was the first time I'd ever heard a Black Country accent on national telly.

I'd religiously watch *Top of the Pops* every week and enjoy bands like Freddie and the Dreamers, Cliff Richard and the Shadows, and the Tremeloes. I'd buy singles in Walsall from W. H. Smith, or a posh music shop called Taylor's, which had a grand piano in the window.

But really, like so many people, my love affair with music began with the Beatles.

I liked their early singles, but it was *Sgt. Pepper's Lonely Hearts Club Band* and the White Album that got me. The White Album transfixed me. I thought it was cosmic. I spent weeks listening to it, analyzing the lyrics, and Sellotaping the collage of photos that came with it onto my bedroom walls.

I gave my little box room bedroom a radical makeover. I painted the walls dark purple and took the door off its hinges, replacing it with a bright orange curtain. It was a gauche, adolescent attempt to be cool, but its hipness factor was lost on Mom:

"Rob! *What the...* Why have you taken your bedroom door off?!"

"It's my room! I can do what I want!" I huffed, a textbook teenager.

I listened to Radio Luxembourg—when I could get it, with its crackly medium wave transmission—and John Peel's weekend *Top Gear* program on the new Radio 1. I loved the old blues artists he played that I'd never heard of: Muddy Waters, Howlin' Wolf, and Bessie Smith.

If you were an arty youth, as I fancied myself to be, music was all-important at the end of the sixties. I soaked it up. Jimi Hendrix blew me away and I bought all his albums. I liked the Rolling Stones, but I was most drawn to artists with huge, powerful voices, like Joe Cocker or the brilliant Janis Joplin.

You wouldn't call Bob Dylan a vocal powerhouse, but he interested me with the way he used words. Despite that, I didn't like how all his songs seemed to be political. Even when I agreed with him, I felt that music should be a space to escape from stuff like that.

I felt the same about 1967's Summer of Love. I liked the *idea* of peace and love, especially when John Lennon talked about it, yet I looked at the atrocities happening in places like Vietnam, and what was then Rhodesia, and they seemed a million miles from such idealism.

There's a certain downbeat, even *dour* element to the Black Country nature that declines to get swept away by hippy dreams and flower power. I bought *NME* and *Melody Maker* and read all about peace and love in California but, as far as I was concerned, it might as well have been happening on Mars.

I lived in a council house in Walsall and rode my moped to work. I got pissed on barley wine in the Dirty Duck. All that hippy stuff felt out of reach: two different worlds.

Just occasionally, they would meet. I was working a matinee show at the Grand one Sunday afternoon in 1968. I was spotlight operator that day, and the tiny room that I controlled them from used to get so hot that it was like a sauna.

It had a little window, and during the interval I opened it and stuck my head out to cool off. I heard music from the street below and peered down. A long-haired couple were walking along, hand in hand, wearing bell-bottoms, headbands, and fringed suede jackets. They looked like they should be strolling through Haight-Ashbury. They had a transistor radio and, appropriately, the song wafting up to my sweltering lights room was a hit from the year before, Scott McKenzie's "San Francisco (Be Sure to Wear Flowers in Your Hair)." I looked at them, totally astonished, and thought: *Bloody hell! The hippy dream is real! It's even made it to Wolverhampton!*

Years later, I read Ozzy Osbourne saying exactly the same thing: "I used to hear about people in California with flowers in their hair and think: *What the hell's that got to do with me? I'm from Birmingham and I've got holes in my pockets!*"

The first band I saw live certainly weren't hippy dreamers trying to change the world. It was Dave Dee, Dozy, Beaky, Mick & Tich, a West Country pop group with a string of chart hits. They weren't my thing, but when I saw they were playing at a Wolverhampton club called the Silver Web, I went to see them.

"You look a bit young," the bouncer said, looking me up and down.

"Nah, I'm not, mate, I work at the Grand Theatre!"

My blag worked and he let me in. The gig was amazing. It had a bit of an early glam tinge, there was a bar so I got nicely pissed, and I loved being up close and watching a real band playing songs I had seen on *Top of the Pops*.

I went to see the Crazy World of Arthur Brown at a funny little club in Walsall. He was a one-hit wonder, but *what* a hit: "Fire," which he performed on *Top of the Pops* while wearing a flaming helmet. There were only a hundred people at the Walsall gig, but he did his full theatrical stage show, including a papier-mâché galleon.

They were fun, but Dave Dee, Dozy, Beaky, Mick & Tich and the Crazy World of Arthur Brown weren't the music that moved me and reached deep down into my soul. That came at the turn of the decade when I heard people like Led Zeppelin and Deep Purple.

Given where I come from, and the person I am, I was *always* going to get into heavier music. And it came along at the right time for me. Everything was getting louder at the end of the sixties. The process had begun that was to lead to heavy metal.

Jim Marshall had invented his huge amps that made guitars louder, so drummers had to hit their drums harder to be heard. Girls were screaming more loudly; the Beatles couldn't hear themselves play above the screams at Shea Stadium. The volume was shooting up all round.

And as guitars and drums grew louder, so did the singers. I loved huge voices, and hearing Robert Plant and Ian Gillan belting it out *did* things to me.

They were incredibly exciting to hear. I heard them, and I just knew: *This is it. This is the music I want to make.*

Led Zeppelin blew me away. I'll never forget lying on my bed on the Beechdale, between my two speakers, hearing "Whole Lotta Love" for the first time. The left-right, left-right interplay between Robert Plant and Jimmy Page, back and forth between the speakers, amazed me.

Zeppelin and Purple triggered something in me…and changed my thinking. Before them, I still wanted to be an actor. I was side-stage at the Grand every night, watching actors and comedians getting standing ovations, thinking it must be the best feeling in the world. Hearing Plant and Gillan changed that. Now, suddenly, I wanted to be a *singer.*

Thanks to one of my school music teachers, I'd been messing around in local bands for a couple of years. He'd asked me to sing with his band, Thark—weird name!—so I'd go to rehearsals and belt out a few songs. It was just a laugh, and I never saw it leading to anything.

There was a loose scene of musicians around Walsall, and through Thark I met a band called Abraxis. I'd hang out in practices and sing covers with them, too. They morphed into Athens Wood, which was me and three blokes called Mike Cain, Barry Shearu, and Phil Butler. We played bluesy prog rock and took it a bit more seriously.

Interestingly, I had no desire to play guitar or anything else. I had no interest in lugging around a drum kit. Just being the singer felt comfortable: *This is me; I am the instrument.*[*] All I wanted to do was belt out my vocals, as loud as I could.

Music was moving center stage in my life, but I was still pootling off on my moped to the Grand every day. And the incipient feelings of sexual confusion that had vexed me in school were not receding—they were getting worse.

The theater has never been short of friends of Dorothy, and the Grand was no exception. A guy called Roy who worked there was the first gay guy I'd ever met (apart from the perverts who'd preyed on me). He introduced me to his boyfriend, Danny, a professional drag queen.

Danny was booked in to do a show at Butlin's in Skegness, so the three of us made a weekend of it, sharing a one-bed caravan. I slept in the middle: the meat in the sandwich. We did a bit of fumbling, although it didn't go very far.

Well, it must have gone far enough. A week on, back in my bedroom in Kelvin Road, I felt itching in my crotch and pulled my pants down to have a look. My pubes were a wiry, infested jungle of tiny jumping creatures. *Oh, shit! What the fuck was this?* I had no idea what they were, so I went to find my dad.

"Dad, I've got…a birrova problem," I mumbled.

"What is it?"

I pulled down my trousers and showed him. He took one look and knew exactly what the issue was.

"You've got crabs!" he told me. "Who've you been hanging out with?"

---

[*] I considered that as a title for this memoir: *Rob Halford: I Am the Instrument.* But not for very long.

"What do you mean?" I asked, nervously, knowing *exactly* what he meant.

"Well, you can only catch crabs from other people," Dad said. He took pity on me. "Or off a toilet seat."

"Yeah, that'll be it!" I eagerly agreed. "Off a toilet seat!" But I was mortified beyond words.

Dad saw a doctor for me and came back with a bottle of what looked like milk, and instructions to put some on cotton wool and dab it on my pubes every day. It burned like acid. I had those fucking crabs for months: they wouldn't go away. And I never did dare tell Roy.

My sexual confusion deepened. The gay world remained a mystery to me. I was curious about it—*how could I not be?*—yet also scared of it, after my previous bad experiences. I was a little boy lost, but I was desperate to dip my toe into that world and to try to have a relationship.

In a newspaper, I saw a small ad from a guy looking to meet other men for "friendship, and maybe more." A-ha! I wrote to his PO box, he replied, and we arranged that I'd go down to visit him in Redhill in Surrey.

I'm not sure what I was anticipating on the train down. I didn't necessarily expect to have sex...but it was possible. *Was this to be my first time?* It wasn't. He was a nice guy of my own age, but we didn't click. We went to London shopping, then I got the train home.

At the Grand, when the pantomime season rolled around, we put on a big, lavish production with a full orchestra. The musical director had a major crush on me and just wouldn't leave me alone. He could not have been more obvious. The guy was a lot older than me, and I guess he was a step up on the factory guy, and my dad's creepy mate, in that he didn't try to cop a feel or molest me. He was respectful, but he never stopped trying to flirt with me.

I hated it. By now, I knew what he was up to, and what he was after, but I didn't fancy him and I needed it to stop. It was driving me nuts. One day, after he hit on me yet again, I'd had enough. I knew I had to do something…but what?

And then the strangest thing happened. I have no idea where it came from, or why, but an urgent thought came into my head: *I have to go to church.*

So, I did. That lunchtime, I left the Grand and walked down Lichfield Street to St. Peter's Collegiate Church. It is a big, ornate old Catholic church in the city center, but it was empty when I got there. I walked up to a statue of the Virgin Mary and…*communicated with her.* I am not even sure if I spoke out loud, or just thought hard, but this was what I told Our Lady of Lourdes:

I really need some help here. I'm so confused about how I feel and what I'm going through. I don't know whether it's right, whether it's sinful, whether it's evil, or whether it's OK. I don't know what to do!

And an extraordinary thing happened. As I spoke—or thought?—the words, a wave of peace washed over me. It was like all my angst and frustration had lifted. I smelled the fragrance of roses. I looked around the church, but there were no flowers to be seen.

What happened in that church in Wolverhampton that lunchtime? Was I *really* blessed by the Virgin Mary? Well, I know how silly this may sound, but fifty years later it still gives me the shivers when I think about it. And, for a bit, my angst went away.

Music helped me. I found a lot of solace in bands like Zeppelin. When I was confused, not wanting to be how I was, and angry at myself and my desires, I would crank up the music. Between Zep and the Virgin Mary, I was just about hanging in there.

In 1970, I went to the Isle of Wight festival to see Hendrix. It was the year after Woodstock had been the defining moment of the hippy generation in America. I went over, with a mate, on the ferry to Ryde, thinking it was our turn: *"This is it! This is our Woodstock!"*

The festival was overwhelming. The Who blinded the crowd with antiaircraft spotlights at the start of their set. Hendrix came on in the middle of the night, when I was paralytic, and was unbelievable. We camped…well, we didn't have a tent. We lay on the ground and passed out.

Music was calling me and I knew it was time to leave the Grand. I had had a brilliant time at the theater but my priorities had changed. I had joined because I longed to be an actor…and now, I didn't. I wanted to be the singer in a band.

Athens Wood rehearsed in the evenings, and I couldn't do that if I was slaving over hot theater lights seven nights a week. I needed a regular day job. So, in 1970, after just under two years at the Grand, I bade *adieu* to the theater and found myself…in the world of fashion retail.

There used to be a nationwide chain of British menswear stores called Harry Fenton. Their shop in Park Street, in the center of Walsall, had an advert for a store junior. *Why not?* I thought. I rang them up, went along for an interview, and got the job.

Before long, I was store manager. I didn't adore selling clothes the way I'd loved the Grand, but the job was OK. The hours suited me, the money was decent, and I liked the banter with the customers. One thing about me has *never* changed: I do love a good natter.

Fenton's had always been a traditional, quite stuffy gents' outfitters, but the company had a rethink and started targeting younger guys who'd usually shop in boutiques. We had a sudden influx of trendier clothes: polyester suits, flared trousers, kipper ties, and stack-heeled shoes.

This new stocking policy suited me down to the ground, as it meant I suddenly had a far better selection of gear to nick. Well, not nick: *borrow*. I was a swine for it. I would grab a new suit, or cool shirt and bell-bottoms, and wear them to go out at the weekend.

The following Monday morning, still hungover, I'd be sticking a suit that stank of booze, cigs, and Old Spice back on the racks, and trying to re-pin a shirt and cram it back into its cellophane wrapper as if it were unused. *Those bloody pins!*

Once I became manager, I could also play whatever music I liked in the shop, so I blasted out Alice Cooper's "School's Out." We got a few complaints, but... *I'm the manager! I'll play what I bloody want!*

Athens Wood managed to get ourselves a gig or two in local pubs. *Playing live!* It was what I wanted, yet I approached the gigs with a weird mix of confidence and terror.

Before the first show, I had a fear that nobody would be there, or people would hear the first song and walk out. I wasn't too far off. A handful of hardened drinkers propped up the bar and silently looked on. If anybody wandered off, I prayed, silently: *Please be going to the bog! Don't be going home!*

But far more important to me was the fact that, when the shows got going, I loved them. Prancing around a stage and wailing at strangers came pretty easily. I quickly realized that when I walked onstage, I grew more confident and outgoing. I wasn't cocky, but I didn't have self-doubt.

That space right at the front, between the guitarist and bassist, fitted me nicely. It felt natural; where I was meant to be.

It wasn't happening for Athens Wood. Soon, things dribbled to a halt and we went our separate ways. I was getting well into heavy metal by now, and I joined a bluesy hard rock band called Lord Lucifer, who had a lot more attitude going on. I was well into this lot. By now I had graduated from my moped to a BSA motorbike, and I painted the band's name on the petrol tank with flames spurting out of it. It looked ace—but Lord Lucifer never played a gig.

When I wasn't doing band stuff myself, I went to see as many groups as I could. I became a regular at a rock club called the Whiskey Villa in an old Methodist church hall in the heart of Walsall. I saw another early hero, Rory Gallagher, there with his first band, Taste.

---

* I still feel the same. I can be onstage in a sold-out arena, and if I see somebody heading for an exit, my heart sinks. We performers are an insecure bunch.

Now my evenings were free, I'd venture into Birmingham to gigs at venues like Henry's Blueshouse, above a pub. I saw some great blues there. One night, I saw Muddy Waters and I couldn't believe he was *there*, in front of me, in Brum. It felt like seeing Mozart!

I'd go with Sue to Mothers in Erdington, the Midlands version of London's Marquee. I saw Zeppelin and Pink Floyd there, and I think that, one pissed night, I saw Earth, before they mutated into Black Sabbath.

On free nights, I'd go down to the Dirty Duck and get wankered. *Totally wankered.* I was a real binge drinker by now, and saw no reason not to knock back barley wine after barley wine and slam the Mogadons. At kicking-out time, my homing-pigeon instincts would kick in and I'd lurch home.

One Friday night, Sue drove me down and I necked six barley wines and a Mogadon. On the way home, I threw up out of her passenger window. I woke up the next morning, with no memory of that at all, to hear a pissed-off Sue downstairs, pleading with Dad:

"Dad, I took Rob down the Duck last night and he puked all over my car door! He's still unconscious and I'm late for work—can you clean it off for me, please?"

He did. God knows why he didn't drag me out of bed to do it.

There again, Sue was no angel. My sister was going through a wild-child phase. On top of the hairdressing, she had started doing some photographic modeling locally, and was getting adept at pouting and wearing hot pants.

I'd gotten a decent record collection by now, and one night when the DJ at the Duck's rock disco was ill, I volunteered to stand in. I arrived to find I was spinning records in between turns by a go-go dancer—Sue! I felt protective toward my little sis, and wasn't sure how I felt about seeing blokes ogling her.[*]

If there was a lock-in at the Dirty Duck, or we went on to some-

---

[*] Dad certainly knew how he felt—he bloody hated it!

one's house, I'd stay out all night and stagger into Harry Fenton's still drunk the next morning. Luckily, as I was the boss, there was nobody to bollock me. And the shop seemed to run itself OK.

One long-standing urban myth about me is that before I became a singer, I worked in a porno cinema. That little nugget is even on Wikipedia, and we *all* know that every word there is gospel, right? Well, not quite. *Here* is the true story.

On my walk to work, I used to pass a row of tatty shops in converted Victorian town houses. They had been there since the year dot and were mostly knick-knack shops and vacuum-cleaner-repair places…but behind one seedy, battered door, with its paint peeling off, was a sex shop.

After my experiences with the holiday gay novel, and the Bob Mizer photo book, I was curious about pornography, so now and then I'd pop in after work. The shop was the size of a sitting room and had risqué books and porno mags from Amsterdam hanging on the walls in plastic bags.

They had a few gay mags, too. Oddly enough, I never bought any of them, but I got matey with the bloke behind the counter and we'd jabber away about music. One night, I called in on the way home from work, and he had a favor to ask.

"Ay, Rob, I'm busy for the next couple of weekends—would yow look after the shop? I'll pay yer!"

"Yeah, all right, then!"

So, for two weekends, I was a porn-shop manager. It was brill.

We got a handful of women coming in, because we also sold dildos and sex toys, but it was mostly men on their own. In no time, I could size up what a bloke was after as soon as he walked in the door: *Ah, he'll go for the big tits mags!* I was rarely wrong.

I certainly had some salubrious stop-offs on my way home from Harry Fenton's. As well as the porn shop, I would often also call in to a public loo for a spot of cruising (I've always preferred that term to the British "cottaging").

Right next to British Home Stores in the middle of Walsall was an old Victorian underground toilet with railings around the entrance. I would loiter nearby until I saw a tasty-looking bloke making his way in, then surreptitiously follow him down.

I'd try to size up whether he just needed a pee, or might be after something else. Ninety-nine times out of a hundred it would be the former, of course, but if I got even the slightest sniff that he might be interested, I'd try to make eye contact and give him a smile.

I was taking a bloody risk. Back in those days, homophobic violence was common, and I knew I was leaving myself open to a bout of gay-bashing. *But, really, what else could I do?* I hated the fact I had to put myself in danger to try to get a bit of male company.

I never came to harm, save the odd suspicious look, or getting asked, *"What the fuck do yow want?"* Once in a blue moon, I'd get lucky and have a panicky, rushed grope. Mostly, I'd trudge back to the Beechdale dispirited, a fisherman who had failed to land any cock.

It was frustrating…as was the fact that I wasn't getting anywhere with my musical endeavors. The lurid flames painted on my BSA's fuel tank had failed to ignite Lord Lucifer, and we'd split up. However, I had higher hopes for my next project.

I'd made mates with a few more blokes on the local gig circuit, and we formed ourselves into a band called Hiroshima. A guy called Paul Watts played guitar, and Ian Charles was on bass, but I was closest to our drummer, a friendly but tightly wound bloke named John Hinch.

Hiroshima played the sort of stuff I listened to all the time: very loud, progressive bluesy rock. Listening to old blues records— and seeing Muddy Waters in Brum—had got me intrigued by the harmonica and I'd bought one. I'd vamp away on the "harp," as we musos call it. I wasn't bad.

John Hinch lived in Lichfield, which was very green and middle-class compared to Walsall, and we spent evenings rehearsing in a church hall over his way. Hiroshima didn't play covers, but I'm not sure our own "songs" had any structure: we specialized in free-form noodling and rambling jams.

This may have been why the one or two pub gigs we got to play were unremarkable. My main memories are blokes holding a pint, having a look at us, shrugging, and heading back to the bar.

So, it was dawning on me that Hiroshima were not my fast-track to musical success…when the greatest opportunity of my life fell into my lap.

It really was as straightforward as that.

Sue had stopped stroking the mane of Brian the Lion and was by now dating a friendly bloke named Ian Hill, whom she'd met down at the Duck. Ian played bass in a band called Judas Priest, who had been knocking around the circuit for a little while.

They had recently hit a few problems. Both their singer and their drummer had walked out and they needed replacements. Sue was telling me about this one day—then stopped, and looked at me.

"You know, Rob, you should try out for Priest," she suggested.

I looked back at Sue, as the possibility ran through my mind. *Hmm.*

"Yeah," I told her. "Yeah, I think I probably should."

4

Joining the Priesthood

As it happened, I already knew a little bit about Judas Priest.

The band had been around for three or four years. Because Sue was dating Ian, I knew some of their history and that they had had their ups and downs. Early on, they had had a guitarist, John Perry, who died in a car crash. A few members had come and gone, like in any band, and they had had their share of bad luck. Right at the start they'd signed a record deal, but the label went bust before they could release anything. Priest had then split before reforming with nearly all new members.

I'd even seen them live once, somewhere in Birmingham a year or so earlier. My main memories were that Ken Downing, the guitarist, was new to the group, and that Ian had looked amazing, a stick-thin bass player with hair down to his waist. I remember thinking that they definitely *had* something.

They had played a lot of Midlands gigs, but now they were going through another rough patch. Their singer, Al Atkins, had been there from the start, but had just told them he had to quit. He was married, had kids, and wasn't making enough money from the band to support them.

It wasn't all rosy in their garden, then, but I liked Judas Priest's sound and look and they seemed to me a way more professional outfit than Hiroshima, who were going nowhere fast. OK, I said to Sue. Could she mention me to Ian and Ken, please?

A week or so later, they came to the Beechdale to meet me. Now, it's fair to say that Ken and I have conflicting memories of this first encounter. Ken says that when Sue opened the door to them in Kelvin Road, and called me, I came downstairs with a harmonica. This sounds feasible: I was always blowing away then. But *here* is our point of difference: he claims that, as I walked down the stairs, I was singing a Doris Day song. *Doris Day?! Why the fuck would I be singing a Doris Day song?* For what it's worth, Ian says it was Ella Fitzgerald, which is a lot better…

Whatever. Ken, Ian, and I sat in the front room and chatted. We got on great right from the start. Ken worshipped Hendrix, so when I told him that I was a huge fan, that was a big plus for both of us. In fact, we had very similar music tastes all round.

Ken was very driven about Judas Priest, which appealed to me. He didn't seem knocked back by having lost their singer, and was talking in optimistic terms about what he wanted the band to achieve. Ian was more laid-back, as I knew already.

Priest hadn't just lost a vocalist. Their drummer, a bloke called Congo Campbell, was also calling it a day, so when Ken and Ian invited me to join them for a jam—or a "knock," as we used to call it—I suggested I should bring John Hinch along.

"Sure," said Ken. "Why not?"

They explained that Judas Priest usually rehearsed in a school hall, nicknamed Holy Joe's, attached to a church in Wednesbury, three miles from Walsall. So, a couple of days later, Hinchy and I headed over there.

Ken, Ian, John, and I just riffed and jammed for three hours or more. We all felt really easy around each other so I wasn't nervous. In fact, I really went for it, giving it plenty of wailing and "Ooh, aah, baby!" and showing off my best Planty and Joplin moves. It felt good from the start.

If I had done my audition in Los Angeles, of course, Ian or Ken might have said, "Wow, dude, that was awesome! With your voice and our guitars, we can rule the world!" But that's not the down-to-earth Walsall way.* Instead, when we were done, Ken gave a satisfied nod of the head.

"That were all right, wor it?" he reflected. "Do you want to have another knock later this week?"

And that was it: it was as low-key and as easy as that. I was now the singer in Judas Priest. I went home feeling really happy.

We quickly got down to a routine of weekend and midweek-evening rehearsals. Our knocks at Holy Joe's had a strange ritual. Holy Joe himself—Father Joe, the elderly vicar of the church next door—lived on the premises and used to drop in to collect our hire money for the hall.

Father Joe looked like a priest who enjoyed a drink, and he made no bones about the fact. "C'mon now, boys, I'm parched!" he'd tell us, as we fiddled in our jeans pockets to find a few notes for him. Once he'd got them, he'd happily vanish off to the pub on the corner.

In Holy Joe's, we'd jam the occasional cover, but right from the start we tried to write original songs. When I joined, Priest already had a few primitive pre-songs, left behind by the old lineup. If I'm honest, I didn't think the songs were that great, but I loved the sound and *feel* of the band.

We didn't talk about it much, but we knew instinctively that if we did loads of covers, we might become known as a covers band. There were lots of those on the circuit, and nothing wrong with that…but it wasn't for us. We wanted to be independent, and original.

It was never discussed that I should be the main lyricist but it made sense. I had my love of literature and words from school and

---

* If Walsall, as a town, had a motto, it would be something like this: "We Dow Like to Mek a Fuss."

the Grand and, anyway, singers in bands write the lyrics: *that's how it works*. It was my first real chance to try to express myself artistically.

Our early songwriting sessions mostly happened in a tatty flat in a block called Meynell House in Handsworth Wood, Birmingham. Ian lived there, and even though it only had one bedroom, most of Priest, plus mates, crashed out there all the time. And, of course, Sue stayed over a lot too.

This scruffy flat was half hippy commune, half rock 'n' roll crash pad, and I spent a lot of time there. Really, a lot. We'd sit around, late at night, smoking, jamming, and looking for cool riffs: "Hang on, Ken, what did you just play? Play it again!" I bet the neighbors *loved* us.

The other big hangout for me was the place that Ken shared with his girlfriend, Carol, in Bloxwich. I'd go home from Harry Fenton's, have my tea, and then head over to Ken's place to watch TV and listen to records.

My hair had got a bit longer by then and I went around in a three-quarter-length herringbone hippy coat. I was walking home from Ken's place one night at about midnight, and had just passed G. & R. Thomas Ltd. when a police car screeched to a halt right next to me. *What the…?*

Two coppers jumped out and grabbed me. "Right, you little toe-rag, we've got you! Thought you'd get away with it, did yer?" one of them said. I was shocked…and scared.

"Eh? What's going on?" I asked.

"Don't bloody talk back to us! You know what you've done!"

"I've not done anything! I was just walking back from my mate's…"

"Oh, yeah? We're taking you back to the house you've just burgled! Now, shut up!" They threw me in the back of the squad car, gave me a slap round the head for good measure, and we set off.

We only drove for about ten minutes but I had no idea where we were. We pulled up outside a house, and the coppers pulled me out of the car and frog-marched me up the path to the front door. They rang the bell and a middle-aged woman answered.

"We've got your burglar, love," one of the policemen said. "Can you just confirm this is him?"

The woman glanced at me. With my shoulder-length hair and herringbone coat, I looked fairly distinctive.

"He is absolutely *nothing* like him!" she said, then turned around and shut the door.

The two coppers looked at each other, shrugged, let go of me, and walked back down the path, with me trailing behind. They opened the front doors of their squad car.

"Eh! What about me?" I asked them.

"What *about* you?"

"I dunno where I am. Can you drop me back where you found me?"

"Not our problem, mate," one of them said, and they got in the car and drove off. I walked around, lost, for thirty minutes until I got my bearings, and got home at two in the morning. *Community policing, seventies-style!*

Even though I knew I was gay, for a while there was a part of me that was in denial about it. I didn't think there was anything *wrong* with gay people, I just didn't want to be one of them—probably because of the confusion and pain I sensed it would bring me in later life.

This meant I still sometimes fooled around with girls. There was a lovely girl called Margie, the sister of a friend of Sue's, who was often around Ken's house at the same time as me. She was a sweet, quiet soul, and she loved Priest.

Margie and I would snog on the sofa and do some heavy petting. I enjoyed it, and I got aroused, but at the same time I never felt *completed* by it. While it was going on, there was always a voice in my head: *Look, what are you doing? You're a gay guy!*

One night, we arranged that Margie and I would stay over at

Ken's, in his spare room. On the way there, I was full of resolve: *OK, so maybe tonight's the night I lose my virginity to a woman!* We all sat around as usual, then, when it came to bedtime, Ken pulled me to one side.

"When you get up to the bedroom, look under your pillow!" he whispered.

While Margie was in the bathroom, I did. Ken had left me a Durex. I didn't know *what* I made of that. I half thought it was presumptuous of him, and half thought he was just being a good mate and helping me out. When Margie came to bed, we did some more petting…but that was all. The Durex remained unused. It was always going to.

It made me realize that it was wrong to lead Margie on: *I was a gay guy, and that was that.* I liked her and I didn't want to hurt her, but I was a sorry hormonal and emotional mess, and totally incapable of communicating that fact to her.

So, like most blokes, I finished it in a shitty way. Shortly after we had spent the night together, I was sitting on my bed in my room in Kelvin Road on a Sunday afternoon, vamping away on my harmonica. The doorbell rang, and Sue called upstairs.

"Rob! Margie's here for you!"

Shit! Now what do I do?

I panicked. "I don't want to see her!" I shouted down.

"Eh? Rob, don't be daft, she's here now! Are you coming down?"

"No, I'm not coming down! I don't want to see her!"

I was twenty-two years old and acting like a pathetic teenager. Luckily, Margie was a lot nicer than I deserved, and she and I stayed friends. But I took the hint that my body and mind were giving me. It was the last time I tried to go with a woman for a very, very long time.

Back in Meynell House in Birmingham, living with Ian in the band's crash-pad flat, was a distinctly eccentric soul who was to become a very significant figure in the Judas Priest story: Dave "Corky" Corke.

Corky was the band's manager, although nobody was quite sure how that had happened. It seemed he had just hung around with them, and then appointed himself to the job. But nobody could deny that he had thrown himself into the role with the utmost relish.

Corky was a real hustler, probably the kind every band needs at the start. A West Bromwich bloke, he was a short, chubby, twitchy guy with curly hair, a strange mustache that never seemed to grow, and terrible eyesight that meant he had to wear bottle-bottom glasses.

Corky could talk the hind legs off a donkey. He was a lovable rogue, and his gift of the gab opened doors that would otherwise have stayed firmly shut. He told us he had offices in Birmingham. He didn't. What he *did* have was a car that he sat in next to a phone box outside the Beacon pub in Great Barr. He gave the phone box's number as his office, and would sit in his motor, with the window down, awaiting incoming calls.

Then he went up in the world—literally! Corky got access to an office block in the center of Brum and somehow managed to rewire the lift phone (which was there to enable people to talk to the engineer in case of emergency) to make external and even international phone calls. He did all of his business zooming between floors.

I heard Corky make a few of his wide boy (wheeler-dealer) phone calls on our behalf, and my jaw would drop. "I'm calling from DCA in Birmingham, and I represent the international artistes Judas Priest!" he would begin. "They are the best rock band in Britain, with a massive following!"

Corky would bang on and on about us, giving the poor bloke on the other end of the phone an earache, until they gave in: "OK! OK! They can play next Thursday! I'll pay 'em a tenner!" I'm sure we got most of our early gigs because people were so desperate to get Corky off the phone.

I had to hand it to him, though—it worked. Corky seemed to know promoters in all the major cities and towns of the UK, and plenty of minor ones. Despite still being an unknown and unsigned band, Priest were playing a shitload of gigs.

We somehow managed to scrape together enough cash to buy a Ford Transit van, and it widened our scope. With transport, and Corky's big gob, we were in business.

God knows how many hours—days!—we spent in that van during those first months. Off we'd trek, to Manchester or Newcastle or Cardiff or Hull. We played a lot of northern pubs and social clubs. We did the Cavern, in Liverpool, which was a buzz. And we always went down well in St. Albans.

We had been to St. Albans the night I disfigured the Transit. We were on the way home from the gig, I was pissed as a skunk and I suddenly felt the urge to purge. I shoved my head out of the window… and sprayed puke all down the outside of the van.

"Bloody hell, what have you had, Rob?" Ken asked me.

"Just a bottle of Beaujolais and three Valium," I mumbled.

When I came to clean the van the next day, my vomit had marked it like paint stripper. Nothing could shift the stain. It became the Transit's distinguishing feature. Nice!

We were paying our dues. We played to crowds of drinkers who had never heard of us and were only there for the beer. We never knew how it would go. Some nights, we would smash it. Others, we'd finish a song to resounding silence…or the sound of a solitary clap.

One clap. It used to make me wonder: *Is that an approving clap? A sarcastic clap? An indignant clap? What kind of clap is it?!*

If we could afford it, we got B&Bs, but normally we were skint and drove back through the night or slept in the Transit. Trying to kip between the guitars and amps was crap, especially as we all smoked, so a fug filled the van. I'd cope by getting blind drunk and passing out.

But those gigs were great for us. Whether we went down well or had a rough one, we were learning. We were getting to know each other's playing better and getting tighter as a band and as mates. We were on a proper learning curve.

I was also finding myself as a singer and outgrowing my influences to develop my own voice. It was an interesting time for music. I still worshipped Plant and Gillan, but I've also always been a bit of a pop tart, and I loved a lot of what was going on in the charts.

The early seventies was the big time for glam rock, and I loved the wham-bam riffs and showmanship of it all. I liked the visual side as much as the music. I've always thought a pop star should look and dress like a pop star, and glam ticked all of those boxes.

I loved Marc Bolan and T. Rex on *Top of the Pops*, and David Bowie blew me away. Those two, plus Roxy Music, seemed to me magical, alien, and *above* everything else going on. They seemed to be pushing the envelope and I gave them some serious attention.

Not all of the glam stuff was so rarefied, and I also liked the more slapstick bands. I loved the camp side of the Sweet: strutting pop peacocks kissing the *Top of the Pops* cameras. Gary Glitter was a fun cartoon, even if subsequent events have made him impossible to listen to.

We had our own local glam-rock hero. Slade mostly came from Wolverhampton, but Noddy Holder was a Walsall lad who had grown up on the Beechdale, two streets from me. I never met him, and he moved away as Slade got famous, but I'd occasionally see his white Rolls-Royce parked on the estate when he called to see his mom.*

However, there was one band from that era that rocked my socks off more than any other, and that still does—Queen.

---

* Nearly fifty years later, I've still never met Noddy. How daft is that?! We've tried to arrange it once or twice but, so far, it's never quite happened. I hope it does—I bet we'd have a right laugh.

I first heard Queen when Alan Freeman played them on his Radio 1 show, and then Kenny Everett did the same. They sounded good, but it wasn't until I saw them on *Top of the Pops* that they blew my mind. Freddie Mercury was a god for me from the start.

It wasn't that he was gay—I didn't even realize that. I used to watch the glam groups and *wonder*. I knew that Noddy wasn't gay, and nor was Brian Connolly from the Sweet, but I wasn't sure about Bolan or Bowie. Freddie didn't even occur to me; I just thought he was a fantastic, extroverted, flamboyant performer.

I saw Queen early in their career at Birmingham Town Hall. They all wore white Zandra Rhodes outfits and they were amazing. They began with "Now I'm Here" and there was Freddie, in silhouette, in a spotlight on the left of the stage.

"Now I'm here…" he sang.

The spotlight went off, one appeared on the right of the stage—and there was Freddie, singing, in that one as well!

"Now I'm there…"

How did they do that?

Was one of them a look-alike? A cardboard cutout? Even as a former lighting man, I had no idea, but it looked brill. The spotlights alternated, with Freddie in both places…then they suddenly went out and *there he was*, center stage, belting out the song. Incredible!

Was it my Freddie fixation that shaped the outrageous thing that our manager, Corky, did next? He had organized a band photo shoot, for which Sue did me a lovely soft perm. A few days later, Corky turned up at Holy Joe's, excitedly waving individual black-and-white shots.

"Hey, I've given you all nicknames!" he announced. "It will help get us some press!"

Corky handed out the photos. Ian was now called Ian "The Skull" Hill, news that he received with his usual benign indifference. Ken had become Ken "K. K." Downing, which he seemed very taken by. Then Corky passed me my photo.

Underneath a shot of me striking an unintentionally camp pose, it said:

Rob "The Queen" Halford

What. The. Fuck?

My first reaction was to snigger, mostly with embarrassment… but I was also insulted.

"What do you think you're fucking *doing*, Corky?" I asked him.

"It's only to get us noticed!" He grinned, his eyes twinkling behind his inch-thick specs.

"Well, *that's* not the way to bloody do it!"

I was mortified, and when I took my photo home, and my dad saw it, he was livid. He went through the roof. "Tear that bloody thing up—now!" he yelled at me. Thankfully, Rob "The Queen" Halford didn't take off in the way that K. K. Downing did.

Ken has said that the rest of Judas Priest knew that I was gay right from the start of the band. As he says that, it must be true, and yet part of me is still perplexed that my orientation was so obvious to them.

In those days, gay men were represented on TV by ridiculous figures like Mr. Humphries in *Are You Being Served?* played by John Inman. They were screaming, mincing queens, camping it up and fancying the pants off every bloke; figures of fun with stupid catch-phrases like "I'm free!"*

I was nothing like that. I knew I was gay but, on the surface, I was just another Walsall bloke. I was as down-to-earth as Ken, Ian, and John. We talked on the same level and we laughed at the same stuff. We got pissed together and were just mates. I didn't feel *different.*

---

* People now deplore Mr. Humphries as an offensive stereotype but I never did. He seemed like a nice bloke, and I liked the fact all of his colleagues in the shop accepted him for what he was. Even Mrs. Slocombe.

Yet Priest clearly knew, and I am grateful that they not only never cared, but never even *mentioned* it to me. In the early seventies, that was incredibly open-minded of them—and a lot of working-class Midlands blokes would not have behaved in the same way.

Despite my affection for glam's image, my own stage look was all over the shop. I bought an outfit at the Oasis clothes market in Brum and felt sure it would make me look mysterious, like Bowie. It didn't. I looked like a cricketer in stacked heels. I can still picture Ken looking at me askance.

I had modeled many haircuts over the years—crops, perms, fringes—according to what I was into at the time, but now it felt like time to grow it longer. I was finally able to do this after I gave in my notice at Harry Fenton's.

It was just getting too hard to get home at four o'clock in the morning from Priest gigs, then drag myself into the clothes shop by nine. It was a gamble, in that I was giving up regular money for a leap in the dark, but it didn't feel like one. I wanted to make a go of the band. Full stop.

Priest continued slogging our guts out up and down the country. Corky's motormouth was still coming up with the goods, and in summer '73 he got us the support slot on a tour by Budgie, a bluesy hard rock trio from Cardiff.

We were impressed by Budgie. They were well ahead of us in that they had albums out, on a major label, and I'd seen them on TV and in *Melody Maker*. For all that, they were great guys and looked after us on the road really well.

Our trips to St. Albans were all very good, but we knew that London gigs were the Holy Grail if Priest were ever going to get anywhere. *That* was where the A&R scouts went to spot new talent, and the journos to write about it. *That* was where we needed to be.

Luckily, the Budgie tour had a big headline date—at the legendary Marquee club in Wardour Street in Soho. It was a thrill to tread the stage that Hendrix, Zep, and the Stones had played, but it was a shock to find the dressing room was a graffiti-covered cupboard. We added our name to its walls, obviously.

As well as getting us gigs, Corky was bending the ears of record label bosses as he whizzed up and down between the first and sixth floors, trying to bag us a deal. He had also managed to land himself a job—at a start-up London label called Gull Records.

Corky persuaded his boss, a guy called David Howells, to check us out at the Marquee. We went down a storm for a support act, and met Howells afterward. He was an affable guy in a suit who seemed to know what he was on about and he didn't try to bullshit us. We liked that.

Howells didn't give a lot away that night, but he did tell Corky, "I don't *mind* how they look, but I love the way they sound." We had done our bit, and all we could do was wait for his decision. In any case, we had something important to do.

Judas Priest were about to play our first foreign dates.

Corky's patter had come true and he had actually turned Priest into international artistes by fixing up two weeks of dates in Holland and Germany. We were full of anticipation on the ferry to Calais and the drive to Holland. Like any young band on their first foreign jaunt, we felt like an invading army. *We are here to rock, and to conquer!*

The shows were great, and I got the impression that European fans *understood* our music better than people at home. We were welcomed, especially in Germany, a big heavy metal country, where we got good at asking for *"Vier Eier und Pommes"*: four eggs and chips.

A few weeks later, in late March '74, we did two weeks in Norway, starting with an overnight ferry from Newcastle to Stavanger. We had no idea that we could have booked a cabin. Instead, we spent all night on deck, shivering in a North Atlantic gale, drinking ourselves stupid to stay alive. *Lovely!*

This tour was an object lesson in flying by the seat of the pants. Corky had stayed behind in the UK and was still booking the dates as we were touring. This was decades before mobile phones, so we had to follow a strange routine to find out where to go next.

Corky would give us a set time to phone him. When he picked up, he would yell, "Got a pen? Quick, here are your next three gigs!" He was working in an office now, but he was still used to blurting out his calls before someone wanted to use his phone box, or he got nicked in the lift.

One of Corky's calls to Norway was a lot more exciting than the others. One afternoon, we called him from a venue, just before soundcheck. He sounded even more manic than usual.

"Eh, lads, lads, guess what?" he gabbled. "I've got you a record deal!"

5

Not even a bloody fiver!

The deal was with Corky's new employers: Gull Records. Gull were a new, small, independent label, but they were distributed by Pye and Decca, which thrilled us because they were two of the biggest labels in the world. The thought bubbles over our heads said: *Yay! This is it! We've made it!*

Gull were offering to pay us a £2,000 advance and to put us in a studio to make our first record. Even in 1974, £2,000 was a bit stingy, but to us, it sounded like a fortune. It felt like two *million* pounds, because it meant we would get the opportunity to record *an actual album!*

When we got back from Norway, we went straight to London to sign the deal. Corky probably tried to talk us through some of the fine print, I can't remember, but all we wanted to do was cut straight to the chase: "Yeah, yeah, whatever, Corky! Where do we sign?"

Now that he was our label boss, David Howells had some…*interesting* ideas for the band. He seemed to feel that no-frills, four-piece rock groups were a bit boring, and suggested we should bring in a fifth member. Would we consider a keyboard player? A saxophonist?

We knocked those airy notions back firmly, but another of his ideas gave us some pause for thought. How about a second guitarist?

Hmm. Maybe now he was talking…

Not even a bloody fiver!

We listened to a lot of music, and one band we were all into was Wishbone Ash. They had two guitarists, Andy Powell and Ted Turner, and their twin-lead guitar harmonies sounded amazing on albums like *Argus*. Ken was a particularly big fan of their sound.

This was important. Obviously, Ken would be the band member most affected if we brought in a second guitarist, and a lot of guitarists are very territorial about their turf. But, hugely to his credit, Ken liked the idea and said he was willing to give it a go.

Which was when Corky suggested Glenn Tipton.

I didn't know Glenn personally, but I knew of him. He played guitar in a Birmingham hard rock trio called the Flying Hat Band who'd done a lot of local shows and had a strong following. I had seen them before and thought they were OK. We decided to approach him.

Ken and I went to a Flying Hat Band gig and had a good, close look. Glenn seemed a bit special. A few days later, Ken, Ian, and I were in a record shop called Wasp Records in Brum when Glenn happened to walk in. Without saying a word to Ian or me, Ken marched up to Glenn, introduced himself, and cut to the chase:

"Hello, Glenn. We're Judas Priest. We've got a record deal. Would you like to join the band?"

We had a chat with him. Glenn listened, quietly, and didn't say much. I could tell one line had piqued his interest, though: *we had a record deal*, which the Flying Hat Band didn't. He thanked us for our interest and said he'd think about it.

As it happened, the Flying Hat Band had run their course, so when Corky gave Glenn a follow-up call a few days later, he got a thumbs-up: he was in. Glenn came down to have a knock with us, hang out, and get to know us.

Background-wise, Glenn was a bit different from us. Where we were all council-estate lads, he came from a nice part of Birmingham and was more middle-class. He seemed like a thoughtful guy, slightly apart, who kept his cards close to his chest.

We all got on, though, and musically it worked from the start. Glenn was palpably a super-talented guitarist, and when he and Ken started riffing together, it instantly took Priest to another level. It gave us so much more heft, and propulsion, and urgency. It was spectacular.

Suddenly, we sounded really fucking exciting.

We got a chance to get used to each other as we spent June touring Britain with Thin Lizzy and our old muckers, Budgie. Lizzy had had a big hit a while earlier with "Whiskey in the Jar" but were easy-going and friendly. I thought they were a cracking band and the tour was a real buzz.

Then it was time to go into the studio and make an album. David Howells had booked us into Basing Street, the West London studio that had been set up by Island Records founder Chris Blackwell. He had also set us up with a producer: Rodger Bain.

Rodger was a quite a big-name producer and, initially at least, we were in awe of him. He had produced the first three Black Sabbath albums, as well as a couple of Budgie records, and was very well established as a heavy metal producer.

It was quite intimidating, as was being in Basing Street, which was a proper top-of-the-range professional studio. It looked like the fucking Starship Enterprise off *Star Trek*. But Rodger was a chill bloke, willing to listen to our ideas, and we gradually relaxed into the environment.

We were making the album in, let's say, *challenging* circumstances. Gull couldn't afford to pay for daytime sessions in Basing Street, so we were on the night shift, beginning work at eight at night when the bigger bands with major deals cleared out. We'd record until the sun came up. We were *vampires*.

We couldn't even afford coffins to rest our vampire heads in. We had no money for B&Bs, so had to crash in our Transit outside the studio. It was a blazing hot summer's week, and Notting Hill is a lively, noisy part of London, so we didn't get a lot of sleep.

I was feeling the pressure inside the studio, far more than I ever had playing live. At first, I got into this daft mindset where I felt panicky whenever the red light came on to show we were recording. *This is it!* I'd think to myself. *Now or never! I only get one go!*

This was daft, as we could always do retakes, but I hated doing those, with Rodger and the other Priest lads staring at me from behind the studio glass. It made me feel a failure—although I think a lot of musicians feel that way their first time in the studio.

One good thing was that Glenn was an experienced songwriter from his Flying Hat Band days and had lots of ideas. He quickly joined up with me and Ken, and we fit into a nice groove as the group's songwriting team.*

I was pulling lyrics out of the air. I was pleased with "Run of the Mill," a song about an old man looking back on having lived a mediocre life. I was pretty hard on the poor old codger, really:

> What have you achieved now you're old?
> Did you fulfill ambition, do as you were told?

Now, I wonder: *Where did those words come from, written by a kid of twenty-two?* I think I was probably scared of doing the same thing and letting life pass me by, as I saw so many people doing every day.

"Dying to Meet You" was another angry number. It was a song about the futility of war and the legalized murders committed in its name, written from a very pacifist, hippy perspective:

> Killer, killer, you keep your thoughts at bay,
> Maiming, destroying every day…

Musically, because heavy metal was so new, we felt as if we were creating it from the ground up. We knew we were in the same club

---

* Glenn was less impressive in Basing Street when he accidentally tipped a pint of beer into a Steinway grand piano! If they'd found out, and made us pay for the damage, it would have bankrupted us.

as Purple, and Zeppelin, and Sabbath, but we wanted our own identity. We were pushing hard toward the sound we had in our heads.

Rodger Bain was a laid-back bloke, and maybe he was a little *too*
laid-back, because on the last night, as we raced to get everything
done, he was fast asleep. He was snoring on a sofa. It was dawn and
the birds were cheeping outside when he came to, sat up, and asked
us, "Are you finished?"

"Yeah, we think so," we told him.

"Right, I'd better go and cut it, then," he said, and sauntered
upstairs.

We looked at each other, flabbergasted. We thought mastering
an LP was a long, careful process, not something you woke up and
knocked off in an hour? Still, Rodger had pedigree. *He must know
what he is doing.* We got in the van and headed back to Walsall.

The album was a disappointment in many ways. We didn't like
the title, *Rocka Rolla*, but that was the name of the first single off it
and, in those days, that was how it worked. We *definitely* didn't like
the cover, a spoof of the Coca-Cola logo on a bottle top. It looked
shit, and not at all heavy metal.

But the biggest disappointment was how the album *sounded.*
When we played it back, it felt weak and diluted. It didn't sound like
the record we'd thought we were making. We had gone for it in the
studio, with me screaming away, and Ken and Glenn firing out riffs
like bullets from dual machine guns. But Rodger's production had
lost that power and left it sounding…tepid.

It was still exciting to have an album out. I remember my
solitary vinyl copy (cheers, Gull!) arriving in the post at Kelvin
Road. I was chuffed to see how proud Mom and Dad were to hold
it in their hands. I was proud, too…but it still felt like a missed
opportunity.

This impression was confirmed when the album died on its

arse. It didn't so much get released as it *escaped* into the rock world. It made absolutely no impression on the charts and got virtually no airplay.

We did a handful of interviews and a fat lot of good they did us. A review in *Sounds* said, "Don't give up the day job," which was unfortunate, as I already had. One female interviewer arrived convinced that we were called Judith Priest. Maybe she was expecting to meet an earnest female singer-songwriter?

In all the interviews, the questions were flat and boring: *Where did you get your name? Who are your influences?* Within Priest, we quickly coined a dismissive new nickname for music journalists: *wrist merchants*. We even had a very expressive hand gesture that went with it!

It was also time for a major life change for me as I said *au revoir* (not in a yam-yam accent) to the Beechdale Estate. Sue had already left to move in with Ian in Meynell House, and here was I, twenty-two and still living with Mom and Dad. It was time to go.

My opportunity came via a mate, Nick, who roadied for the band. He lived in a shared house on Larchwood Road on the Yew Tree Estate, five miles away toward Birmingham, and mentioned that they had a spare room going.

"Oh, really? Do you think *I* could live there?" I asked.

"Yeah, as long as you pay your rent!"

Nick was a nurse at the local hospital in West Bromwich, and the other two rooms were also rented by nurses: Denise and Michael. We were four single people in our early twenties and we liked caning it—drinking to excess. It quickly became a full-on party house.

We all thought we were apart from straight society, *man*, so we made the place as bohemian as possible. In Walsall in 1974, that meant scatter cushions and beanbags (chairs were bourgeois!) and sleeping on a mattress on the floor, to be close to the earth. The house always stank of joss sticks and patchouli.

Nick and Michael were both gay. They weren't out (because nobody *was*, in those days) and we never discussed it, but the three of us knew we were all gay. Even though it went unspoken between us, it felt reassuring: *Phew, I've actually got some mates who are like me!*

Nick and Michael took me to my first-ever gay bar. It was at the Grosvenor House Hotel on the Hagley Road in Birmingham and was a very classy joint, all plush red-velvet drapes and guys discreetly hooking up. I didn't meet anybody, but I was very impressed with the place.

They also took me to a livelier gay bar called the Nightingale in an area of Birmingham called (now, don't laugh!) Camp Hill. And that was where I met Jason.

He was sitting with some friends in a small food area of the bar when I clocked him. He was a good-looking guy, and I waited until he was on his own before I plucked up the courage to go over and introduce myself. We were both fairly sober and had a good chat.

We arranged to meet up again, and slowly, over a few meet-ups, we became an item. He was a cool guy—quite masculine but also a bit of a hippy, very much into Monet, growing wildflowers, and, more than anything, Barbra Streisand.

Jason and I had a very easy relationship. He didn't like rock or heavy metal, but we had enough in common to like each other's company. He wasn't a drinker or smoker, and we were skint, so we didn't go out much. Mostly we stayed home, watched TV…and listened to Barbra Streisand albums.

Jason had to be a secret, of course. My housemates knew about us, but I wouldn't have *dreamed* of introducing him to my family or the band. It just felt nice to be with somebody, and it made being gay make a bit more sense: *Ah, OK, now THIS is what it could be like!*

We had a very comfortable relationship, but I'm not sure we were ever all that serious about each other. I never went to his home—I think he still lived with his mom and dad. He'd stay over with me at the Yew Tree but our sex, such as it was, was no more than fumbling.

Not even a bloody fiver!

I saw Jason for months, maybe a year, and then we just… fizzled out. There was no big scene—I don't think we had a cross word in our entire time together. It was no great passionate affair, but at least it taught me what it could be like to have a boyfriend.

A *partner*.

In the autumn of '74, Judas Priest went out on the road to promote *Rocka Rolla*. There were highlights. We made a return trip to the Marquee, as well as playing the prestigious Barbarella's in Birmingham.

It was a tour tinged with disappointment that the album had done so badly. When we returned to mainland Europe at the start of '75, we eagerly visited every local record store, hoping to find *Rocka Rolla* nestling in the racks. We never saw it once.

What the fuck were Gull playing at?

This was a European jaunt that had more than its fair share of mishaps—including Ian and me very nearly freezing to death in an ice storm in Germany. It is not a tale for the faint-hearted.

By now, we had flogged the Transit and managed to get a second-hand Mercedes tour van. It was a definite upgrade…until a bitter February afternoon when John Hinch was valiantly trying to drive us through a blizzard, with the temperature outside down to −25°F.

We were on our way to a gig in Stuttgart, but trouble in the Middle East meant there was an oil embargo, so only heavy goods trucks and working vehicles were allowed on the autobahns. The road was like an ice rink as we inched through snowdrifts at 20 miles per hour.

It was so cold that the diesel froze in the engine. The van did one last slide across the sheet of ice and stopped dead. *Fuck! NOW what do we do?*

Ken, Glenn, and John bravely volunteered to be Captain Oates and step out into the subzero temperatures in search of help. Ian and I stayed behind in the van to look after the gear and wait for them.

They were gone for bloody yonks—forever. Ian and I started off sitting in the front, staring at the snowstorm around us. It got too cold to bear, so we crawled into the back of the van and buried ourselves under mountains of blankets on a couple of mattresses.

Hours went by. Then more hours. We had nothing to eat or drink and were nearing hypothermia. We passed out and slept. When I came to, it was like waking up in an igloo. Frost crystals sparkled inside the van. I looked at Ian, still asleep. His long hair was frozen solid across his face.

Where the hell were they? Had they perished in the storm?

Ian woke up, we crawled back into the front of the van… and then we saw them. Three silhouettes appeared on the snowy horizon, staggering back toward us. And they seemed to be carrying items. Was it…a box? And a bottle?

Ken, Glenn, and John opened the door and fell into the van. They stank of booze, and were carrying a bottle of Scotch and a box of chocolates.

"We found a hippy café!" Ken happily explained. "The people in there were really cool—it was bostin'! They gave us some food, then we had a few drinks and a bit of a party. I think we fell asleep …and then it was morning! Anyroad, here we are! A mechanic is on the way! You two been OK?"

He should have been grateful we didn't throttle him.

I was blameless in that instance, but our next grisly moment on that tour was very much down to me—or, rather, to my troublesome arse. It was not, in truth, my finest moment.

We were driving through Amsterdam. I was dying for a crap, and one thing about the Netherlands, great country that it is, is that there are never any public toilets to be found. I was touching cloth and, as we say in Walsall, *when you've gorra gew, you've gorra gew*! I took emergency measures.

Not even a bloody fiver!

As Hinchy drove along, I crawled into the back of the van, where I saw a manila envelope. I crouched over it and silently pooed into the top. Luckily, it was a whistler, where you don't even need toilet paper. It shot out like an Olympic sprinter from the starting line.

Well, great...except that I was now in the delicate situation of holding a manila envelope full of my own shit. I crawled back up to the front of the van, wound down the window, and discreetly lobbed the package into one of Amsterdam's famous canals.

Maybe the rest of the band wouldn't notice what I'd done? Fat chance! They were on to me as my rotten stink suddenly filled the van. "Ugh, Rob, you dirty bastard!" they moaned, as my poo floated happily up the 'Dam.

We made our first TV appearance on that tour, in Ostend (yet again!). It was a family variety show, and Corky wangled it by telling the producers we were like Cliff Richard and the Shadows. We blasted out "Never Satisfied" to an audience of smartly dressed, middle-aged Belgians who didn't know what had hit them.

A far more exciting television break came back in England, when we were invited to appear on *The Old Grey Whistle Test*. I'd religiously watched BBC 2's weekly music show since my early teens. It focused on albums, rather than *Top of the Pops'* glittery fixation with the singles chart, and seemed more *serious* about what it covered and how it covered it.

We had assumed we'd go down to London to film our appearance at BBC Television Centre in White City. I was looking forward to this, as I was dying to meet the show's legendary presenter, "Whispering" Bob Harris, who always talked as if he was sharing a sacred secret.

So, I was disappointed when Corky told me we were doing our bit at the Beeb's Pebble Mill Studios in Brum. We arrived to find lengths of carpet draped over the speaker stacks to keep the noise levels of that awful *loud* heavy metal music down.

Our first instinct was to remove the rugs. No chance! The unions ruled the roost back then, and we weren't allowed to touch a thing. A cardboard box stood on a nearby table, with a piece of paper advising the production staff to:

GET YOUR EAR PLUGS HERE

I was going on British telly for the first time and I didn't have a *clue* what to wear. So, I rummaged through Sue's clothes and borrowed a pleated pink blouse with a belt, which I wore with a pair of spangly black flares. I looked like Jim Morrison on a budget.

We didn't coordinate our look. Ken wore a vivid paisley shirt that Carol had made him with tight, flared loon pants, and a white fedora. Ian was all in white, like an emaciated Jesus. We looked like three bands in one: a tin of heavy metal Quality Street.

We did two songs. Gull made us play the title track from *Rocka Rolla*, and we did "Dreamer Deceiver," a wistful, Zeppelin-like six-minute prog number with a line about "purple hazy clouds" that paid tribute to Hendrix. It was a big, serious song, so I unbuttoned my—sorry, Sue's—blouse and let rip.

It was over in no time but I enjoyed doing it, and the modern miracle of YouTube means you can still see our immortal performance today. There I am, posing in Sue's shiny top, staring at the cameras through twin curtains of hair (ah, those were the days!).

I hated watching my performance back, though. As a performer, you expose a very intimate side of yourself, and whenever I had to watch a recording of myself performing, I would always think: *Should I really be doing this?* Even today, I can't stand watching myself on telly.

The good part about seeing the final program was that there was good old Whispering Bob, buck-toothed, bearded, and earnest as ever, murmuring "Judas Priest, there!" in a voice like a slight breeze two miles away. At least he never called us Judith.

We toured all through that summer of '75, from Cleethorpes Winter Gardens to the Nags Head in High Wycombe—the staples of the beer-and-bands seventies rock circuit. Despite having no cash, we tried to introduce an element of spectacle to our live show.

I wanted to strut around stage with a microphone without having to hold the mic itself, so I took a broomstick, painted it red, filed it down, and glued the microphone clip to the top. *Voilà!* A mic-holding posing stick! I stuck little rectangular mirrors to it with Bostik, like Noddy Holder's hat on *Top of the Pops*. It took me hours.

We also experimented with rudimentary dry ice, made with zero regard for health and safety from smoke bombs from the Army & Navy Store. A mate called Kosha, who sometimes helped out as a roadie, would light a tray of powder behind John's drums and waft the smoke across the stage.

Ken's pride and joy at the time was the white fedora hat he'd worn on TV, which even had its own box to travel with us in the van. At one gig, I suddenly heard Ken shouting furiously mid-song, and glanced around to see him bawling his head off at Kosha.

Kosha was using Ken's fedora to fan the gas across the stage. Like all good roadies, he hadn't washed his hands for a few days. They were grimy, and Ken's usually pristine hat now looked very stained and crumpled. I tried to keep a straight face. I failed.

It was during this run of gigs that we got the highly surprising news that we were to play the Reading Festival.

This appearance came about by a rather left-field route, and I have to tell this story very carefully. At a northern show on the tour, a mate who had come with us met a guy in the crowd who said the promoters of Reading Festival had asked him to recommend good new bands. It wasn't until we were driving home in the van after the gig that our friend admitted they had clinched a deal in the venue bogs (toilets).

"Guess what? You're playing Reading Festival," he told us.

What? We were stunned, amazed, incredulous, and the van filled with whoops and cheers. "How did you manage *that?*" one of us asked him, when the noise had died down.

"The bloke said that if I'd let him give me a blow job, you could play Reading. So, I did!"

Ahem. Ah well, I suppose you get your breaks any way you can... even via a casting couch!

I immediately became obsessed with what I would wear for Reading and went out and sourced an outfit. After we'd met in a club, I had got friendly with a fashion designer called Fid, who lived in a bedsit (a rented room) opposite Malcolm McLaren and Vivienne Westwood's shop, Sex, on the King's Road in London. I'd go down and crash on her couch.

Fid made clothes for Rod Stewart and Elton John and she designed a corker for me. I've always liked the idea of rock musicians being like medieval minstrels—*heavy metal minstrels!*—traveling from town to town, and I'd found a picture in a book of a medieval lute player in a long-sleeved jerkin. I asked Fid to replicate it.

She made me a fantastic red jerkin and a pair of black-and-gold-striped trousers. Reading Festival would not know what had hit it.*

I had the idea to use a family heirloom as a finishing touch. Dad had a lovely old silver-topped walking cane that had belonged to his grandad. I could imagine myself twirling it around as I flounced around the big festival stage, so I asked if I could borrow it.

"What do you want it for?" he asked.

"Just for a stage prop, Dad."

He looked at me, considering.

"Yeah, go on then. But don't break it!"

Reading Festival was ace. We opened the bill on the first day on the main stage, going on in bright sunshine at two in the afternoon. I hated playing in the daytime—I still do—but the adrenaline was kicking in big-time and I went for it.

---

* Fid also made me a pair of...well, the only thing to call them is hairy trousers. She assured me they'd be the next big thing, but I looked like a bear from the waist down. I never dared to wear them.

Actually, it wasn't just adrenaline. I'd necked a few drinks in the tatty old backstage caravan we got given as a dressing room, and was tipsy when we got onstage. That was why, under a cloudless, bright blue sky, I greeted the crowd with "Good evening!"

The Dutch courage worked a treat as I pirouetted around the stage in Fid's flamboyant ensemble, bare-chested and waving Dad's cane as if conducting an invisible orchestra. We went down great and got a lot of raucous cheers. We made a lot of friends that day.

Again, the wonders of YouTube mean this Priest performance is preserved for posterity. Now, forty-five years on, it looks bonkers. A guy in the crowd shot it on Super 8, and the cine film is so jumpy that I am jerking around stage like a pantomime dame on crack. Which was about right.

I was desperate to make an impression. Toward the end of our set, for no reason, I began berating the crowd, who were warmly applauding us: "You might enjoy this one, if you can be bothered to take the needles out of your arms!" *Huh? What do they say about the arrogance of youth?*

After our set, I carried on drinking and got paralytic. I stayed pissed the whole weekend as we partied hard and watched groups like UFO, Hawkwind, Wishbone Ash, and Yes. Sharing backstage space with bands that I had idolized and read about for years was amazing.

This is it! I thought. *This is where we want to be!*

The festival had one downside. Like a dickhead, I spent the weekend posing with Dad's cane. One night, I had a row with someone, and in my drunken rage I smashed the cane, hard, against a caravan door. It snapped in two.

Oh, fucking hell! I thought. *NOW what have I done?* I dreaded breaking the news to Dad. When I did, he just sighed and looked disappointed. I felt worse than if he had bollocked me.

Yet after Reading, we felt as if we had grown massively in that one performance. We were used to playing pubs, dive bars, and little clubs, but now we had rocked a huge festival crowd. We were inching into the big time.

When I wasn't on the road with Priest, I was getting used to life in my new home on the Yew Tree Estate. It was a fucking hoot. There was a lot of drinking—mostly vodka and tonics—and a lot of spliff-smoking in Larchwood Road. I had never been much of a dopehead, but soon I found myself getting partial.

We threw a cracking party with a theme of "Dare to Be Different." We told all our mates to come in mad fancy dress, the crazier the better—and it had to be in some way *different*. I hired a policeman's outfit: helmet, uniform, truncheon, handcuffs, whistle. But it wasn't really *different*. It was just dressing up as a copper.

So, I accessorized . . . with frilly knickers, black lacy tights, and a towering pair of stilettos. I have to say, I was very pleased with the end result. And the party was bedlam.

The Yew Tree was a peaceful estate and most of the houses on Larchwood Road had a car outside, which meant that our mates couldn't find anywhere to park. There was a lot of honking of horns and shouting as they drove around and around.

Already pissed, I thought: *Who could resolve this situation better than a traffic policeman?* So, I ran outside, in my copper's uniform, lacy tights, and six-inch heels, and began directing traffic and blowing my whistle. Every net curtain in the street was twitching.

Once the party got going, dope smoke filled the house. I didn't know the spliffs were homegrown. Nick was growing cannabis plants in our greenhouse.

I had no idea until the day I found him drying them out in the oven. "What you cooking, mate?" I asked him. "It smells like a joint!"

"I'm doing my gardening," he grinned. And *then* the penny dropped.

At first, I was worried because growing marijuana was a serious crime and we could all have gone to jail. But the boys in blue never knocked on our door (in stilettos or otherwise) and I grew fond of our line of supply being so convenient.

Nick loved his spliff. He liked connecting a lump of hash to the two wires of a car battery and putting it inside a big hospital bell jar with a hole in the top to make a giant bong. He'd light the dope, the jar would fill with smoke, and he'd stick a straw in the hole and inhale the lot in one go. He'd never even cough. I rarely dared try it—and when I did, I choked and spluttered like a consumptive.

Because Denise, Nick, and Michael were hospital nurses, they would often be on call even if we were sitting at home relaxing. One Saturday night at about two in the morning, we were all sprawled around the front room drinking and smoking joints when the phone rang.

Denise answered it. It was the hospital. "We've got to go in," she told the other two. "There's been a road accident and they've got to do some operations." As they sighed and staggered up from their beanbags, I must have looked disappointed that our night was over.

Denise looked at me. "You can come with us if you like, Rob?" she suggested.

"Yeah, OK then!"

I was buzzing on the way there, from the joints, the booze, and the excitement. *What would I see?* When we got there, they showed me how to scrub up, gave me a uniform, including a surgical mask, and led me into the operating theater.

I stood in a corner as they helped the surgeon try to save the leg of a car-crash victim. It was mangled and all folded back on itself and yet I didn't feel squeamish at all. *I love that stuff.* Whenever the BBC had TV shows that broadcast operations, I watched them avidly.

I stood alone, swaying slightly, fascinated by what I was seeing.

The surgeon spotted me—I suppose pissed, stoned strangers stand out in an operating theater—and asked, "Who's that?" When Denise said, "Oh, he's with us," he ignored me and got on with saving the guy's leg.

The *Rocka Rolla* tour had gone great, but there was no denying that the album had been a flop—and, worst of all, we were skint.

That £2,000 advance had long gone and the money coming in from record sales wasn't even a trickle. I had spent my savings from Harry Fenton's. I flogged off my precious record collection to my mates, and some of the band found cash-in-hand work to pay the rent.

Ken got a weird part-time job in a factory where he clocked in, played cards, and never had to do anything. Ian built office furniture for £5 a day. Glenn sold Mr. Sizzle hot dogs outside Birmingham Town Hall. I bumped into him there once. The stingy git didn't even give me a free sausage.

It was rubbish, and we decided to talk to Gull and see if they would put us on a weekly wage. They had had a windfall that summer—a number one single called "Barbados," a cod-reggae kids' song by a duo called Typically Tropical, so we hoped they might be flush and able to help us.

We got in the van, drove down to London, met David Howells in his office in Carnaby Street, and made our pitch.

"If you could give each of us a fiver a week, that would be amazing," we told him. "It would only be £25 a week. We can live off that, just about, and it will give us more time to write songs, rehearse, do gigs, and commit to the band."

"Sorry, lads," Howells told us. "I can't do it. We just don't have the money." And that was that.

They couldn't even spare a bloody fiver. We couldn't believe it.

We grumbled in the van halfway back to Brum, then just sat there in gloomy silence.

Not even a bloody fiver.

The only saving grace was that Gull didn't want to drop us after the failure of *Rocka Rolla,* and stumped up the cash for a second album. It was the same terms as the first: £2,000 up front. By now, we knew this was rubbish—we called the Gull deal "four-fifths of five-eighths of fuck all!"—but it was Hobson's choice.

Before we went back into the studio, we knew we needed a change in the band's lineup. We were developing musically, and we wanted a more adventurous drummer to complement what we were doing. We didn't think John Hinch was up to it.

Rehearsals had got frustrating. "John, mate, can you try something a bit different?" we'd ask, as he pounded out the same old rhythms. "Maybe try it like *this*? Or *this*?" John was trying his best, but he just wasn't doing what we wanted or, if I am honest, sounding like he ever would.

It was a shame to lose John, because I'd been with him ever since Hiroshima. A band is like a family. Yet, ultimately, the music comes first. We knew we had to do it. Glenn drew the short straw, and drove over to Hinchy's house in Lichfield to break the bad news.

Glenn returned with quite a tale. He hadn't told John in advance that he was coming so, when he knocked on the door, John was surprised to see him: "Hello, Glenn! What are you doing here?"

"I need to have a word with you," Glenn said.

Glenn said that, at this point, John's face suddenly dropped and he looked shocked, as if he knew what was coming. He must have done because, as Glenn stepped into the house, John ran upstairs, without saying a word, to compose himself.

When he came back down, a couple of minutes later, Glenn gave it to him straight: "I'm sorry, but I've got bad news. You've been voted out of the band."

John was good at carpentry, and he had made a nifty little box to keep some of the band's cables in when we were on the road. It was lying on the floor in his lounge. As soon as Glenn broke the bad news, John began booting the box around the room.

"Well, you're not having *this*, then!" he told Glenn. He gave the cables box a few hefty kicks against the skirting board, burst into tears, and ran back upstairs. Glenn could hear him sobbing. "Er, I'm going now, John!" he shouted from the hall, and made a quick exit.

It was a sad story, and I felt upset for John when I heard it. It's crap getting kicked out of a band.

We needed to find a quick replacement and, luckily, one was at hand: Alan "Skip" Moore, an early Priest drummer from before my time, stepped back in. I had never met Skip* but he was a great guy, chill and laid-back, and he slotted in seamlessly.

OK. Now it was time for that second album—at which point, we were given some bombshell news. David Howells informed us that he wanted the record to be produced by…Typically Tropical, who had had Gull's novelty reggae number one that summer!

Initially, we were outraged by this mad suggestion. *We're a heavy metal band! We don't play fucking Caribbean joke-pop!* But when we calmed down, we realized it made more sense than we had thought.

Typically Tropical were actually two studio producers and engineers called Max West and Jeffrey Calvert. When we met them in Rockfield Studios in Monmouthshire in Wales, where we were to record the album, they leveled with us.

Max and Jeffrey confessed they knew nothing about metal, but said they knew how to make an album technically: where to put the mics, how to work the mixing desk, and so on. That's fine, we said, because *we know* how we want to sound.

Rockfield was a live-in studio and we stayed there as we made

---

* I've no idea why we called Alan Moore "Skip." He was a really solid drummer and I never heard him skip a beat!

Sad Wings of Destiny. We never left the complex: we had no money to go anywhere. When we switched to Morgan Studios, in London, to mix the record, Gull gave us 50p a day to spend in the studio canteen. *50p! We felt like Oliver Twist!* We could only afford one meal a day.

Yet making the album was a great experience. Max and Jeffrey were good guys, true to their word, and they let us shape the sound of the album. I felt far more confident in the studio than I had doing *Rocka Rolla*, and was pleased with the vocals I was laying down.

I worked hard at my lyrics. I hated how so many heavy rock songs were about getting drunk, or fucking women: lame, predictable stuff. I was reading a lot of sci-fi, by writers like Isaac Asimov, and I loved incorporating that influence into songs like "Island of Domination."

We came up with a couple of belting songs. "Victim of Change" is still one of the most popular Priest numbers of all, yet it had a very strange birth. We had two songs knocking around—"Whiskey Woman," a Priest song from before my time, and one I'd just written called "Red Light Lady."

We were jamming on them both but neither felt quite right. "Why don't we take bits from each song and stick them together?" Glenn suggested.

"Eh? We can't do *that*!" I said. "They're two separate songs!" But we did, and it sounded great.

One day in the studio, a package arrived from Gull with a single that David Howells wanted us to cover on the album. It was "Diamonds and Rust," a song about Bob Dylan that had been a big US hit early that year for American folk singer Joan Baez.

We fell about. *Are they having a laugh? We're Judas fucking Priest! This ain't us!* Then we sat down, listened to it closely, and realized it was a brilliant, sensitive song. "OK," we decided. "Let's show them what we can do with this…" In the end, the song didn't make it onto the album—it didn't fit the mood, so we kept it back for future use.

When we played *Sad Wings of Destiny* back, we were delighted with it. And it bore a very important credit: "Co-produced by Judas Priest." It's a credit we have had on every single album since.

We had just finished recording *Sad Wings of Destiny*, and I was back on the Yew Tree Estate just before Christmas 1975 when I saw a TV film that absolutely knocked me backward.

The Naked Civil Servant was a dramatized biography starring John Hurt as Quentin Crisp, a flamboyant homosexual who had emerged from a suburban British upbringing to become a male model, rent boy, and Oscar Wilde–like socialite and *bon viveur*. He never hid his sexuality and was beaten up almost daily.

This film captured the trauma, pain, heartache, and defiant joy of his life, and I watched transfixed by his honesty and courage. *To be gay so openly!* It seemed unthinkable, and a million miles from my own limited existence.

Quentin's liking for straight guys and men in uniform mirrored a few stirrings I could already feel in me, and *The Naked Civil Servant* was full of unforgettable lines. My favorite was his description of why he never reacted to the gay-bashings meted out to him: "Love is never closing your hand. Love is never making a fist."

In 1976, Ian Hill became my brother-in-law. He and Sue married in a church in Bloxwich. In those days, stag dos were the night before the wedding, and Ian's was a riot. We went to a club called Bogart's in Birmingham. Skip got so drunk that he fell asleep in the bog. We never noticed.

Skip woke up in the early hours to find the club shut and in darkness. He tried to force his way out, set off the alarm, and got nicked by the police, who thought he was breaking *in*! He spent the night in the cells and missed the wedding.

I was Ian's best man, but I remember little about the day except having a stinking hangover and wearing a kipper tie. I bottled out of making my best man's speech—turns out I find it easier prancing around onstage than making a speech at a wedding!

Thanks to stuff like *The Old Grey Whistle Test* and the Reading Festival, Judas Priest's name was steadily growing. When *Sad Wings of Destiny* came out in spring '76, it squeezed into the album chart...at number forty-eight, for one week. It was hardly an earth-shattering triumph but it *was* a confidence boost: *"Fucking hell! We're in the charts!"*

We toured the arse off that album through that year's long, hot summer. The gigs were great, as they always were by now, but we were still broke and we all felt as if something needed to happen. We had gone as far as we could with Gull—so what the hell did we do now?

Luckily, an answer quickly presented itself. Because Judas Priest were about to get ourselves a proper, grown-up, major-label record deal.

6

Superman in a fur coat

We knew we were stagnating with Gull and Corky. The label didn't have the resources or ideas to move us forward, and while we were grateful for everything that Corky had done for us with his wide boy antics, he didn't feel like the man to take us to the next level.

We needed a break…and it came surprisingly easily. Glenn knew a Birmingham guy named David Hemmings, who had a new job at a London management agency, Arnakata. Hemmings and his bosses came to see us play, and Arnakata agreed to take Priest on. It was hard to break the news to Corky. He didn't take it at all well.

Arnakata was run by two brothers with different surnames— Mike Dolan and Jim Dawson. That seemed a bit odd to me, and nor was I entirely convinced that Arnakata *got* metal, or were steeped enough in the music to know what we were doing.

Still, they clearly had the contacts, clout, and professionalism we had lacked until then. They knew an A&R man, Robbie Blanchflower, at CBS Records, who liked what we were doing and recommended us upward to his chairman, Maurice "Obie" Oberstein.

Obie was an American guy who was later to become a music-industry legend. He came to see Priest play a gig in Southampton and liked us enough to offer us a deal. He seemed to think we were punk rockers, though, telling David Hemmings: "I was surprised I didn't get spat at!"

Unfortunately, Gull were as angry as Corky over our departure and refused to let us buy back the rights to our two albums with them. Arnakata and CBS both tried to negotiate with them on our behalf and got nowhere.

In subsequent years, we went back to David Howells many times, offering more and more money for *Rocka Rolla* and *Sad Wings of Destiny*, but the answer was always a flat no. It's a shame: those first two albums are an important part of Priest history, and are totally out of our control.

Once we had signed the deal with CBS, we knew we were dealing with the big boys now. Where Gull had advanced us £2,000 for each of those first two records, CBS handed us £60,000 to make the follow-up. *Ker-ching!*

In truth, £60,000 probably wasn't all that exceptional for a five-man band recording an album in an expensive, top-of-the-range studio, but to us it felt like a small fortune. It also gave us a big confidence boost that a major label was willing to spend so much on us.

Yet we also felt that we deserved it. Bands hit their stride as they make their third album and, by now, we knew what we were about and we were in tune with our abilities. We were a tight unit, and Glenn particularly was introducing some good new musical ideas.

So, we were on a high as we went into Ramport Studios in south London at the start of 1977 to make the album that was to become *Sin After Sin*... not least because of the identity of the producer.

CBS had fixed us up with Roger Glover, the former bassist with one of our favorite bands, Deep Purple, and the man who had come up with the title for "Smoke on the Water." His first task was to help us solve a personnel issue.

Alan Moore had done an OK job on *Sad Wings of Destiny*, but we still weren't totally satisfied. This meant we were going into our third album without a drummer. Roger Glover got us out of that predicament by fixing us up with a young prodigy named Simon Phillips. Simon was basically a session player, but he was a truly brilliant drummer who would twig exactly what we wanted at the start of each song and nail it first go. He was also likable, level-headed, and a dream to work with, despite being only fifteen years old.

"Would you like me to try that again?" Simon would ask, after turning in yet another faultless first take on a track. "No, you're all right, mate, that was fine!" we'd tell him. Simon was by a long way the most mature musician—and human being—in that studio.

We started the *Sin After Sin* sessions quite in awe of Roger Glover and feeling privileged to have the chance to work with him. Within a week, we had sacked him.

It wasn't Roger's fault. He was doing nothing wrong, but after coproducing *Sad Wings of Destiny* with Typically Tropical, we felt that we knew how to capture the band's sound better than anyone else. Glenn was particularly exercised on this subject.

Well, maybe we didn't know as much as we thought we did, because after we had farted around ineffectually in the studio for three or four weeks, we had to ask Roger if he would come back and take the reins again. We were lucky that he was not a man to bear a grudge.

Once Roger was back in place and coproducing with us, we hit our stride. I was determined to write my best lyrics yet for this album…a resolution that initially led to Roger forming a wrong impression of me.

When I wasn't recording vocals, I was low-profile in the studio and usually sitting on my own in the corner, studying hard from a book. Roger was obviously curious, and after a few days he wandered over to have a word with me.

"You're very engrossed in that book, Rob," he noted. "Is it a… Bible?"

"Hardly!" I laughed, showing him the book. "It's *Roget's Thesaurus!*" Roger looked pretty relieved.

Mr. Roget and I were coming up trumps. I have always been keen to widen my songwriting vocabulary and still have that same tome today. I was pleased with my lyrics on *Sin After Sin*, as I honed my natural style of tackling psychological and philosophical traumas via dramatic, apocalyptic tales of gods, devils, and warriors fighting epic battles, in which Good—and heavy metal!—always vanquishes Evil.

"Sinner" was a great example of this. I love painting word pictures, and if I can be a bit poncy for a minute, I'd like to think the first lines had an almost Blakean air of flamboyant doom:

> Sinner rider, rides in with the storm,
> The devil rides beside him
> The devil is his god, God help you mourn

Yet, beyond a doubt, the most important song for me, personally, on *Sin After Sin* was "Raw Deal."

"Raw Deal" was a song about cruising gay bars on Fire Island, the hip homosexual hangout just outside New York. Not that I had been to Fire Island in my life, or cruised any gay bars besides the odd dolly bop (as we used to call dancing) in the Nightingale in Birmingham. It came (im)purely from my lustful imagination:

> All eyes hit me as I walked into the bar
> Them steely leather guys were fooling with the denim dudes
> A coupla colts played rough stuff
> New York, Fire Island

I thought it was completely overt and obvious, a bald statement of my sexual need for "heavy bodies ducking, stealing, eager for some action." Yet the song also had a hard, dark edge. Its grim last line concluded that life was just a "goddamn, rotten, steaming, raw deal."

"Raw Deal" was a coming-out song, a vent of my angst as a gay man in the closet. I thought I might have gone too far, and people would pick up on the lyrics and put two and two together. It could open doors for me, or, more likely, slam them shut in my face.

Yet…nothing happened. The band said nothing about the words—they have always had tremendous respect for my lyrics and left them to me—and probably thought I was just telling a story. Nor did critics or fans notice anything. It was a howl of rage that nobody heard.

I didn't know if I was disappointed or relieved.

If that was a howl of rage, "Here Come the Tears" was a cry for help. Glenn and I wrote this gentle, bruised song, and it was cathartic for me as I poured out my lonely heart about my compromised life:

> Once I dreamed that life would come and sweep me up away,
> Now it seems life's passed me by, I'm still alone today
> Here come the tears

Again, nobody noticed! It went completely over their heads. Critics were more interested that we had put "Diamonds and Rust," the Joan Baez cover that hadn't made it onto *Sad Wings of Destiny*, on this album.

The playback for *Sin After Sin* to the suits from CBS felt like a disaster. For reasons unknown, Roger Glover turned the volume up to eleven and hit our new corporate bosses with sheer noise. I had my hands over my ears: not a good look when you are listening to your new album!

What the fuck are you doing, Roger? I was sure that CBS would be horrified, but at the end the executives just congratulated us and said it was great. They must have wanted a roaring, full-on, heavy metal assault, and that was what we gave them.

Roger always claims he never got paid for producing the album. I have no idea why that would be, but it was nothing to do with us.

Fifty years on, he still occasionally jokingly bugs me to send him a check.

The big fear that we all had when *Sin After Sin* came out was that nobody would listen to it—because punk rock was ruling the roost. In 1977, punk was everywhere. There was nothing else in the music papers, and it seemed like nothing else mattered—including heavy metal.

That seemed dumb to me. I liked some of the punk bands, and went to see the Sex Pistols in Wolverhampton around this time. It was a secret gig, which they had to play under a pseudonym as the Spots, because venues up and down the country were banning them due to tabloid outrage.

Johnny Rotten came out and, drowned in a sea of spit, said, "I don't even know if we're going to play for you! We've got your fucking money, now you can all fuck off! We don't care!" They *did* play, and I liked them—to me, they sounded like heavy metal. But punk was very hyped. It was never going to last…and it didn't.

Johnny Rotten would have hated what I did in 1977, anyway! Ever since seeing the Queen in Walsall Arboretum when I was six, I had been an arch royalist, and I went to Windsor for her Silver Jubilee. She did a long walk from the castle through the crowds and, as ever, had a wave just for me. Or so I imagined, anyway.

When it came out, *Sin After Sin* did well. The magazines that weren't obsessing about punk liked it, and it went into the Top 30. It was a strong album, and had the promotional and marketing weight of CBS behind it, rather than some bloke making phone calls from a lift. And now, it was time to take it on the road.

Simon Phillips didn't want to come on tour with us—he probably had to do his O levels, or something—so we auditioned drummers in London. We chose a Belfast guy called Les Binks, who was a great player, easy to get on with…and could start straight away.

We rehearsed for the tour at the famous Pinewood Studios, west of London. On the first day, after we'd set up our gear, we went in search of our hotel. Around ten at night, we found ourselves in front of a Gothic Hammer Horror mansion.

Huh? Was this it?

We rang the bell…and a tiny nun opened the door. *Oops!* We began to apologize, thinking we had the wrong place, but she stopped us, and smiled: *No, we were staying here, and she'd been waiting for us.* She led us up creaky old stairways to our rooms.

The next morning, I got woken up at five o'clock by a low, humming noise. It turned out that we were staying in a convalescent home run by Swedish nuns—well, it was cheap—and they were beginning their morning chants. I heard them every day for a week.

We had breakfast with the nuns at seven each morning and dinner with them at eight every night. It was lovely grub but we were a bit intimidated by them, so we sat and ate our meals in silence. At the end of the room sat a venerable old nun. She looked about a hundred years old.

One night, she gestured toward us. "Who are they?" she asked.

"They're a musical group," one of the other nuns explained.

"They don't speak much, do they?" said the ancient nun. "Are they a bunch of bigheads?" It was a very good question.

While we were at Pinewood, they were filming the first *Superman* movie. One day, I had a gawp at the set. They were preparing to film the famous scene where Superman rescues Lois Lane when a helicopter falls from the top of the *Daily Planet* skyscraper.

I was walking back toward our sound stage when I saw something heading toward me. *Was it a bird? Was it a plane?* No, it was a huge bloke and, as he neared, I saw it was Christopher Reeve. It was cold, so he was wearing a fur coat…on top of his Superman costume.

It just blurted out of my gob: "Oh, hello, Superman!"

"Hey!" said the Man of Steel. "What's up?"

"I'm here rehearsing with my band," I told him.

"Oh, yeah? What's their name?"

"Judas Priest."

"Awesome! Well, good luck with it!"

"Thanks!" And, with that, Clark Kent strode past me to change out of his fur coat and rescue Lois Lane from a plunging chopper.

Now Priest were on a major label, our tour transport had gone up a notch. It was bye-bye stinky Mercedes van and hello to a second-hand, bright orange Volvo, which we drove to gigs while our road crew (another new addition!) went ahead in the van. Good! It all felt like progress.

Our Volvo got a chunk taken out of it one of the very first times we used it. We had been to a record-label meeting in London and Ian was driving us down Wardour Street in Soho. Glenn was chomping on a sandwich, and as we waited at traffic lights, he had had his fill.

Glenn opened his window and whanged his lunch into the street. We all watched as, seemingly in slow motion, the half-eaten sandwich arced through the air before hitting a massive biker guy in the back of the neck. The biker spun around and glared at us.

The lights changed. "Go, go!" we yelled at Ian as we sped away. We were laughing, thinking we'd got away with it, but a minute later— *shit!*—the biker was alongside, snarling at us, and smashing the Volvo with a metal chain. The big dent he put in the boot never came out.

The British dates went well and we were playing—and selling out—bigger venues. Headlining Birmingham Town Hall was a highlight, as was the Apollo Victoria Theatre in London. Yet we were counting down to June and an almost unbelievably exciting prospect. We were going to America.

Even on the flight over, I couldn't believe it was happening. I'd been enamored with America ever since I was a boy: the music, the movies, the iconography, the very *idea* of the place. It felt beyond a dream that I was actually going there.

The drive from JFK Airport into Manhattan blew my mind. There were all the sights I'd gawped at on TV all of my life: the towering skyscrapers, the beeping yellow taxis, the steam billowing up from the drains in the sidewalks. I felt like I had walked into a movie.

New York in '77 was more tense, brittle, and exciting than ever. It was a sweltering hot summer and everyone was avoiding Central Park because a serial killer, later known as the Son of Sam, was prowling the streets. He shot six people dead before being arrested that August. He said his neighbor's dog had ordered him to do it.

We got driven to a hotel on Columbus Circle, next to Central Park, where I was sharing with my usual roommate, Ken. Jet-lagged, we put our bags on the floor and went straight out to soak up New York City.

It was phenomenal. The city was so wild, and huge, and overwhelming that I could hardly take it in. We went to our US record label HQ, which felt like a big deal. Standing in Times Square, I looked around me and drank it all in: *Whoa! I'm not in Walsall now!*

That part of New York was still all sleazy sex shops and porn cinemas then. I felt like Robert De Niro in *Taxi Driver*, except that I absolutely *loved* all the animals, whores, and queens in that human zoo. Ken and I went to see *Deep Throat*, which I'd heard all about. It was a big turn-on.

New Yorkers are like nobody else on earth. We went into a deli to get some food. There was so much choice my head was spinning. I hadn't decided what I wanted when I got to the front of the queue. The owner yelled at me—"C'mon, already! Get outta here!"—and served the guy behind me.

The next night, I went on my own to Studio 54. I'd heard so much about this legendary anything-goes nightclub, and I suppose I was secretly hoping to score some guy-on-guy action. I didn't, but I loved its full-on hedonistic disco vibe. I knew I'd be back.

After a few days of bliss in NYC, it was time to begin the tour. We were flying the longer journeys between dates and getting hire cars for the rest. The vastness of America, and crossing between time zones, took some getting used to.

We were the opening act for REO Speedwagon and Foreigner. They were both big American bands but I wasn't very excited about either of them. The feeling was clearly mutual as, off the stage, we hardly saw them or exchanged a word. Support acts were way down their list of priorities, and it showed. At some gigs we were only given enough space onstage to use half of our equipment. We were at the bottom of the food chain.

Still—fuck it! We didn't care! We were Judas Priest and we were on tour in America!

The first five dates were in Texas, where we already had a following, mainly because a local radio DJ, Joe Anthony, loved *Sad Wings of Destiny* and played us to death. When we went on his show to do an interview, he was as excited as if we were the Beatles.

In most cities, we'd emerge to deathly silence, plug in, and try to blow their heads off. There would be a stunned silence as a thought bubble rose over the crowd's heads—*What the fuck are these guys?*— then we'd win them over through sheer brute force and volume.

Because REO Speedwagon and Foreigner were huge, we did some mega-venues. In St. Louis, we played to 45,000 people at a stadium show headlined by Ted Nugent. Ted swung onstage with a flaming bow and arrow, like Tarzan, because…well, because that's the sort of thing that Ted Nugent does.

The crowd seemed to stretch as far as I could see…but I didn't enjoy that show. I had been nervous and got no sleep the night before, and the blazing sun was so hot that it burned my feet in my steel-toe-capped leather boots. I felt like I was hallucinating.

But you get through these things, and I thought back to something I had learned at the Wolverhampton Grand: *When you are doing a show, try to reach the guy at the back.* So, I jumped and waved and exaggerated every movement, and it seemed to work.

We loved crisscrossing the States, but I couldn't wait to get back to New York, which was our hub for the last couple of dates of the tour. We flew back in on July 13, 1977, and got caught up in one of the most notorious nights in the city's history.

I had no sooner gotten back to our poky hotel by Central Park when the lights in our windowless twentieth-floor room went out. *Huh?* I ran to the fire escape, where I bumped into Ian, and peered out. The whole city was in darkness. *Was I in some kind of surreal dream?*

Lighting matches to see our way, we stumbled down the fire escape. When we got to the ground, the hotel bar was packed with people. Someone drove their car onto the sidewalk and put their headlights on full beam to light the room. Then we all got stuck into the booze.

That felt very New York: making a party out of a disaster.

New York was already paranoid due to the Son of Sam, and it got worse as riots and looting broke out across the city. We heard gunshots all night, and the next day I found out that whole blocks of Broadway had been burned down and more than four thousand rioters arrested.

Glenn had gotten a later flight than the rest of us, and arrived at the hotel looking ashen-faced. In his cab from JFK, he had seen looters with baseball bats smashing windscreens and robbing drivers in the tunnels from the airport. He'd escaped unscathed but was really shaken up.

The lights came on the next day and we ended the tour at New York Palladium, which was a total buzz. Then we got an even bigger high. Arnakata called from London with a crazy message. Robert Plant had heard that Judas Priest were touring the States.

Did we want to open up two shows for Led Zeppelin?

Did we…? Shit, what did they *think* the answer was going to be? We were beside ourselves with excitement. Supporting Led Zep in America…Christ, this really was fairy-tale stuff! The only drawback was the logistics.

The gigs were part of the Day on the Green festival at the Oakland–Alameda County Coliseum in California. There was nearly a week before the shows and we had virtually no money left. So, we flew to California and shared one room in a fleapit hotel near the stadium.

The festival was a Bill Graham production and, beforehand, we wondered if we would meet the legendary tour promoter. We sure did! On the day of the first show, we were lounging around the backstage hospitality area. Glenn, uncouthly, had his feet on a table. Bill Graham appeared, strode over to where we were sitting, and slapped Glenn's feet off the table. "What the fucking hell are *you* doing here?" he asked. He had assumed we were just a bunch of layabouts (he was clearly an astute judge of character).

"This is Judas Priest, sir!" one of his security men informed him. Bill apologized and was a whole lot nicer after that. We got to know him very well, and he always looked after the band brilliantly in America.

The show was extraordinary, a real out-of-body experience. Because the festival had an early-evening curfew, we played at some ungodly early hour. The fog rolls in over Oakland, so when we went on, I could only see the front of the crowd. The back of the stadium was lost in the mist.

We only did twenty minutes, but during that time the fog burned off rapidly. By the end, I could see a sea of 80,000 people, reaching right to the back of the far bleachers. It was mind-blowing, exhilarating, and an unforgettable way to round off an amazing debut tour of America.

It was *such* a prestigious gig for us to play, and it really announced Priest in America. Sadly, it was to be Led Zeppelin's last-ever show in the States, as Robert's young son, Karac, died suddenly from a virus, and Zep pulled the rest of their tour and flew home.

The morning after Day on the Green, Judas Priest also headed back to Britain, after six weeks in America. I felt as if, somehow, everything had changed. Life would never be the same again for the band...nor for me.

7

The Shirley Bassey leather years

When you wake up from a vivid, vibrant dream, dull reality can feel seriously deflating. Touring America had been like living a fever dream—or, if I am honest, a wet dream! When I got back home, for a few days I hit a major slump.

After weeks of traversing the States, running wide-eyed around the fleshpots of Times Square and jumping around for 80,000 Zep fans, I couldn't help but feel flat when I was waiting in the piddling rain to get the bus to the Dirty Duck. I'd been out and seen the world, and the Yew Tree Estate in Walsall suddenly felt very small.

Coming off tour can be *such* a comedown. One minute you are wowing crowds, signing autographs, and being interviewed on the radio. The next, you are trudging to the corner shop and coming back to be told off by your housemates for forgetting the Rizlas.

You feel like you want to tell people everything you have done, but they don't always want to hear it. "How was America, Rob?" a mate would ask me down at the Duck.

"Oh, God, amazing!" I'd say. "New York was incredible, and St. Louis, and Robert Plant is such a great guy…"

"Oh, yer? Sounds great!" they'd say. "I'm tekkin' the motor in for its MOT tomorrow…"

I was young, and precocious, and it was frustrating—but now I'm older, I can see that that downbeat, matter-of-fact Black Country nature, that deadpan refusal to blow smoke up anyone's arse, has been a blessing for me. Because, without it, I might have turned into a right dickhead.

But I didn't have too much time to feel sorry for myself—because Priest had another album to make.

CBS gave us a new producer for the album that was to become *Stained Class*: Dennis Mackay, who had an eclectic CV that included producing Curved Air, Gong, and Tommy Bolin. We began work at the live-in Chipping Norton Recording Studios in the Cotswolds.

Those sessions were the first time I became aware of tensions within our twin-guitar attack of Glenn and Ken. They normally rubbed along OK, on the surface at least, but there was no denying that they were very different characters.

Glenn was—and always has been—a very confident, assured, driven individual. He knows what he wants to do and how he wants to do it. From the start, he had a very strong vision for how he wanted the band to sound, and that was coming to the fore on *Stained Class*.

He and I wrote the title track to the album and "Exciter," and he wrote "White Heat, Red Hot" on his own. Yet probably my favorite track on the album was penned by me and Les Binks.

Les had settled in well as Priest's drummer, and he and I wrote "Beyond the Realms of Death" (that *Roget's Thesaurus* was worth its weight in gold!) together. It was a song about a protagonist who was struggling through the world, at the end of his tether. It had some very personal lines:

> I'm safe here in my mind
> I'm free to speak with my own kind

With my own kind. Because, in 1978, the idea of being able to talk to other gay men, openly, freely, and without stigma, seemed as likely as pole-vaulting to Mars. I just knew: *It will never bloody happen*.

Dennis Mackay did a good job on the album. We were still

prone to prog-rock noodling, and he saw our songs could go on a bit. He pointed out that we didn't have to make a musical statement, then keep repeating it. *Shear off the waste! Hit people with the sharp end!*

CBS were keen to include a track that might pick up serious play on American rock radio, and suggested a cover of Spooky Tooth's "Better by You, Better than Me." It was a last-minute addition to the album at the mixing stage, and James Guthrie, who came recommended by CBS, produced it, as Dennis Mackay was unavailable.

Released early in '78, *Stained Class* was well received and within two months of recording it, we were back on tour. The venues went up a notch again—Hello, Hammersmith Odeon! Good evening, Birmingham Odeon!—and something else had notably changed.

As Priest began to get bigger, and our tracks got more airplay, the makeup of our crowds was beginning to change. The rabid, headbanging blokes that were our core following were as loyal as ever, but we also started to get more women followers…and our first groupies.

Well, I didn't. None of our fans knew that I was gay at this point, of course. If any misguided girls made a play for me, I could politely brush them off. But if I wanted some action on the road—and I really, *really* did—how the hell was I supposed to go about it?

For straight blokes, the ritual was easy. They could invite a girl to come backstage. Would you like a drink? Would you like to come to our hotel? Would you like to see my room?

I couldn't do *any* of that. If I fancied a guy in the crowd, how did I go about it? What were the chances of him being gay (or, if he was, of admitting it)? What if I got it wrong, made a misjudged pass, and got a smack in the mouth? And, of course, the overriding fear that was to limit my existence for decades:

What if it got out that I was gay, fans didn't want anything to do with a band fronted by a queer, and it killed Judas Priest stone-dead?

Priest was the most important thing in my life, and even if I were willing to sacrifice it for my sexuality—which I *wasn't*—I simply couldn't do it to Ken, or Glenn, or Ian. It wouldn't be fair on them. It was my problem, not theirs.

No, the safest thing, the *only* thing, to do was to remain firmly in the closet. And that meant our fans were off-limits.

The other main change in Priest-world during the course of 1978 was the complete and total revamp of our image. Ken had the idea, and I quickly bought into it. He and I went down to London and got fitted for bespoke leather outfits. Ken reckons as soon as the guy took my inside leg, I was up for it, but I like to think I'm not *quite* that cheap.

Not quite.

When we got back to Walsall and showed the others our new black leather cut-off shirts and trousers, they were all into the idea. So, we all trekked down to London again to order the gear.

Some of the outfitters we visited were hilarious. One place in Soho was run by a tall, very camp, middle-aged queen with long hair and a Guy Fawkes–like goatee beard. Every time we went into his shop, he would pirouette and clap his hands with excitement.

"Yay! Here they are, *my boys!*" he'd squeal. His party piece was doing an impressive Tiller Girls kick—his foot would go way up over his head. "Not bad for a man of fifty-eight, eh, boys?" he'd ask us. I had to give it to him, he was very flexible…and quite possibly double-jointed.

Suzi Watkins, a Canadian who worked at Arnakata, took us to an S&M and fetish shop in Wandsworth. As well as leather trousers, caps, boots, and wristbands, it had cock rings, chains, and whips! I thought that one or two of the Priest lads looked a little uncomfortable in there.

Our leather-and-studs image came together gradually over the next few weeks and felt very natural. I thought we were channeling all sorts of things, from macho culture to Marlon Brando, but the end result was that suddenly we *looked* like a heavy metal band.

The biggest myth about this new stage gear is that I had

somehow masterminded the image as a cover and a vent for my homosexuality—that I was getting a thrill from dressing onstage as I'd like to dress in the street, or the bedroom. This is utter bollocks.

I had no interest in S&M, domination, or the whole queer subcult of leather and chains. It just didn't do it for me. My sexual preference was for men, sure, but I was—and still am—pretty vanilla. I've never used a whip in the boudoir in my life.

Or, have I? Hang on, let me think for a minute…

Les was the slowest to fall into line with our new look. He didn't seem to have gotten the memo. We would turn up for photo shoots with Ken, Glenn, Ian, and I clad head to toe in leather, and Les would be grinning away in jeans and a scruffy cowboy shirt.

It did my head in: *Les! We're trying to get an image together here!* But I never knew how to broach the topic with him. *At least he's hidden behind the drums*, I thought. Eventually, he half-heartedly fell into line and bought himself a biker jacket.

Our fans, male and female, certainly didn't detect any secret, cryptic gay element to our new image. They just thought we looked macho, and butch, and alpha male. Imitation outfits started springing up in our crowds, a sure sign that the look was a success.

I must admit, I still occasionally look back at Priest photos of that late seventies era, and suspect that they were our Shirley Bassey leather years. But that is probably just me being me.

I had been eager to get back to America and the big moment came in March when we began two months of dates. We flew into JFK again and kicked off by headlining two nights at a biggish theater near Union Square called the Palladium. They were not to get off to the best of starts.

CBS were sending a limo to our hotel before the first of the shows but it never showed up. We were getting more and more agitated in the foyer as our stage time ticked ever nearer. There were no taxis to be seen, so I asked the front desk staff the quickest way to the venue.

"Well, sir, the bus leaves from right over *there…*"

We had no choice but to pile on to a commuter bus. New Yorkers have seen it all, but even they were taken aback to share their journey home with a gang of sweaty, panicking Brits, in studs and leather, speaking a strange, unknown tongue: "We'm never gonna mek it!"

I took advantage of a free day in New York before the second show to sneak off back to Times Square and pick up some gay porn mags from the sex shops. You could get stuff there I'd never seen in the UK and my eyes were on stalks. In fact, *everything* was sticking out!

I would hide those mags in flight cases to get them home at the end of the tour. I don't think they were actually illegal, but I'd have been embarrassed to have them brandished at customs. I hated having to feel guilty about them…but, well, that was just how it was.

After the Palladium shows, we took off on another nationwide jaunt, this time with Foghat and Bachman-Turner Overdrive. It was the same as our first US tour—no contact with the headliners, and treated like shit. At one show, they gave us one solitary light, on me, as the band played in darkness.

We traveled between shows on a tour bus. At first, we were wildly impressed at our big, sleek coach, which had bunk beds and even a lounge area: *Whoa! This is the future!* It could get claustrophobic, but I liked how I could get pissed and fall into my bunk.

We wended our way through Texas to California, and one particular date was circled in red on my personal calendar. We were heading for San Francisco, a city renowned for its gay culture and thriving homosexual community. I imagined it as a land of plenty.

Ever since I had read about it in some rag in the Nightingale back in Brum, I'd wanted to get hold of *The Advocate*, a campaigning gay newspaper published in San Francisco. Priest were staying in a Holiday Inn at Fisherman's Wharf, and I emerged from the hotel to see a row of newspaper vending machines slap-bang outside the entrance.

The New York Times, the *Washington Post*…wait, there it was! *The Advocate!*

It felt like I had found the Holy Grail. I needed a quarter to open the box and get a copy, so I scrabbled through the pockets of my leather trousers for coins. Damn! I only had a dollar bill.

A well-dressed, middle-aged woman was just passing by, and in my excitement, I jumped toward her. "Excuse me, but haveyowgorraquarterorfourquartersforadollar, like?" I gabbled.

She stared at me with eyebrows raised. "Ex-cuse me?" At which point, it occurred to me that they probably didn't speak fluent yam-yam in northern California. I slowed down and tried again: "I'm very sorry, but could you possibly give me four quarters for a dollar?"

She could, and I took *The Advocate* back to my room and read it from cover to cover. There were pages of gay events, and talks, and discos, and dating ads. I compared it to my sordid life in Walsall, scuttling nervously into public bogs. *I was in the Promised Land!*

San Francisco's main gay neighborhood is the Castro, and I longed to go see it…but I didn't. I had my usual fear. We were getting bigger in the US, and I'd occasionally get recognized—what if a fan saw me, and word got out that Rob Halford was sneaking around gay areas?

Another piece of gay literature I picked up in San Francisco was *Bob Damron's Address Book.* This was a slim, discreet volume, just the right size to slip in your jeans back pocket, and listed gay bars, bathhouses, and cruising areas in hundreds of cities and towns across America.

As our tour bus pulled through the night, I would lie on my

bunk, my light on and curtain closed, memorizing its info. It told me the Fire Pit was the best gay bar in Birmingham, Alabama. If I were in Covington, Kentucky, I should go to Jouche Bo's. On the pull in Hollywood, I should try Annex West on Melrose.

I never went to *one* of them. The most I ever dared to do was stroll around any gay areas that happened to be near to the band's hotel, or quickly press my nose against a gay club's windows, like a Dickensian ragamuffin ogling out-of-reach cakes.*

Playing support in big venues, I was being deliberately flamboyant, and worked out a few spectacular moves with the mic stand. It backfired in the Agora Ballroom, in Cleveland, where I crashed it off the ceiling and a whole load of plaster fell on my bonce.

After Cleveland, we had a brief, one-night return to New York to play the Bottom Line. I was looking forward to this…as I had some possible action lined up for afterward. A knowing gay guy at CBS had put me in touch with his friends "who wanted to meet me."

We got together after the show and they took me to a big house by Central Park. I was feeling good—I had a drink in my hand as soon as I got there and the guys were chatting me up, telling me how much they loved Priest and how great I was onstage.

Somebody refilled my glass, and I began to feel woozy. Then I felt *very* woozy: *What the fuck is going on?* A couple of guys led me into a different room, then all I can remember is hands all over me… and an older guy giving me a blow job.

I knew he was older, as he took out his false teeth to finish me off.

I stumbled back to my hotel. It was the next day before I realized my drink must have been spiked. It left me feeling conned, upset, and angry…and nursing horrible flashbacks to Dad's mate "who liked the theater."

---

* "Cakes" is US gay slang for bum cheeks, so my analogy is extremely accurate.

Priest were quickly realizing just how much the world could open up for us now we were signed to a major label. After the American jaunt, we were only back in the Midlands for two months before it was time for our next big adventure—our first trip to Japan.

It was mind-blowing. I loved Japanese society from the start. My first visit to New York had been amazing, but the city had seemed spookily familiar as I'd seen it on so many TV shows and movies. Landing in Tokyo, it felt as if we had touched down on a fresh planet.

On that first trip, CBS had booked us into a tiny little hotel that was basically for Japanese businessmen. The rooms were the size of postage stamps. If you stood in the middle and stretched your arms out, you could touch two opposing walls.

I didn't travel light in those days. For some ungodly reason, I used to take every item of clothing I owned away with me, both for onstage and off—I'd change my clothes three or four times a day because, I dunno, *that's what rock stars do, right?* I'd cram them all into a huge aluminum trunk like people had on the bloody *Titanic*.

The first night, I ordered a three-course meal on room service. My door was half-open and a waiter came in, struggling under the weight of two laden trays. He didn't see my monster trunk just inside the room.

BANG! SPLAT!

The guy went flying. It was pure slapstick. He went sprawling over my luggage, and loads of plates of Japanese food arced through the air and landed on every single surface. The bed, the walls, the floor, the telly. It was even all over me!

It was a comedy sketch, and I was laughing my arse off...until I saw how mortified the poor guy was. He was bowing, up and down from the waist, so fast that his torso was a blur, and apologizing frantically.

I immediately became a cartoon Englishman abroad. "IT'S OK!" I barked at him, at three times my normal volume, as that would *obviously* help him to understand me better. I gave him a grin, and a reassuring thumbs-up. "NO PROBLEM!"

The guy was not remotely reassured. He backed out of the room, still apologizing, and scurried off to find the cleaning staff.

I wish I could say that I equaled the hotel's standards of respect and decorum…but I didn't. The Japanese shows all kicked off at six in the evening, meaning that we were back in the hotel by nine with a few drinks inside us and time to kill. It was a lethal combination.

I've never been one for smashing up hotel rooms—as a working-class lad, I knew somebody's poor mom would have to clean up the mess—but I had a phase of having a big thing for fire extinguishers.

On the *Stained Class* tour, I had taken one into an empty lift, set it off, pushed the buttons for every floor, and then run out as the doors closed. The writhing, out-of-control extinguisher traveled up and down the hotel, soaking the people waiting outside the lift on every single floor. It was the most fun anybody had had with a lift since Corky and his phone calls.

Priest always had ongoing pranks with our road crew. When I found out that one of them was staying two doors along from me on our corridor in Tokyo, it seemed the perfect opportunity to strike—and to take my love for fire extinguishers international.

I grabbed an extinguisher from the wall, pointed the nozzle under his door, hit the top, and scarpered back to my room. I had my door ajar and was peeping out to watch the fun, when I suddenly heard a load of furious shouting…in *Japanese?*

I had gotten the wrong room! The door shot open, and out stumbled a Japanese businessman covered from head to toe in pink powder. I could see the same powder all over the walls and carpet behind him. I'd thought all fire extinguishers were full of water, but it seemed the Japanese did things differently!

I eased my door shut. The offended pink guy carried on howling,

I heard shouts, and people running up and down the corridor, then, five minutes later, a siren. Through my window, I saw a police car pulling up downstairs.

Shit!

When I heard people coming down my corridor, knocking on every door, I quickly put on my complimentary kimono and shoveled my hair up into clumps. When they banged on my door, I asked, "Who is it?"

"Police! Police!" came a voice. "We need to speak with you!"

I opened the door, yawning theatrically. "Yeah?"

It was two policemen and an English-speaking member of the hotel management. "Someone let off a fire extinguisher!" he said. "You know anything?"

"How awful!" I said. "No, nothing at all. I was fast asleep. I'm sorry, I have to get back to sleep now. I have a show tomorrow."

"Sorry to disturb!" said the manager. We bowed to each other, and I went back to bed to kill myself laughing under the sheets.

The actual shows were amazing. The first was in a theater called the Nakano Sun Plaza, which was twice the size of the Wolverhampton Grand. We were gobsmacked to find that Priest already had a bit of a following in Japan. I found this humbling and hardly conceivable.

I had had what I thought was a bit of a brainwave for the opening of our set. For our intro, we were using Mussorgsky's "The Great Gate of Kiev," which is a beautiful piece of classical music. Then, when the curtain came up...

"Wouldn't it be great if, right at the start, we had our backs to the audience?" I suggested to the band.

"What the bloody hell do you want to do that for?" they inquired, not unreasonably.

I explained my grand concept. The crowd would get excited when the intro started. They'd be even more excited when the curtain rose and they glimpsed our backs through the dry ice...

then most excited of all when we turned to face them! Three thrills in one!

The others didn't look totally convinced but they went along with it. So, on the first night, we took our places, the gorgeous strains of Mussorgsky drifted through the theater, the curtain rose and…behind us, Beatlemania broke out. Or, rather, Priestmania.

It was extraordinary. In the late seventies, Western pop and rock was just starting to break into Japan. There was a perception in the country that this music was just for girls, so the crowd was three-quarters female. And screaming their heads off.

It was Beatlemania in more ways than one. As we launched into the first song, small objects began whizzing past my head. It was like the Beatles' early days, when George Harrison said the band liked jelly babies, so their fans started pelting the group with them at gigs.

So, there we were, trying to play "The Ripper" while a couple of thousand Japanese girls shrieked themselves crazy and lumps of food, sweets, cuddly toys, and other little gifts shot all around us and into the dry ice. What an experience!

Japan was *full* of mad adventures like that. As well as the sleek modernism of Tokyo, we saw the ancient city of Kyoto with its amazing ruins, where I picked up some little dolls in national costume for Mom. I always took dolls home for her and knew these would take pride of place in her Beechdale cabinet.

It had been an unbelievable year for Priest and, as we jetted back to Heathrow, the sensible thing would have been to take some time out, unwind, relax, and take stock of everything that had happened. We deserved a break.

So, we went straight back into the studio to make another album.

8

A whip-round for Marie Osmond

Judas Priest's work rate was incredible in the late seventies. We would think nothing of playing a huge US and European tour for months, coming home, taking no more than a week off, and then going back into the studio to make a new album.

This was partly driven by our label. "You are really picking up speed now!" CBS would tell us. "You're up against some big bands, so you can't afford to stop or let this fizzle out. There's no time to slow down. You have to stay on the radar!"

It was hard work…but it didn't feel like a hardship. We were totally up for it. We saw our arduous schedule as a test, and as proof of our tenacity and determination as a band. Going straight into the studio after a tour felt very natural, and the right thing to do.

So, the jet lag from our flight home from Japan had hardly worn off when we went to London to make our second album of 1978. The producer was to be James Guthrie, because we had liked his work on the Spooky Tooth cover (despite the short notice).

When we got into the studio, we hit the ground running. I suppose that was one advantage of our punishing, nonstop recording and touring schedule. We were always together, never off duty, and it was turning us into a well-oiled metal machine.

Plus, we felt like we were really going somewhere. We were getting more solid, more confident, and utterly focused on making the band as powerful as we could. Nowadays, I have to lie down if I even *think* about our workload in those days. Back then, it was second nature.

Priest never wrote on the road, so we would always go into the studio with nothing prepared and start from scratch. That never bothered us, and this time around, songs came together remarkably quickly. We were on a roll and we made the most of it.

There is a thin line between being "influenced" and being "inspired" by another band. Being "influenced" often means you just copy other artists and try to sound like them. But I was definitely *inspired* by Queen's "We Are the Champions" when we wrote "Take on the World."

When Glenn came up with a killer riff, it felt perfect to me to pen a similar lyric along classic Priest themes: optimism, believing in yourself, and triumphing against the odds. Yet "Take on the World" was also more than that. It was us making a strong connection with, and commitment to, our fans. Metal was still routinely derided back then, and here was an anthemic statement of our faith in the value of the music that we, and our fans, believed in. *We were in this together:*

> Put yourself in our hands, so our voices can be heard
> And together we will take on all the world!

When we finish writing a song, I can always hear in my head what it will sound like when we play it live. As we recorded it, I could already hear thousands of fans bellowing along to that one with us. The prospect made me tingle.

Glenn was on fire and came up with a track that was to become an all-time Priest classic. I was still glued to my trusty thesaurus in the studio, and a phrase jumped out at me: "Hey, lads, listen to this: Hell bent for leather! Wow! How Priest is *that*?" Glenn ran with it and did the rest—and *what* a riff!

One night, we took a break from recording to watch Muhammad Ali fight Leon Spinks for the world heavyweight boxing crown on the TV in the studio bar. The band were still working as I watched the prefight preamble, and had asked me to call them in when it was about to start.

As Ali and Spinks climbed into the ring, I ran to the control room and, in my excitement, leapt through the doorway: "Hey, lads, the fight is starti—"

CRACK! I had leapt too high. I smacked the top of my head hard against the soundproofed metal door frame, and collapsed flat on my back as if I'd been sucker-punched by Ali myself. *Ouch!*

"Don't worry, it's just a scratch," I guessed, staggering groggily to my feet as blood trickled down my face.

"No, it bloody isn't!" said Glenn. "I can see your skull, mate!" Cue a couple of hours in the emergency room, a few stitches, and me missing the big fight. Still, at least I have a scar to remember Ali's victory by.

Glenn had written a number called "Killing Machine," and we went with it as the album title because it captured just where we were as a band: a sleek, relentless metallic machine. It made perfect sense to us...but then we got a phone call from Arnakata.

Our management told us that CBS were fine with the name in the UK, but the American label were not. There had been a spate of mass shootings in the States in recent months, and they felt the title was too controversial and would garner too much negative publicity.

Glenn was the most annoyed. "We're referencing ourselves— *we're* a killing machine!" he moaned. "We're not killing people: the machine is our music. Judas Priest is a killing machine, with the power of metal. Don't they *get* that?"

The irony was, of course, that the alternative title that the US label chose, *Hell Bent for Leather*, was a masterstroke that paid dividends for both them and us.

Killing Machine was released to good reviews in the UK and was our third consecutive album to get into the Top 40. We always watched our chart positions closely. Every artist does. Any band who say they don't are lying, basically!

So, we were dumbfounded by what happened next. Our previous singles had never even had a sniff at the charts. We never expected them to: we were a metal band, it wasn't our world. But the first single off this album was a different story.

We were gobsmacked when "Take on the World" went into the Top 40 at number thirty-one, and couldn't believe it when it continued to rise all the way to number fourteen. *Number fourteen!* But the biggest surprise of all was what came with it: an invitation to go on *Top of the Pops*.

Wow! Now *this* was something! We'd done a bit of TV, and loads of radio, by now, but … *Top of the Pops?* The show that I had watched religiously every week as a kid, thrilling to Hendrix, Bolan, Bowie, and Queen? Now we had *really* arrived!

I was incredibly excited on the drive down to Shepherd's Bush to BBC Television Centre. Mom, Dad, Sue, and Nigel were just as buzzed to watch it on telly. You can make albums, play gigs, even tour America, but it's when you go on *Top of the Pops* that your family and friends know you're getting somewhere!

The show wasn't quite what I expected. The studio was poky and there were no more than thirty kids in the audience. Our fellow artists on the day were Dr. Feelgood, a band that I liked, and Donny and Marie Osmond, who I was rather less concerned about.

The band's leather image was still a work in progress, but I had fully embraced it. I was a vision in black leather from my toes to my peaked cap, with a bullet belt, long studded armlets, and the latest addition to my wardrobe: a bull whip, courtesy of the Wandsworth emporium.

This last item was to prove an issue. I might not have been terribly concerned about Marie Osmond, but it seemed she was taking more interest in me. Priest were hanging around our dressing room during rehearsals when one of the show's producers came in with bad news.

"Rob, you're going to have to lose the whip, I'm afraid," he said.

"Eh? What for?" I asked him. "It's part of my act!"

"Marie Osmond has complained. She's not very happy about it."

What? I have always been essentially an easy-going soul, who hates confrontation, but this information had me seriously riled.

"Hang on a minute! We're a British heavy metal band, on a British TV show, and some American artist is telling us what we can do?"

"Well, um…" stammered the producer. "It's just that…"

"Out of my way!"

It wasn't hard to find the Osmonds' dressing room. When I burst in, bull whip in hand, Marie had huge rollers in her hair and was being made up. I was too cross to notice if there were any paper roses.

"Marie, I'm Rob from Judas Priest!" I introduced myself.

"Oh! Hi, Rob!"

"What's this that you don't want me to use my whip?"

"Oh, er, well…"

I didn't give her a chance to finish her answer.

"I'm using the whip because it is part of our show, and it's *what we do!*" I declared, in a tone that brooked no argument. Marie smiled awkwardly, and nodded. Priest 1; Osmonds 0.

After a couple of swift ones from the BBC bar, I belted out my vocal live as the band mimed along to a playback. The irony was that I forgot to crack my bull whip, in the end, but I loved doing the show. We felt like we were ambassadors for metal.

Some of the more hard-line Priest fans disagreed. They thought that *Top of the Pops* was soppy, a weak show full of lightweight pop crap, and that it was virtually an act of betrayal for us to go on there. We heard a few vague grumbles that we had "sold out."

I had no time for this argument. I've always thought we should do whatever it takes to promote the band and our music—and promote metal as a whole. *Top of the Pops* were willing to let us showcase our single on the BBC to 15 million people? Brilliant—bring it on!

It was by far the most mainstream thing we had ever done, and I wondered if the exposure would change my daily life. Would I become a public figure, a *celebrity*, signing autographs nonstop and unable to walk around Walsall without being mobbed?

I needn't have worried. *Nobody cared.* Even today I get stopped and asked for selfies in America, but it *never* happens in Walsall. People clock me, but think: *Ah, don't bother the bloke! He's off duty—let's leave him alone!* It's a beautiful thing, and I'm grateful for it.

In any case, I had no time to bask in my (ahem) newfound popstar status. We were to be on the road for virtually the whole of 1979. I looked at the calendar, and nearly 140 live shows lay ahead of us.

Because we would not have time to make a new album in '79, CBS came up with a contingency plan. We were starting in Japan, and they arranged to record two of the Tokyo shows to be mixed into a live album—*Unleashed in the East*—to be released later that year.

I had no objections to doing a live album but I had misgivings about the timing. My voice wasn't in great shape in Japan, partly because I had had no sleep. I've always suffered from insomnia and that trip saw me endure probably the worst jet lag I'd ever had.

Before one of the shows, I had literally been awake all night without even one minute's shut-eye. Like a trouper, I struggled through the performances, but I was a bit wary as to what the tapes would throw up.

After this, it was back to America for two months of dates across the States. The majority of these shows were supporting UFO who, to put it mildly, were an absolute fucking riot. We partied with them every single night. *Hard*. Priest had our moments as party animals, but UFO were nuts.

Onstage, I was dialing up the theatricality. Priest's music was so loud and powerful and strong and dynamic, and I wanted to match up to it, and with it, physically. I'd run around the stage and wave my arms around, and started to develop a few signature moves.

I was brandishing my bull whip every night and would pretend to lash at the front row. Ever alert to a merchandising opportunity, CBS and Arnakata soon started flogging provocative T-shirts and badges:

I'VE BEEN WHIPPED BY ROB HALFORD!

I took my onstage arsenal one step further and got ahold of a machine gun, from which I'd fire blanks at the audience, usually at the end of "Genocide." We didn't play it every night, but when we did, we went to town on it. Some nights it would last nearly fifteen minutes.

Ken, Glenn, and I would also line up and do some synchronized headbanging and posing at certain points of the set. It was all part of the Priest experience. We knew we had the music to blow people away, but we also wanted to put on a *show*.

This went up yet another level when we flew back home in May to play our UK tour dates. We pushed the boundaries of our live performance a bit further somewhere in the Midlands, on the first few dates of that tour. I think we were in Derby.

We had arrived at the venue for our afternoon soundcheck and were watching our crew load in the gear via a narrow alley down the side of the theater. I saw a few motorbikes parked farther down the alley, and *PING!* A light bulb came on over my head.

"Eh, lads!" I said. "Wouldn't it be great if tonight, when we do 'Hell Bent for Leather,' I rode out onstage on a motorbike?"

"You're bloody mad, you are!" was the general response. "Let's do it!"

I hung around outside and when a biker showed up to check on his bike, I told him my plan and asked if I could borrow it. He was a big Priest fan so he was bang into it. We wheeled it into the venue and parked it in the wings of the stage.

The effect it had was electric. When I sat on the bike and revved the throttle up full at the start of the song, the audience didn't know what had hit them. I rode it out to a sea of shocked faces:

"Eh? What's that noise? It sounds like…fuck me, he's riding onstage on a motorbike!"

The place went mad. From that moment, the motorbike was one of our rituals and our fans came to love it, and to expect it. It gave Arnakata a few headaches as they had to negotiate with individual venues to get permission for us to do it, but it was worth it—it was such a great spectacle.

After the success of "Take on the World," CBS put out "Evening Star" from *Killing Machine* as its follow-up. Its release brought an invitation to return to *Top of the Pops*. We had a gig the same day, at Birmingham Odeon, but we figured we would have no problem doing both.

Wrong.

There was an awful lot of farting around at *Top of the Pops* that day.

We kicked our heels for hours. There were sound rehearsals; dress rehearsals; live run-throughs. They were having technical issues: God knows what they were. Time was ticking by.

We were getting more and more worried: "Bloody hell, have yow sin the time?"

I collared a passing producer: "Look, mate, what time are we doing this? We've got a gig to get to!"

"Yes, yes, any minute now!" he assured me, and vanished. Another half hour passed.

It got to six o'clock and we knew we wouldn't be able to make it through rush-hour London traffic and up the M1 and M6 to

Brum in time. A woman from Arnakata was at the studio, glued to a phone. Could we hire a plane? A helicopter? Get a police escort? She drew a blank.

Eventually we were done, but by the time we got to Birmingham Odeon, it was an hour after we were due onstage. Some fans had given up and gone home, thinking we weren't going to show, and there were isolated boos when we finally came out. *In our hometown!* We felt awful about the whole fiasco.

We had a rare month free of gigs after the UK dates, which gave us a chance to mix the *Unleashed in the East* album. When we listened back to the Tokyo show recordings, my worst fears were realized.

CBS hooked us up with a guy called Tom Allom to produce the album. Over the next few years, we were to become blood brothers, and have a long, happy, and productive relationship with Tom— which didn't look likely from our first impressions.

A few years older than me, Tom Allom had an immaculate cut-glass accent and was the poshest person I had ever met. He could have been a minor member of the royal family, or a military man— hence his nickname, the "Colonel."

Yet, once we saw past his aristocratic demeanor, Tom was a great bloke and very rock 'n' roll. He was into Priest, and metal, and *got* the band from the start. Unlike some producers, he could read music and play the piano, which highly impressed us.

Tom became a member of the Priest family from our first meeting, but he had his work cut out mixing *Unleashed in the East*. The band were on point but my vocals were all over the shop. You could hear the jet lag and the fatigue as I strained for notes and fell short.

We were remixing it in Ringo Starr's studio complex in Titten-hurst Park, a gorgeous Georgian country house just outside Ascot. Ringo had bought the place from John Lennon and Yoko Ono. It was a thrill to be there—but we had no time to gawp. We had a crisis.

Tom was doing his best, but even he couldn't polish a turd, and I couldn't bear the thought of Priest fans hearing me so below form and out of tune. Wincing as I listened back to the tapes, I made a decision.

"Listen, lads," I said. "I'm going to go into the front room with a mic and I'm going to sing the album from start to finish. Let's record it, and let's see if we can do anything with it."

I did exactly that. The vocals were infinitely better and Tom mixed them in with the band's Tokyo performance. We kept that quiet for years, and when it came out—because Big Gob here let it slip in an interview!—fans began calling the album *Unleashed in the Studio*.

My rerecorded vocals were controversial for a short while—but our consciences were clear. We hadn't tried to cheat our fans: we just wouldn't release an inferior Priest product. Because that would have been cheating them far more.

Our long year on the road picked up again, and we made our first trip to Ireland, to play a Dublin festival with Status Quo. We had met Quo before and they were nice guys, but we nearly didn't go on to support them, because the day degenerated into a standoff.

The Irish promoters and police told us there was no way I could ride my motorbike onstage. They seemed to think it would provoke a riot in the crowd. I thought this was bollocks. The fans were expecting the bike and we didn't want to let them down.

Nobody in Priest has ever been a prima donna, *not even me*, but this time, we made a stand: *If we can't use the bike, we're not going on.* The impasse went on right up to showtime...when the organizers suddenly relented. The crowd's roar as I vroomed onstage showed we'd done the right thing.

Dublin was to be the last show Les Binks played with us. Suddenly, our drummer was gone. It was a surprise and I wasn't too sure what was behind it, although Les was to tell Ken years later that it was down to arguments over money with Arnakata.

I liked Les, and he had even ditched his cowboy shirts by the end, but to be honest, I wasn't too sorry to see him go. I thought he was a bit of a *drummer's drummer*, who could be more concerned with honing his technique than locking into the heart and soul of Priest's music.

His replacement, Dave Holland, had been playing in Trapeze, a band we liked, but was happy to switch to us when we sounded him out. As soon as he arrived, I appreciated the difference between him and Les. Les had given us complexity, sure, but Dave gave us simplicity, drive, and *power*—and that was what we needed.

Dave was in place that autumn when we headed back to the States for another string of dates, this time to promote *Unleashed in the East*. The first shows were playing arenas and the odd stadium in support of true American rock royalty: Kiss.

When we were offered these dates, we pondered hard. Kiss weren't a metal band and we weren't musical soulmates. But Gene Simmons and Paul Stanley loved Priest and had personally requested us, which was flattering, and the opportunity to reach hundreds of thousands of new fans was impossible to refuse.

The Kiss Army are notoriously hard to please but we went down well with them. We were only doing thirty minutes per night, so we just went for it, with a full-on metal assault. The crowds accepted us because we were fierce and committed, and we had a strong image.

Gene and Paul may have been into our music but we didn't see a lot of them offstage. However, it thrilled me that Gene was dating Cher, who is a very big deal for gay guys. I kept concocting feeble excuses to hang around near her just so I could say, "Hi!"

While we were playing the Kiss dates, CBS released the *Unleashed in the East* album. We had no idea how it would sell—I suppose we had nothing to measure it against—so we were amazed when it went into the Top 10 in the UK, and even crept into the Billboard 200 in America!

What? A live album? Really? It felt as if everything we touched was turning to gold. It was almost too much to take in.

I was about to have an experience that was even more difficult to assimilate. After the Kiss dates ended, we had some headline dates in theaters and arenas in Texas, Canada, and the West, finishing up with a show in an old stomping ground: the Palladium in New York.

CBS had arranged an end-of-tour music-industry party for us at a nightclub called the Mudd Club, where we had played earlier in the tour. We did a short set after midnight, and while I was wailing away, I couldn't help but notice the guy taking photos right in front of me.

He was a small, older guy with peroxide-white hair. He had a tiny Olympus camera, and he looked the spitting image of…

Hang on, that doesn't look like him, that IS him! Andy Warhol!

I knew all about Warhol, and was a big fan of his pop art and his avant-garde movies. To me, he *was* New York, in the purest, most artistic sense. To be frank, when I was introduced to him after our set, I was pretty star-struck.

"Hello, Andy!" I began. "Thanks for coming! Nice place, isn't it? We've played the Mudd Club before!"

"Oh, really?" drawled Andy, still photographing me as we spoke. CLICK!

"Yeah! We sold out the Palladium earlier tonight, as well!"

"Oh, really?" CLICK!

"Yes. And I'm a big fan of your work! I love it!"

"Oh, really?" CLICK!

I'd had a couple of drinks and his monosyllabic conversational style was starting to get on my tits. I'd always heard that Warhol was very awkward socially, and said very little, and this was clearly the case. But even so… *I was talking to fucking Andy Warhol!*

I tried a fresh conversational gambit.

"I always love coming to New York!"

"Oh, really?" CLICK!

Right. That was it! I'd had enough! Alongside my bull whip, I had recently incorporated handcuffs into my stage gear, and I had a pair hanging from my studded belt. For whatever reason, I took them off, put one cuff on my wrist, and fastened the other around Warhol's.

He looked at me, and laughed nervously.

"I've got some bad news for you, Andy," I told him.

"Oh, really?"

"I've lost the key!"

"OH, REALLY?" They were the same words, but his voice definitely went up in tone and intensity that time!

"No, I'm only kidding you, mate! I've got them here!" I said, producing them from my pocket. Warhol looked very relieved.

"Oh, really!" He smiled.

Warhol then varied his conversational repertoire enough to suggest that we should go to Studio 54. The two of us went outside, hailed a yellow cab, and I sat in the back with him as we pulled through the early-hours Manhattan traffic.

I gazed out of the window as it sank in just where I was and who I was with. *Was this really happening?* I wasn't in Kansas—or Bloxwich—anymore! When we got to Studio 54, Andy Warhol hung out with me for two minutes…then he was gone. He vanished into the crowd. I never saw him again.

I still have photos of that famous night, and when I look at them, one thing jumps out at me. My T-shirt. It had a picture by a famed gay erotic artist, Tom of Finland, and it was a full-on homosexual orgy: a riot of erect cocks, bum cheeks, fellatio, and anal penetration.

Now I just wonder: *What the hell was I thinking?* I was still firmly in the closet, and terrified to come out, yet that shirt might as well have been a neon sign over my head, bearing the legend "I AM GAY!"

If you want one image of the angst and turmoil that gripped me for decades in Judas Priest, you could do no better than those photos of me and Warhol. I longed to come out, and to stop living a lie, but I could see no way that it could ever happen.

No wonder I used to fucking drink…

Our year on the road was about to come to an end. I had less than a week back at Larchwood Road, gabbling on to Nick, Michael, and Denise about meeting Cher and handcuffing myself to Andy Warhol, before it was time for the last leg of our odyssey: going to Europe to support AC/DC on their *Highway to Hell* tour.

This was a big one for us. We were huge fans of the Aussie rockers, who were already massive. And, like the Kiss tour, we knew this was a chance to introduce ourselves to hundreds of thousands of metal fans who might not know us yet. We had to make it count.

Rather than waste money on hotels, we decided to hire a tour van for this jaunt across Belgium, Holland, Germany—a LOT of dates in Germany—and France. We got one that was big enough to hold the band, our road crew, and all of the gear.

It would be fair to describe this decision as a false economy. It's OK to tour like that for two or three days, but living on top of each other for weeks on end gets to you. We were like trapped animals crammed into that van, and we started to lose our minds.

We hated that fucking van.

We were going down well with AC/DC's fans, but we didn't see a lot of the headliners. We normally finished our set, then had to drive through the night to the next town. After a few days of doing this, Angus Young came and sought us out.

"Don't you guys *like* us?" he asked us.

"Huh? What do you mean?"

"You never hang out with us!"

"Oh, we'd love to!" we assured him. "It's nothing personal! We have to leave right after the shows because we're in a stupid bloody van!"

"Oh, forget that!" said Angus. "Travel with us on *our* van, and have a beer!"

When we realized that their "van" was a top-of-the-range luxury coach, with air-conditioning and all the modern conveniences, we were bang up for it.

So, most nights, we started doing that. AC/DC were all lovely guys, really generous blokes who were fantastic company. Bon Scott and I got on like a house on fire, two metal singers who would talk up a storm on their tour bus (which really was a *lot* more luxurious than ours).

Angus Young hardly drank. I asked him why he never touched a drop. "It's because if I have one drink, I'm off my tits," he told me. I didn't know if he was joking, but then one night I witnessed it and saw that he wasn't. He had literally one glass of champagne and was utterly legless within seconds. He changed before my eyes.

Bon Scott was the complete opposite. He was *always* drinking: he was a bottomless pit for alcohol. He would drink until he fell on his bed and passed out, then the next day he would get out of his bunk and walk straight onto a stage. That was how he worked.

Bon never looked rough, either. He seemed indestructible. At the end of the *Highway to Hell* tour, AC/DC and Priest all hugged each other and promised we would tour together again. Four weeks later, Bon had OD'd and was dead. It really shook us up.

Priest finished up '79 exhausted but elated. *What a year!* We'd had a hit album and singles, toured the globe with some of the biggest rock acts in the world, won countless new fans…and I had handcuffed myself to Andy Warhol.

I remember thinking that it was hard to imagine things going any better. How wrong I was. Because we were about to make the album that would take us supernova.

9

Mine eyes have seen the glory hole

Sometimes, there is nothing quite like getting your shit together in the country.

After we had decompressed in Walsall and Brum over Christmas 1979, it was, as usual, time to go back into the studio. To my delight, we were all heading back with Tom Allom to Tittenhurst Park, Ringo Starr's country pile, where we had mixed *Unleashed in the East*.

Last time we had been there, it had been a flying visit and, for me, panic stations as I salvaged my Tokyo vocals, so I hadn't had much of a chance to have a good look at the place. Now we were going to be there for a month, I got to inspect it—and I loved what I saw.

Glenn and I were both Beatles fanatics, so it meant a lot to us that Ringo had bought it from John and Yoko, and that they had lived there. We would take off separately around the mansion on recons, then meet up to breathlessly tell each other what we had found.

On the first day there, Glenn said to me, "You've got to come and see this." He showed me a fairly ordinary bedroom—but the kicker was the en suite bathroom. It had two toilets, a couple of feet apart, side by side, with nameplates behind each one:

JOHN   YOKO

I tried to imagine them sitting side by side, holding hands, having a poo. Truly, sometimes love knows no bounds.

We were super-excited to be eating our meals, and writing, in the big room in which John and Yoko had filmed the "Imagine" video. The white Steinway piano that John had played was long gone, but the floor-to-ceiling shutters that Yoko had opened in the vid were still there.

One day, the band and Tom were all sitting having a meal in there, watching TV, when that video came on. It blew my mind to look around me as it was playing, thinking, *Wow! I'm in the same frigging room!* Well, they say simple things please simple minds…

Ringo didn't seem to have made any mark on the house at all, except for the main sitting room, where he'd torn out the period fireplace and replaced it with one that looked like a huge stainless steel ring. It looked totally out of place…but I guess he must have liked it.*

I claimed the bedroom over the "Imagine" room because I wanted a view of the lake where John and Yoko rowed a boat in the "Jealous Guy" video. I was going through a fitness phase, and went jogging around the lake most mornings. Every time, I pictured them on the water.

The album that was to become *British Steel* came together like a dream from day one. The stars were aligned. Tom Allom was highly organized and on top of things as a producer, but he was also very astute and in touch with Priest's strengths and sensibilities.

Tom knew playing live was Priest's strength and where many of our best ideas sprang up. On previous albums, we'd put the drums down first and then piled everything on top. Tom scrapped that and had us all playing together in the studio. We'd never done it before and it was magical.

---

* Maybe he hoped that people would say, "It's a ring—oh!"

As well as being a great producer, Tom was also an excellent audio engineer who knew how to use space to its maximum effect. I did most of my vocals in a broom cupboard. I must admit, I couldn't help but see a certain irony in me singing in the closet!

Ken, Glenn, and I began writing as a team for the first time. That was a real quantum leap. Previously, we had come in with song ideas individually, or in pairs, and then doled out the songwriting credits accordingly. Now, all credits were to run: Tipton/Halford/ Downing. This was important in terms of eliminating potential friction if one of us thought our ideas were getting ignored or over- looked. I'd guess that more bands break up over resentment about songwriting royalties than any other reason.

Priest had always been aware of what was going on around us musically. We were not remotely part of the punk movement but we had paid attention to it, and I think its short-sharp-shock, two- and-a-half- or three-minute songs planted a seed for *British Steel*.

Tom helped us to hone the process that we had begun on *Sin After Sin*: cutting off the fleshy bits of our songs until what was left was a raw, glistening, metallic core. We pared everything down to the bone: our ethos was "minimal is maximal."

One very punky-sounding song that we wrote on the spot early on was "Breaking the Law." Judas Priest have never been a political band—it's not our bag—but this song was, without question, a slice of acute social commentary.

As an apolitical soul, I had been fairly indifferent when Margaret Thatcher came to power the previous year, beyond vague awareness that it was a big deal to have a woman prime minister. Yet a few months into her government, it was obvious a lot of bad stuff was going on.

The heavy industry and the car makers in the Midlands and around the country were struggling, and there was already talk of factory closures. Unemployment was shooting up. Worst of all, millions of young people had no hope and felt they were being ignored.

Writing the lyrics for "Breaking the Law," I tried to put myself in the mind of a jobless young bloke at his wits' end:

> There I was completely wasted, out of work and down,
> All inside it's so frustrating as I drift from town to town,
> Feel as though nobody cares if I live or die

I wasn't trying to be any kind of spokesman: I never have. But I saw a lot of disenfranchisement and anger and anarchy around me, and I wanted to document and reflect it.

"Grinder" was another bout of social commentary, about how people get lied to, used as puppets, fed into the machine of capitalism, and spat out the other end. I also fed in more sexual tension: "Grinder, looking for meat…"*

One fateful night, at four in the morning, I was trying to get to sleep as Glenn had his amp set up and was working through some riffs in the "Imagine" room beneath me. I sighed, put on my dressing gown, and went down to have a word.

"What you bloody doing, Glenn?" I inquired.

"Oh, sorry, did I wake you up?"

"Yeah. I'm trying to sleep!"

"I'll turn it down," he said, fiddling with his amp.

As I turned to go, I hit him with a parting shot: "You're living after midnight down here, you are!"

I stopped dead. We grinned at each other. "*That* is a fucking great title for this song!" he said. The next day, I wrote a lyric for it, about partying and having a good time. Tom got the feel of it straight away, and we had the track done and dusted by teatime.

---

* Why the gay dating app has never asked to use this song in their ads is simply beyond me!

For "Metal Gods," I took inspiration from the giant robot on the cover of Queen's *News of the World* album, as well as from *The War of the Worlds* and the sci-fi I was still devouring. It was a song about metal monsters obliterating mankind. Who'd have thought it would lend me my nickname?

We covered such a wide range of subjects on that record, from rock and roll party songs like "Living After Midnight," to social protest, to an us-against-the-world anthem like "United." I loved what a well-rounded album it was.

Tom Allom liked us to experiment sonically. The breaking glass in the background of "Breaking the Law" was Glenn smashing milk and beer bottles against the studio's outside wall. In "Metal Gods," I conjured up marching robots by shaking a drawer of knives and forks next to a mic. It was work, but it felt like play.

Hearing the playbacks, we knew it was all coming off. "Bloody hell, it's bloody marvelous!" Tom would rave, in his plummy tones. We felt the same. We knew that this was *special*.

Now we just needed an album title—and I knew precisely what I wanted. En route to a gig up north, I had glanced out of the car window and seen a huge sign outside a factory: BRITISH STEEL. It seemed to me to sum up our album in every way.

A Polish designer, Rozlaw Szaybo, who had already done the covers for *Stained Class* and *Killing Machine*, gave us the sleeve image of a hand holding a razor blade emblazoned with our name and the album title. His initial design had blood oozing from the fingers as the razor blade cut into them, but we thought the image looked tougher without blood:

We're a heavy metal band! We're so tough that we don't bleed!

We had written, recorded, produced, mixed, and mastered *British Steel* inside thirty days! It was a stupendous performance and yet it never felt rushed. It took exactly as long as it needed to take.

As Priest left Tittenhurst Park, we could not have been more pleased with our new baby—and I couldn't bear to leave without a souvenir of our time in John and Yoko's love nest.

The closet where I had poured out my angst and laid down my vocals had all sorts of Beatles and Lennon paraphernalia stored in it. There were photos, gold discs, even master tapes—plus an object I had recognized immediately.

It was an ornament, a Perspex obelisk about eighteen inches tall…and it had been in the "Imagine" video. As John played piano, it was on a plinth beside Yoko as she opened the shutters behind him.

Wow! And here it was!

I couldn't quite believe what I was looking at. I picked it up, and felt as if I was holding a piece of musical history in my hands. I have to admit that I snuck it out of the mansion to show it to a few of my mates, back in Walsall. Forty years on, I somehow appear to still have it.*

British Steel was to emerge into a changed media environment. We had grown used to the wrist merchants of the music press routinely mocking and ridiculing heavy metal. Now, to our surprise, they had concocted a scene celebrating it.

Sounds newspaper were the main movers behind the New Wave of British Heavy Metal. The main bands that it looked to champion were Iron Maiden, Def Leppard, Motörhead, Saxon, Samson…and Judas Priest.

Now, a lot of bands dislike being co-opted into music journalists' manufactured movements and lazily pigeonholed, but I liked the idea of the New Wave. I figured, after years of being ignored, it was nice for metal to get a bit of attention for a change. It felt like validation.

Our support on the UK leg of the *British Steel* tour was to be Iron Maiden, one of the new bands being championed by the press. On the eve of the tour, they did a music-press interview in which their then-singer, Paul Di'Anno, said they would blow Judas Priest off stage every night.

* I really must take it back someday.

I wasn't remotely bothered by this, because a) they were wrong, and b) that was the kind of thing cocky young bands were *supposed* to say! We had tried to do it to every major band *we* had supported, so why shouldn't they? I found it funny.

Ken didn't agree. He was offended and outraged by the comment, and demanded that we kick Maiden off the tour. The rest of us said that would be a daft overreaction to a flippant remark, but he was absolutely livid.

I love Ken to bits, but he will never let go of a grudge and he stewed about the Iron Maiden slight forever. When they sat and watched us soundcheck before an early gig on the tour, he took it as a personal affront, for reasons I didn't begin to understand.

We didn't really hang out and banter with Maiden much on that tour, but maybe I took Di'Anno's comment that he would blow Priest offstage too literally…because the one night we got drunk together, I tried to seduce him! We went to my room to carry on drinking, but I was too pissed to try anything, and he was too pissed to even know what I wanted to try.

I think that was *definitely* for the best.

We were already on tour when CBS put out "Living After Midnight" as the lead single from *British Steel*. It went into the singles chart, which brought a third invite to *Top of the Pops* at the end of March. *Brill!* One problem. We had a gig the same night…at Birmingham Odeon.

What?!

Absolutely not! After showing up an hour late the year before, there was no way we were going to risk a second disaster! We asked Arnakata to tell the Beeb: "Thanks, but no thanks. We're on tour, and we can't do it."

This didn't go down well. *Nobody* turned down *Top of the Pops!* CBS and our management were horrified by our stand and immediately mounted a charm offensive to get us to change our minds.

Didn't we *know* what a boost it could give *British Steel*? They would make sure the producers knew our situation. We'd be away from there by six o'clock, latest.

There was no way it would happen again. Honest.

They were totally adamant and, against our better judgment, we gave in to their silver-tongued persuasion. *OK, OK! We'll do it!* On March 27, 1980, we made a return trip to BBC Television Centre.

And it happened again.

It was an absolute fucking bad dream. It was exactly the same story as before: gormless producers fannying about, technical hitches, hours and hours of waiting in the dressing room, then worrying, then going out of our minds with sheer panic.

How can this be happening again? Who can we fire? Who can we KILL?

It was even worse than the previous time, because we didn't get away from Shepherds Bush until nine in the evening. By the time we reached Birmingham Odeon, it was eleven—the time we should have been coming *offstage. Shit!*

As our car pulled up down the side of the venue, some Priest fans were outside, having a fag. They let us have it with both barrels.

"Oh, here you *fucking* are! About time!"

"This is twice you've done this to us now! *Twice!*"

"You don't care about your fans—you think *Top of the Pops* is more fucking important than us!"

All we could do was say sorry, again and again, and feel absolutely shit. We made a band rule, there and then, that we would never again do *Top of the Pops* on a day we had a gig. And we never broke it.

When *British Steel* appeared, two weeks later, it received the best reviews we had ever had. And it wasn't just the critics who loved it. In its week of release, the record rocketed into the albums chart... at number four.

Wow! We had not seen *that* coming! We had tentatively thought the album might do well, but this was something else! With my eyes glued to the chart in *Melody Maker*, I took in the artists around us in the Top 10: Genesis, Status Quo, and, um, Boney M. No mistake, this was the big league.

It heralded the start of a lot of new experiences—one of which was making videos. After "Living After Midnight" had peaked just outside the Top 10, CBS were putting out "Breaking the Law" as its follow-up. They hooked us up with Julien Temple to shoot a vid.

Temple had already shot a live video for "Living After Midnight" but was most closely associated with punk. He had made the vid for the Sex Pistols' "God Save the Queen" and just finished work on their full-length movie, *The Great Rock 'n' Roll Swindle*.

A bit like Tom Allom, Julien was posh, knew exactly what he was doing, and was great to work with. He presented us with a storyboard for "Breaking the Law": we were to be outlaws, robbing a bank armed with no more than our trusty guitars and the power of metal.

It was fantastic. Julien filmed me miming my vocals in the back of a brown Cadillac convertible driving down the Westway into London, then had the band wielding guitars like machine guns as we terrified customers in a disused Barclays Bank in Soho.

Shooting the video rekindled all the thespian urges that had first led me to the Wolverhampton Grand. I hammed it up like a good 'un, not afraid to be cheesy—ham, with a side order of cheese!

As "Breaking the Law" hovered just outside the Top 10—bloody hell, this was getting to be a habit!—we played a slew of spring European dates. It wasn't hard to work out which part of the continent loved Priest the most. We did eleven shows; nine of them were in Germany.

Things were going great at home, but I think even at that stage we could tell that America was going to be the most significant place for us in terms of success. Theater dates were now giving way to arenas and *British Steel* followed *Unleashed in the East* into the Billboard 200.

We flew in to do ten weeks of gigs that summer—which gave me the chance to indulge one of my edgier sexual proclivities.

I was in a strange place in 1980. I adored being in Priest more than ever; we had made what I genuinely thought was a masterpiece of an album; and we were getting seriously successful on both sides of the Atlantic. Our career could hardly have been going better.

Yet away from the gold discs, and the sellout crowds…when I turned off the light each night and fell (pissed, always pissed) into bed in yet another anonymous hotel room, or (occasionally) in my bedroom on the Yew Tree Estate, I was frustrated and unhappy. And lonely.

It was five years since I'd been seeing Jason. Apart from the odd snatched, random fumble, I had been alone ever since…not just *alone*, but forced to suppress my longings, my needs, my*self*. I had to live a stifling lie, or kill the band I loved.

Outside of that bedroom door, I was Rob Halford from Judas Priest, macho talisman and emergent metal god. Inside it, I was Robert John Arthur Halford, a sad, confused late-twenties bloke from the Black Country, longing for the forbidden fruit of intimate male company.

It was impossible for me to have a partner like *normal*, heterosexual, non-famous people—I knew *that*. The most I could hope for was the occasional sexual tryst with strangers. And it was time for me to go on the hunt.

The first ten dates of our latest US tour were again in Texas. I was looking forward to headlining Fort Worth's Will Rogers Auditorium, Austin Opera House, and El Paso County Coliseum, but I was looking forward just as much to visiting a few Texas truck-stop toilets.

US truck-stop toilets are hunting grounds for gay men seeking random sexual encounters. American guys cruise there because the stops are remote, and a safe distance away from their friends or (often) wives and families. There is little chance of being spotted or recognized.

There is even less chance if you never see the face of the guy you're blowing, or being blown by! Cruising in toilets is the ultimate zipless fuck, as Erica Jong called it. It must have been impossible being gay in red-blooded Texas back then, which was why—I had read in *Bob Damron's Address Book*—their truck stops were particularly active.

It was hardly romantic...but I felt like it was the best option I had open to me. In fact, it was the *only* option.

Through trial and error, and my furtive trips to the public loo next to British Home Stores in Walsall, I had learned the cruising ritual. First, you find a cubicle with a glory hole—a small hole through to the next cubicle, drilled at crotch level. You bolt the door, sit on the toilet, and wait.

You wait, and you wait, then you wait some more. Eventually, a guy will come in and go into the next cubicle. You give him a few seconds to sit himself down, and then you tap your foot. Just gently.

TAP-TAP-TAP.

Usually, there is no response. But if the other guy does the same—TAP-TAP-TAP—you move your foot slightly nearer to his cubicle and repeat. If it happens three or four times, your feet will be touching under the partition. *Then*, you are in business.

You stand up and put your cock through the glory hole. The other guy grabs it, makes you hard and sucks you off. When you've come, he puts his dick through the hole and you do the same to him.

You have to stay silent throughout the whole transaction (and, believe me, a transaction is what it is). Passersby could innocently stroll into the loo for a piss at any minute. If that happens, you freeze to avoid arousing suspicion. And you pray that they are not cops.

There's an etiquette. Once you have blown each other, one of you stays in the cubicle until the other has gone out, washed his hands, and left. It's the ultimate human contact that involves absolutely no real human contact.

But beggars can't be choosers…

On that tour, if Priest broke off a journey at a truck stop for lunch, I made a beeline for the toilets. I don't know if the rest of the band knew what I was up to. They may have suspected. I never said; they never asked. Like proper mates, they gave me space.

You score more action in those places at night, and once or twice I even got a cab to a truck stop after a Priest gig. As the others grabbed a beer backstage (or one of the many groupies), I made an excuse that I was going back to the hotel…and headed into the night.

In the cab, I'd think about how the Priest fans who'd just seen me strutting across stage to conduct a mass chorus of "Take on the World" would boggle if they knew what I was on the way to do. *Please God, they would never find out.*

When I got to the stop, I would sit on a cold loo seat, heart beating fast, in the middle of nowhere. Usually, nothing would happen, then I would go home. But occasionally, just occasionally, someone would sit in the next cubicle. Another poor sod, on the same lonely quest as me.

TAP-TAP-TAP.

When it happened…*it was something*. It wasn't an emotional release, but at least it was a physical one. And it felt like the most I could ever hope for.

The *British Steel* American tour was a good one. The venues were sold out and the dates were a blast. We bonded well with Def Leppard, who played with us at the last few shows. The Scorpions were also on the bill and were a lovely bunch of lads.

At the time, Priest had a British PR guy named Tony Brainsby, who was very resourceful when it came to getting press coverage. He always had a few ideas to drum up news stories, and wasn't overly concerned whether they were true or not.

While we were touring *British Steel*, Tony suggested planting a story in the papers that I had made a porno film. It seemed a bit daft to me. The album and tour were going so well that I didn't think we needed any hype. But I went along with it: "OK, go on, then…"

Tony put the story out there, but the only paper that ran with it was the *News of the World*, the now-defunct Sunday scandal sheet… and, unfortunately, a rag that my parents had read ever since I was a lad.

Wherever I was in the world, I always phoned Mom and Dad on Sundays. I had totally forgotten Tony's confected story on the Sunday that I phoned home from somewhere in the Midwest.

RING! RING! My dad picked up.

"Hello, Dad! It's Rob!"

"Hello." He sounded unusually curt and brusque.

"What's up? You all right, Dad?"

"I am, yeah," he said. "But your mom's not."

"Why not?"

"The *News of the World*."

The penny still didn't drop. "Eh? What about it?"

"Your porno film."

Oh, fuck! Dad explained that he and Mom had opened the paper to be confronted by my supposed X-rated exploits. Mom had recently started working part-time at a local school, and was dreading facing her colleagues the next day.

"I didn't do it!" I assured him. "It's all bloody made up!" I think that Dad believed me because, after thirty years of loyal readership, he and Mom never took the *News of the Screws* again. So, at least *some* good came out of it.

Priest rounded off the touring year with one final heavy rock festival in Nuremberg...and after that, I knew exactly what I needed. *A holiday.*

The only people I could be openly gay with were Michael, Nick, and Denise in the house on Larchwood Road. That summer of 1980, Michael had blagged himself a job as a receptionist in a hotel in Mykonos, the Greek island that gays went to for sun, sea, and sex. I decided to fly out and join him.

I had a night in Athens before getting the boat to Mykonos, so I went to a gay bar I had read about. It was absolutely rammed, and I was having a drink in a corner when, just across from me, on the other side of the bar, I spotted...Freddie Mercury.

It's weird, but although Freddie was a hero, I had mixed feelings about him then. Queen had just had a big hit with "Crazy Little Thing Called Love," and in the video Freddie got off a motorbike, all in black leather, and threw his biker's cap away. It had niggled me: Was he ripping me off?

I'd also read one or two interviews where Queen had been asked if they were a heavy metal band and Freddie had said they weren't. It had bothered me. It sounds preposterous now, and it *is*, but those things were on my mind when I clocked him.

Freddie saw me across the bar and gave me a wave and a wink. I'd have liked to go across to talk to him, but you couldn't move in the bar and, if I am honest, I was nervous. By the time I got my courage up, he had gone.

Michael and I had a great time on Mykonos. I got a boat every day to a gay nudist beach called Super Paradise. It was only a fifteen-minute ride, but all the hot guys would strip stark bollock naked on the boat. I thought I *had* died and gone to Super Paradise!

While I was on the beach, I saw Freddie again. He was kind of hard to miss. He had a big yacht, festooned with pink balloons, and he was sailing round and round the island with scores of buff gay guys in thongs sprawled all around him on the deck like courtiers. *Amazing!*

Freddie Mercury later sang that he wanted to break free. Going by what was going down on that boat, I reckon he was doing a pretty fucking good job of it.

Back in Walsall, I wanted to buy my parents a new house. By now, they had been living on the Beechdale Estate for nearly thirty years. Mom, especially, was tired of it and wanted out. She didn't hate it: she just really fancied a change.

Through local estate agents, I found a nice place on the Birmingham Road up by the Arboretum, in the posh bit of Walsall. Sue and I told Mom and Dad we were taking them for a Sunday afternoon drive, and pulled up with them outside the house in Sue's car.

"Do you two like that for-sale house?" I asked them.

"Yeah!" said Mom. "It's lovely, isn't it?"

"Well, I'd like to get it for you," I said. "It's yours, if you want it."

They both stared at me, horrified, and shook their heads. "Don't be daft, Rob!" said Mom. "We're not going to let you do *that*!" Dad was equally adamant. He was a proud man. As he saw it, it was down to him to provide for his kids, not down to them to provide for him.

"But you looked after *me* for twenty years—I want to do something for *you* now!" I argued. They weren't having it. Sue and I took them back to Kelvin Road and we had a cuppa. *To be continued*, I thought…

However, if Mom and Dad wouldn't let me buy them a house, at least I could get myself one. I had been living the peripatetic life of a working musician for six years. The transitory lifestyle that would seem freakish and strange to 90 percent of the population had become a routine for me:

Weeks in a studio. Days of interviews. Months and months of living out of a suitcase (or, in my case, a trunk), sleeping in hotels or on a bus, and crisscrossing the globe, with all the madness that goes with it. A few days off. Weeks in a studio…

And repeat.

This wasn't a complaint. It was the life I had always wanted, and I still felt like a missionary, spreading the word of metal. But it did occur to me that it might be nice to spend my few, rare days off not crammed into a box room in a shared house on a council estate.

I loved Nick, Michael, and Denise and I had had a fantastic time living with them. Sharing with two other gay guys had been a life-saver for me, at a time when I was the most insecure and vulnerable about myself and my sexuality.

But now, after the success of *British Steel*, I was beginning to get checks that were more money than I had seen before in my entire life. It didn't go to my head, and I didn't go mad, but nor did I see the need to go on living like a penniless student.

Like anybody, I fancied having a place of my own where I could stretch out and relax in my downtime. And one day, when I was just back from Mykonos, Nick came home from work. "I've just seen this lovely little house for sale," he said. "I wish I could buy it. It might suit you?"

We jumped in his car and went to have a look. It was a pretty little place, an old coach house, tucked discreetly behind a fence in an OK area about ten minutes' walk from the center of Walsall. It needed a lot done to it but, well, at least I had a bit of dosh now.

I knew the second I saw the coach house that I was going to buy it, and I did, for £30,000 cash. Was it a good investment? Well, forty years on, I still spend large chunks of every year living there. So, yeah, I think it was.

I was always going to buy in Walsall. The fleeting thought crossed my mind to get a place in London instead, because I spent a lot of time there for work *and* play, but I quickly dismissed it.

Walsall was where I was from, where my family lived, and where I wanted to be. *Where I belonged.* It was as simple as that.

10

By the time I get to Phoenix...

It was time for us to begin working on the follow-up to *British Steel*. It was to be a very different process. In October 1980, Priest flew to the Balearic holiday island of Ibiza and reconvened with "Colonel" Tom Allom in Ibiza Sound Studios.

This was to prove a mistake—and, if I am frank, with hindsight I think we should have gone back to Ringo's place. In Tittenhurst Park, we had knuckled down and focused on making the best album that we could. In Ibiza, there were way too many distractions.

The island hadn't yet gone into its Balearic beat, acid house, and ecstasy phase, and was still basically the mellow hippy retreat it had been since the sixties. But holidaymakers still flocked there, and there were all-night bars and clubs aplenty.

I don't know if all of the band would agree but, for me, Priest lost our way making the album that became *Point of Entry*. Lost it badly. We were coming out of a huge record and we had to make something to equal or even better it, and we simply didn't do it.

We had a writing schedule, of sorts, and we would get together with Tom in the studio in the afternoon or evening, but it felt like the most important thing was to finish up and get down to Ibiza Town for a piss-up. And we certainly had plenty of those.

There were little bars close to the studio, but nine times out of ten we'd finish up in town at Pacha. The huge club was rocking seven nights a week and if we'd had a loyalty card, we would have filled it up.

The sun would be up when we staggered back to the villa from our nights of partying. My insomnia was getting worse, so I'd asked for a room at the far end of the complex, away from the social area. I got one, although it wasn't much more than a cupboard.

Unfortunately, it was also right by the swimming pool! I'd fall into bed at dawn, pissed, and writhe around trying to get a few hours of shallow, sweaty sleep. I'd come to with a start, woken by the rest of the band and our crew laughing and splashing about in the pool.

What the fuck?! I'm trying to sleep! Selfish, noisy bastards…!

I'd look at my alarm clock. It would be half four in the afternoon.

There were other distractions. We would rent Bultaco motocross bikes and tear up the island's hills and mountains on them. We nearly lost one of our road crew for good after he had a horrible crash.

We rented cars and got obsessed with trying to change gears in them without using the clutch. Unsurprisingly, they kept conking out and we kept having to take them back and change them. It went on and on until, one day, the owner of the car-hire place turned up at our villa.

"No more cars! No more cars for you!" he shouted, as we sat at a table, drinking beer by the pool.

"Eh? Why not?"

The guy was carrying an envelope, and he opened it and tipped the contents onto the table. Out fell a pile of gray dust that looked like asbestos. It was the important gear-change component of his cars, which we had reduced to flakes of metal powder.

"Because of this!" he proclaimed. It was kind of hard to argue with him.

By the time I get to Phoenix…

We couldn't blame the bloke for losing his rag. After a long drinking session, Ian had accidentally driven one of the cars into a deep pond that stood outside the villa. It lay there for two or three days before the poor guy came and towed it out.

Somehow, out of this carnage, an album emerged. It had its strong moments. I still like "Heading Out to the Highway," which is a proper bikers' anthem. "Desert Plains" and "Hot Rocking" kind of work. Even without trying, we stumbled across our mojo every now and then.

But too many songs fell short. We should have been building on the success of *British Steel*, but listening now to tracks like "Don't Go," "You Say Yes," and "All the Way," there was a big drop in terms of quality. I think we half-knew it at the time…but we all kept quiet and went along with it.

We were just wrapping the album up at the start of December when we heard John Lennon had been shot dead. The news hit me hard. All of those teenage hours in my bedroom in Kelvin Road, poring over the White Album, came rushing back to me.

No! Why?! What kind of moron would kill one of the Beatles?

I didn't know how to process my grief, so I went up on the roof of the studio on my own…and the strangest thing happened. A mini-storm blew up on the horizon, vanished as soon as it started, and a rainbow appeared and went right over the studio.

Now, I'm not going to be so daft as to say it was a message to me from John Lennon. But the important thing was that it felt like one. And maybe the message was:

Next time, make a better bloody album!

Point of Entry was Priest on autopilot. Even the title and the sleeve were half-arsed. What does *Point of Entry* even bloody *mean*? I've thought up most of Priest's album titles, and I can't even *remember* thinking of that one! The airplane-wing cover was horrible, too, like a crap Pink Floyd rip-off.

I didn't fly home from Ibiza thinking our new album was a disaster. I just knew I didn't feel the same satisfaction that I had after finishing *British Steel*. We hadn't taken a step forward: we'd gone backward.

Point of Entry came out, in February 1981, to the reviews it deserved: underwhelming, and slightly disappointed. And we set out to tour it across the world for the rest of the year.

Saxon were the support band for the first, European leg of what we called the *World Wide Blitz* tour. They were down-to-earth, gritty Barnsley lads, like a Yorkshire version of ourselves, and we formed a close friendship with them that lasts to this day.

When we swung into America, we started in the Midwest, where by now we were routinely playing arenas with 8–10,000 seats: a convention center here, a civic auditorium there. We were used to taking these aircraft hangars in our stride: it was rare not to see a HOUSE FULL sign at the show.

Our management advised us that we needed to get a security guy. We were quite chuffed about this: *Cool! We're big enough to need security!* They told us that a guy called Jim Silvia, a former New York cop with Secret Service connections, would be along to see us.

We were told to meet him in a hotel bar at seven thirty in the evening. We were all knocking back beers and peering around us in search of some kind of gorilla in combat gear when a dapper, diminutive guy in a suit sidled up to us.

"Youse guys are Judas Priest, right?" he asked, in the gruffest Noo Yawk accent I had ever heard. It sounded like it had been dredged up from the bottom of the Hudson.

He wasn't what we'd been expecting, but we hit it off with Jim Silvia straight away. He joined us, rapidly moved from being our security man to our tour manager, and ruled us with a rod of iron. He was to be part of the Judas Priest family for the next thirty-five years.

By the time I get to Phoenix…

A month into the tour, at the beginning of June, Iron Maiden joined us as our support, to Ken's utter delight. Their first date with us was at the Aladdin Theatre in Las Vegas, a city we had never visited before, and whose brash, garish bad taste left us gobsmacked.

Before we left home, I had bought a cheap plastic cine camera from Argos in Walsall. As our tour bus pulled down the Vegas Strip, I shot footage of the neon fountains and the huge boards advertising the old-school icons wooing the casino theaters: Frank Sinatra, Dean Martin, Sammy Davis Jr.…

Obviously, Judas Priest felt *right* at home in that company. And, somewhere, I still have a cartridge with that grainy footage. I must watch it again one day.

From Vegas, we had an overnight drive to Phoenix, Arizona, where we had a show the next night. We arrived in the city at four in the morning, yet it was still 100°F outside. Phoenix is notoriously arid in the summer, and as I stepped off the bus into the night, the heat hit me as if I had walked into a sauna or turned a hairdryer on my face.

Bloody hell! It was unbelievable! The next morning, we woke up on the bus in the Valley, gazing out at a wild vista of mountains, desert, and giant cacti, to the soundtrack of a vast, invisible choir of chirping crickets. I'd seen a lot of America by now, but *this* was something else. It felt very special.

At that precise moment, something in me *clicked*. At some strange, instinctive level, I thought that this city, this state, would keep pulling me back for years to come. There was no way of knowing then just how right I was…

That afternoon, Priest had an in-store signing session before our gig at the Arizona Veterans Memorial Coliseum. These events were like second nature to us now and, as usual, we sat in a line behind a long table, chatting to fans and writing our names on albums, shirts, arms, and whatever else they held out to us.

As Jim Silvia kept the fans in order, a guy wandered down the line and held out a copy of *Sin After Sin* to me. As I signed it, he leaned over the table and whispered in my ear: "Is that song 'Raw Deal' on this record about gay guys?"

What?! His words hit me like a hammer. Had this guy listened to my gay venting song, my Fire Island cruising song, and picked up on what all the fans and critics had missed four years ago?! Had I connected, for the first time ever, with an American gay guy?

I looked up at the man. He was a few years younger than me, maybe early twenties, rugged, handsome, with a twinkle in his eye. And he was waiting for an answer.

"Um…why don't you stick around, and I'll talk to you afterward?" I suggested.

He did. He hung around, and after Priest had done our soundcheck, he came back to our hotel for a chat in the bar. His name was David Johnson, he had moved to Phoenix from California, and he worked in a hardware shop.

I liked David straightaway. As well as being good-looking, in that all-American way, he was smart, and funny, and interesting. We got on well in the hotel bar, where I told him he was right about "Raw Deal." I saw him again later, after the show.

David was athletic, and told me how much he loved playing baseball. I wasn't sure if he was gay, but our chat seemed very flirtatious, and I cheekily asked for a keepsake to remember him by.

In fact, I was very specific. "What about a jockstrap?" I suggested (I had a bit of a fetish for them at the time). The next morning, before the band bus left for El Paso, David dropped by the hotel. He seemed a bit awkward, and maybe embarrassed, but when nobody was looking, he slipped me a jockstrap in the elevator.

A-ha! Now THIS was promising…

David and I kept in touch and wrote letters as the tour headed down south, then east to New York. Our correspondence wasn't intimate, but it was warm, and affectionate, and sweet. We had definitely made a connection.

Our communication continued when the tour ended and I returned to Walsall and settled into my new home. I grew to look forward to David's airmail envelopes, with his distinctive handwriting, dropping into my letter box.

One topic I often wrote to him about was how I had been blown away by Phoenix, and had fallen in love with its sultry temperatures and wild, blasted, almost lunar landscapes. The reply that David sent back to me stopped me in my tracks: "Why don't you come and live here, then?"

I used to be very impulsive in those days, and as soon as I read David's suggestion, it felt like absolute common sense to me.

Yeah, why not?

I loved the city, and America. Priest were getting bigger there and it would be handy to have a base. I had the money to do it, it would be a great experience...and if I got a full-on romance with David out of it as well, so much the better!

Moving across the Atlantic at the drop of a hat may sound extreme to a lot of people, but back then, I was traveling so much week after week that a flight to America felt almost as routine as a bus to Brum. I didn't think of it as emigrating: I could divide the time between my two new homes.

Yeah, OK, I wrote back to David. *You're on!*

David offered to help me find a place, and it wasn't long before he phoned me and said he had found a cool town house to the north of Phoenix. He could sort everything out now and get it ready for when I was able to come over a few weeks later.

Brill! All systems go! I've always been a very grounded bloke, but for a few days, I floated around in a happy haze. This could be a fantastic new life—a beautiful coach house in Walsall, a home (and maybe a man?) in Phoenix, hopping between the two at 35,000 feet whenever I felt like it. The idea felt exotic and sophisticated.

At the end of '81, the *World Wide Blitz* tour closed with dates in Britain and Europe. It seemed like Priest, and all heavy metal bands, always toured in the deepest, darkest, bleakest depths of winter. Maybe that was when the music sounded the best, and made the most sense.

Those British dates were good. We did two nights at Birmingham Odeon, getting to both of them *firmly* on time, and two at Hammersmith. The European leg was also great, especially as, by now, we were even filling decent-sized venues that weren't in Germany.

Through it all, though, in the back of my mind, I couldn't wait for my Phoenix adventure to begin. David's letters remained affectionate and he had posted me photos of the town house, which looked smart. At the end of the tour, in mid-December, I flew to the States.

It was great. At least Arizona was less like a giant sauna at Christmas, and the town house was as neat as David had described. It was a two-up, two-down in a cool neighborhood called Tapatio Cliffs. It looked like a place where I could happily live.

Things with David weren't quite as I'd hoped. He was still friendly, and we got on. I'd go over to see him and he spent a lot of time at my town house. If we had a few drinks, he might crash out and, once or twice, we even ended up in bed together, although nothing much happened there.

So what? I was fine with this…for now, anyway. Truth was, I guess I was infatuated with David, who was just the kind of guy I go for. I felt content, we were having a good laugh hanging out together, and if he wanted to take it slow, that was fine by me. We had all the time in the world to ramp things up, as and when he felt ready.

In any case, we didn't have more than a month together on that first trip to Phoenix—because it was time for Priest to go into the studio and get our recording career back on track.

11

I love a man in uniform

In January '82, Priest got together with "Colonel" Tom at the Ibiza Sound Studios again. Given the slack job we'd done on *Point of Entry*, going back to Ibiza could have been a case of returning to the scene of the crime. This time, though, it was to be different.

We knew we'd taken our eyes off the ball on *Point of Entry* and we weren't about to let it happen again. We didn't put our hair shirts on: we still had plenty of fun and games in Ibiza. But this time, we headed off to party each night knowing we had put in a good, honest shift in the studio first.

Our plan worked. Our record label had been emphasizing to us that we were on the cusp of getting very big indeed in the US. If we made an album that fans there could appreciate and relate to, America was a golden chalice that was there for the taking.

That was exactly what we did with *Screaming for Vengeance*. Tom cracked the whip a little (it was my job onstage, and his off!) and we focused as hard on the writing and the music as we had on *British Steel*. We put the elbow grease in, and the songs all came together.

The title track was one of the first numbers to fall into place. I liked the idea of a song that was a howl of disgust at a venal, corrupted planet:

We are screaming for vengeance,
The world is a manacled place

Ken and Glenn were riffing up a storm on that track, and right at the end Glenn went off on one, doing a load of crazy whammy-bar squealing that sounded absolutely fantastic. This was extremely fortunate, as Glenn had not even intended to do it. Ibiza was rife with blood-sucking mosquitos, even in January, and Glenn had heard the dreaded buzz of one zooming in to attack him just as he finished the song. The inspired whammy-bar magic was Glenn jiggling and twitching around, trying his best not to get bitten.

Having recorded most of the album in Ibiza, we adjourned to a studio in Florida, where Tom Allom now lived, to finish and mix it.

We had been playing around with a song called "You've Got Another Thing Coming" in Ibiza but we hadn't really nailed it. It was buried down on side two of the album. At one stage, we weren't sure it would make it onto the track listing. It was a number about classic Priest themes of determination, and never giving up, and believing in yourself, and as we re-listened to it in the Florida sunshine, we realized there might be more to it than we'd thought. "Hmm," we said. "It's quite a good *driving* song, ay it?"

While we were finishing off the album in Florida, I became friendly with Yul Vazquez and his girlfriend, Gigi Fredy. Yul later became a big Hollywood name in movies like *American Gangster*, but back then he played in a local band, Roxx, who did a few Priest covers in their set.

I'd knock off recording in the early hours and then go along to a rock club, the Treehouse, in nearby Fort Lauderdale. It would fill up at three in the morning when the local strip clubs closed and the girls all headed down. Roxx would play, and I'd get up and belt out Priest songs with them.

I would get *so* pissed down at the Treehouse. My specialty, my party piece, was taking off Gigi's or the strippers' high-heeled shoes, and knocking back beer or champagne out of them. It was always open until six in the morning. I was always there till the bitter end. I don't think poor Gigi ever went home with dry feet.

When we wrapped up *Screaming for Vengeance*, we thought it was a storming album: powerful, compact, and honed for maximum effect from the first track to the last. It was coherent, and connected, and basically the album that we should have made after *British Steel*.

The music press agreed, flexing their wrists to applaud us and hail *Screaming for Vengeance*. While we were doing promo for it in England, Julien Temple shot a video for "You've Got Another Thing Coming" at Kempton Park Waterworks. We mimed and posed away, and I decapitated a bowler-hatted bureaucrat with the power of heavy metal. Good old Julien!

When it came time to take the album on the road, on a jaunt we called the *World Vengeance* tour, it became clear how much our label was focusing on America. They lined up well over a hundred US dates for us—with none in Britain or Europe.

We were wary of this. Was it cheating our British fans? We felt as if we were ambassadors for heavy metal, and breaking America would be great for British metal as a whole, but our fans at home had been with us from the very start and we didn't want to cheat them.

Ultimately, though, we had no choice. The US label said they couldn't wait for a month for us to play UK shows, they needed us in America *right now*, and Arnakata had gone along with it. So, we trusted our management.

I snatched a few days in Phoenix before the tour began. I was looking forward to seeing David again, but I was increasingly beginning to wonder whether this feeling was reciprocated on his side.

I knew that I fancied David—after all, although I loved Phoenix, *he* was the primary reason I had moved to the States. It had been at his suggestion, but I had not needed much encouragement. Now I was here, I was confused as to exactly what he wanted from me.

David seemed to have feelings for me. He was affectionate,

and eager to help as I got used to living in this strange new land, thousands of miles from home. It would be fair to describe him as protective of me...and yet we were hardly ever intimate.

Despite this, we had a good time together. Having been in Phoenix for a few years, he knew all the best bars and clubs to hang out at, and he happily introduced me to his social circle. They were all nice guys, and as keen on getting stupidly pissed as we were.

If David and I ended up back at my town house, sharing a bottle of wine or whiskey, and I tried to make a tipsy move on him, he would either politely rebuff me and head for the spare bedroom, or ignore me and pretend that it wasn't happening. As was my nature, I would respond to this rejection by quietly getting blind stinking drunk.

On the rare occasions that we *did* end up in bed together, David didn't seem to want to be there and would generally turn his back and immediately go to sleep. I was beginning to wonder:

Was it possible that he was really straight?

What did he want from our relationship? Was he, at heart, just a Priest fan who was stoked to be hanging out with the band's lead singer and enjoyed being seen around town with me?

I didn't know. All I knew was that the situation was confusing and frustrating, emotionally and physically. I hadn't known exactly what to expect from my move to Phoenix, but it certainly had *not* been to be kept at arm's length by the man that I had hoped would become my lover.

Yet in some ways, David behaved as if we *were* an item. At times, he seemed possessive—or was that just my wishful thinking? As he bade me a fond farewell when I left for the *World Vengeance* tour, I was deeply confused.

America was going mad for Priest. As the band met in Pennsylvania in August '82 to launch into our seven-month-long tour schedule, *Screaming for Vengeance* was flying out of the shops. It was to massively outsell anything we had done before.

It all went up a notch further when we released "You've Got Another Thing Coming" as a single as the tour started. MTV had just launched and was ruling the music world, and they loved Julien's out-there video, sticking it on heavy rotation.

As the single sped up the Billboard rock chart to number four, it felt as if we couldn't turn on the radio and flick the dial without hearing it blasting out of an FM rock station. It quickly picked up so much momentum that it became unstoppable—as did we.

This was our moment. We had built up a following as we slogged our guts out across the States over the last five years, and now we suddenly had a hit song blaring out of TV screens and drive-time radio programs. We had reached our tipping point.

We were no longer a cult British heavy metal act. We had crossed over and we were a full-on, arena-filling hard-rock band. In America, Judas Priest had entered our imperial period.

The tour was not without its mishaps. The bus-hire company we used had given us an early prototype of a new model that was essentially two buses joined together, with a concertina bit in the middle: in Britain, we'd call it a bendy bus. The back bus held the bunks and the front one had our sitting room and socializing area.

It all worked fine until two weeks into the tour, on Labor Day, when the air-conditioning malfunctioned on the way to San Antonio, with the air temperature well over 100°F. It was unbearable. We had all the windows open and I was lying on the floor of the bus to try to get cool as we sped along the Texas freeway. Just when we thought things couldn't get any worse, the bus broke down.

We pulled over onto the hard shoulder, fifty miles from our show at the San Antonio Convention Center. Jim Silvia sprang into action. He gave the sharp edge of his tongue to the bus-hire people, who rushed a repair guy out to us…with the wrong parts. At which point, Jim somehow magicked up a helicopter.

The helicopter landed on the freeway next to us. We all piled in…and it wouldn't take off. The pilot radioed for another chopper with an engineer, which also duly arrived. Sirens wailed and cops sped up the freeway to us to see what the hell was going on.

A big broken-down concertina bus, two helicopters, a rock band...it was no surprise drivers were slowing down for a looky-loo. *Were we ever going to get out of here?* I was getting flashbacks to our late arrivals at the Birmingham Odeon—but now we had five times more fans waiting, in a sold-out arena!

Eventually, the engineer fixed our helicopter and we all bundled in. The pilot said that he would be able to land on a heliport on top of a skyscraper next to the arena. *Phew!* Then, as we took off, we learned we'd have to detour to San Antonio Airport as the helipad was busy.

Our chopper touched down at the airport...and was surrounded by armed security, who assumed we were Mexican drug smugglers. We got a police escort to the arena, ran backstage, put on our leathers, and were onstage a minute later. Fifteen thousand whooping Texans had no idea what we'd just been through.

The transformation of our fan base continued. The front row at our US shows was no longer just headbanging blokes. Suddenly, we had gum-chewing Madonna-look-alike chicks in fingerless lace gloves, with bows in their moussed hair, winking, and waving their tits at us.

The rest of the band were naturally delighted by this development, and made it their mission to get up close and personal with as many of our new female followers as possible. Yet while they were getting their rocks off, my sexual frustrations were as acute as ever.

In my mind, the bigger Priest got—and we were now *huge*—the greater the damage I would do to the band, and to our career, if it emerged that I was gay. I imagined a mass chorus of the voices of our hard-won fans in the Midwest and Texas: *Fuck! I ain't gonna see no band with a goddamn faggot singer!*

I'd hoped to find quiet, discreet contentment and satisfaction in a relationship with David, but that was looking increasingly unlikely as we drifted along in our platonic friendship.

So, he just wants to be mates, yeah? I figured. *Well, at least that gives me carte blanche to do whatever I want…*

It was time for Plan B.

I was still carrying my secret *Bob Damron's Address Book* with me. I began visiting adult bookstores in big cities like Chicago and Detroit. At the back of these stores were cubicles where you could knock one out to a gay video—or, if you got lucky, meet someone to *help* you knock one out.

I rarely got lucky. In fact, you could probably count the number of times on the fingers of one sticky hand.

More daringly, and dangerously, I began advertising for sexual partners onstage. I was well versed in the bandanna code, in which gay men hang handkerchiefs on their bodies to send a signal about their sexual preferences, and try to cop off.

A hankie or bandanna on the left side of your body means you are a "top," or a giver. On the right, you are a "bottom," or a receiver. The colors provide further clues. Light blue means you're up for blow jobs. Dark blue is anal sex. Orange says you're game for anything. *I may as well try it,* I thought. *You never know!*

Glenn, Ken, Ian, and Dave would have no idea, as I pranced across stage before 5,000 people in Houston or St. Louis singing "Victim of Change," that the bandannas on my leather-studded leg guards were telling the cognoscenti that I was bang up for a bit of water sports or fisting.*

It was yet another fishing trip for cock—and, yet again, I'd retreat to my tour bunk or hotel room frustrated, my keepnet empty.

At least, outside of my personal purgatory, the tour was going great. It seemed Priest could do no wrong. And as we worked our

---

* I had never tried either, but I was curious. Who knows? I figured. They might be fun!

way through our never-ending itinerary, I was counting down the days to October 2, 1982: the night we were to play Madison Square Garden.

I had known about this iconic New York venue ever since I was a wide-eyed kid reading *NME* and *Melody Maker* behind my curtain in my bedroom on the Beechdale. *Madison Square Garden!* It was where the Rolling Stones had played, Hendrix, Led Zeppelin…and now, Judas Priest!

I was going to make the most of it. I was phoning home regularly to speak to Mom and Dad, and when I rang two days before the New York show, Dad told me how proud he was of me headlining such a major venue. *Even Dad had heard of it!* His pride was touching…and, suddenly, I wanted him to be there.

I told Dad I would fly the family out the next day to see the show, get them a hotel, and fly them back the day after. He was thrilled and went off to have a confab with Mom. I said I'd call him back in ten minutes.

When I did, Mom had decided a two-day trip would be too hectic for her, and she'd wait and do a more leisurely visit to Phoenix when the tour was over. Sue had already been out on the tour with Ian and didn't want to come out again so soon, so I got tickets for just Dad and Nigel to fly in.

It was the first time either of them had been to America, and they ran around New York like kids, taking in the Empire State Building, Statue of Liberty, and Central Park. They saw more city landmarks in one afternoon than I had in ten visits!

And, while they were doing that, we had a band crisis to deal with.

Jim Dawson from Arnakata was by now based full-time in New York. He called a band meeting, in our hotel, just before we left for the show. It was unusual, but I guessed he wanted to give us a pep talk or make a short, congratulatory speech. I couldn't have been more wrong.

I love a man in uniform

Jim arrived at the hotel looking sweaty and agitated, with very well-chewed lips. He was twitchy as he talked to us.

"Guys, I've got to stop managing you," he said. "I'm sorry, but I'm having personal issues. You're getting really big and I just can't do this any longer!"

We all stared at each other, gobsmacked.

Fucking hell! Pick your moment, why don't you, mate?

Despite that pre-gig bombshell, the Madison Square Garden show was unbelievable. The cheer as I revved onstage on my Harley nearly took the roof off. Staring out at the Garden at the end of the show, as 20,000 fans roared their approval, I pinched myself.

Was this a dream? And if it was, could I please never wake up?

It felt as if our whole career had been leading to this point. And it had all been worth it. We had reached the top—and now, the trick was to keep climbing.

Night after night, day after day, week after week, our tour rolled on across America. Everything was going great, we were playing huge venues, and the crowds loved us. Offstage, it was a different story. I was increasingly drinking myself unconscious to alleviate the frustration of constantly trying to hook up for secret, sordid sexual encounters...and (mostly) failing.

Except for the nights that I *didn't* fail...

In Pittsburgh, like so many nights on the tour, I had ended the night having a drink on my own in the hotel bar. There were some military guys in there. As I've said, I have always had a big thing for men in uniform—and trying to get them out of them—and that has gotten me into trouble at various points in my life. But one soldier in the bar that night was so hot, he was off the chart.

The guy was having a drink with a bunch of Roman Catholic priests in their dog collars. They were having a laugh and a joke, but the soldier also kept glancing over at me. We made eye contact a few times. *Did we? Or was I imagining it?*

The soldier went off to the bathroom, and I followed him in. He was having a piss, and I went and stood next to him at the urinals.

"Hey!" I said to him.

"Hey, how's it going?" he asked me.

"Pretty good. How's it going with you?"

"Awesome!" he told me. "Except that those Catholic priests keep trying to molest me."

"Oh, really?" I replied, channeling Andy Warhol.

"Yeah! They just want to fool around all the time!"

"There's nothing wrong with fooling around…" I smiled.

He smiled back. "That's true, man! Hey, you want to fool around with me?"

And that was it. *Done deal*! That's the thing with gay cruising. You either spend hours, lonely and desperate, getting nowhere, or it happens as quickly and easily as that. He gave me his room number and, separately, we went back to the bar.

Twenty minutes later, the guy left the bar, giving me a wink as he went. I followed him out shortly afterward.

The soldier answered his door as soon as I knocked. He was still in his uniform—*great*! I noticed there was a half-eaten meal and a bunch of roses on his dining table.

"Oh, I didn't know that you had company?" I asked him.

"My girlfriend was here earlier."

That uniform was soon off, and we went at it lustily for an hour. When I fell into my own bed, exhausted but delighted, a couple of hours later, I could not have been more pleased that my chance military hookup had had his privates on parade.

Now that Jim Dawson had abruptly quit, Priest needed a new manager. Playing a US arena tour, and all over MTV, we were hot property at the time, and a few people were keen to manage us.

But what we needed was a proper *rock* manager. Enter "Wild" Bill Curbishley.

Bill flew out from London to one of the last dates on our US tour. He was already managing the Who, and when we met, he gave us a very astute, straight-talking assessment of where he thought we were as a band, and what we needed to do next.

It was clear from Bill's cut-the-crap demeanor that he wouldn't take shit from anyone. I've always had a sneaking regard for the hard-man school of band management, à la Peter Grant and Led Zeppelin, and Bill seemed to, well, fit the bill. We were impressed by him, and the decision to hire him was unanimous.

We had no idea then about Bill's colorful background: that he had done time for armed robbery (he says he was innocent) and was friendly with the Kray twins, who were known for their involvement in organized crime in East London. But when we found out, it sure didn't put us off.

I did notice that Bill had part of a finger missing, and wondered if he had lost it in some East End gang fight. It transpired that he had done it climbing over a wire fence on an old bomb site when he was a kid.

Bill was already in place when we rounded off the *Vengeance* tour in May 1983 with an appearance at a major heavy metal event—the US Festival in San Bernardino, California.

This was a big deal. The festival had been launched the previous year by Apple cofounder Steve Wozniak and promoted by Bill Graham. This four-day follow-up, over Memorial Day weekend, boasted a new wave day, a rock day, a country day—with headliners the Clash, David Bowie, and Willie Nelson, respectively—and a heavy metal day.

The heavy metal day, on the Sunday, attracted more than the other three days added together. Also on the bill were Mötley Crüe, Ozzy, Scorpions, and Quiet Riot. The headliners were Van Halen, who would later that year go nuclear with their US number one single, "Jump."

The audience? Oh, just a cool third of a million people...

The US Festival metal day was being called heavy metal's Woodstock and it wasn't hard to see why. The traffic around the purpose-built amphitheater was so ridiculous that people were abandoning their cars and walking. Every band was getting helicoptered in and out.

It was only a short chopper flight from our hotel, but I'll never forget it. As we neared the show, the first things we saw were the cars. Everybody in the States has a car, and 150,000 of them had driven to San Bernardino. Gleaming American automobiles stretched to the horizon.

Then, we saw the people—the mass of humanity. *Oh my God!* It was like Woodstock *and* Isle of Wight 1970 rolled into one. I had never seen so many people in my life, and I found it so moving that they were all there for one reason, the best reason I knew—heavy metal.

Judas Priest deserved to be there. We had earned it, by now. It was where we belonged. We knew it was a huge opportunity that we had to seize and we did.

In the scorching sunshine, I vroomed onstage on my Harley and we powered into "Hell Bent for Leather." With a crowd that vast, it was impossible to focus on individuals or even groups of people. We knew we were up on the big screens, so we let rip and tried to blow everybody's fucking heads off.

I felt as if we were on and off in a matter of seconds, and yet those twenty minutes were amazing; transcendent; unforgettable. In terms of establishing Judas Priest on the West Coast, it was up there with supporting Zeppelin at Oakland. *What a day!* I will never forget how exciting it was until the day I die.

We got helicoptered back to our hotel, and the next morning Priest did our usual end-of-tour hugs and scattered in different directions. The tour had been a spectacular triumph and the rest of the band—with the possible exception of poor Ian, who had just split up with Sue—couldn't wait to get home to their loved ones and decompress.

For my part, I sighed deeply and got a flight back to Phoenix. I would have loved to have been going home to a partner who would wrap me in his loving arms—but it was looking pretty fucking certain that David was never going to be that man.

12

Ladies and Gentlemen,
take your seats!

If I was flying home to sexual frustration, at least it would be in more luxurious surroundings.

Now I knew Phoenix a bit better, I fancied an upgrade in my living situation. The town house was nothing special, and I liked the look of an area called Paradise Valley, a little out of the city in the midst of the wild, raw landscapes that had first exhilarated me and drawn me to Arizona.

I found myself a big ranch-style house, with a pool, near the foot of the towering Mummy Mountain. The monthly rent was as steep as the mountain, but I liked the place, and by the time I flew home from the US Festival, it was all mine.

David and I just picked up where we had left off…which was nowhere much. We hung out, shopped, ate, and, most of all, *drank* together every day—but we had not a hint of physical intimacy. By now, I'd given up even trying to get it on with him. Effectively, I was a horny, frustrated, young gay bloke, in the closet…and living like a eunuch.

This was NOT what I fucking wanted from my life!

Luckily, David and I still had a decent social life. Phoenix was a hub for US rock and metal bands in those days. LA was so full of groups trying to make it, and all trying to play the same handful of Sunset Strip clubs, that some came to Phoenix as an alternative.

The focal point of that scene was a rock club and venue called the Mason Jar, where David and I saw countless bands and got royally pissed many, many times. And the Mason Jar was where we got tight with a band called Surgical Steel.

Well known in Phoenix but nowhere else, Surgical Steel were the kind of hard rock/metal band you found in every provincial US city back then. They were local heroes who rehearsed and rehearsed, and gigged and gigged. They tried so hard, but never got a break.

Surgical Steel were lovely, good-natured guys and their singer, Jeff Martin, and guitarist, Jim Keeler, became major drinking buddies. Jeff was a hard-core gun freak and would take me out into the wilds of Arizona, hunting and fishing.

Our other big hangout was a bar called Rockers, on the west side of Phoenix. I loved that place, not least because the two brothers who ran it would always have a pitcher of beer on the table in front of me as soon as I walked in and sat down. Some weeks, I would be in that bar every night.

There was always something happening in Rockers. Once, a guy was sitting there with a giant python around his neck. Animals have never scared me, so I asked, "Can I touch your snake, mate?" (He wasn't the first bloke I'd ever said that to!)

"Sure!" the guy replied and put the python on my shoulders. It was heavy…and then it slowly started constricting around my throat and cutting off my airflow. I tried to loosen it, but it was just too strong.

"I've had him for years, dude! I feed him mice…" his owner was telling me.

"Yeah, that's great," I gasped, "but can you get him off? I'm losing my air supply, and I don't mean the band!" The guy and his pal had to literally wrench the snake from round my neck to stop me from being asphyxiated. I needed another fucking pitcher of beer after that!

The Surgical Steel guys were always up at my new Mummy Mountain house, which quickly became the scene of some wild drinking and drugging pool parties. I am not sure what they made of David and me: Did they think we were a couple? Or just good mates?

They didn't ask, and I was glad about that. Because I was feeling increasingly silly for having ever hoped that we might become an item.

Priest were to fly out to Ibiza that September to record the follow-up to *Screaming for Vengeance*. On the way, I spent time in Walsall…and my parents finally let me buy them a new house. After watching me headline Madison Square Garden, Dad had finally relented and accepted that it *was* OK for me to help them out a little bit.

It was nothing like the previous, posh place I had shown them, but Mom and Dad let me move them off the Beechdale into a bungalow in a cul-de-sac around the corner from the coach house. When I was home, they would be five minutes away. It was perfect for all of us.

Dad also agreed to accept a new car. I would've got him anything, but he is a Walsall bloke, and so he didn't ask me for a Ferrari, or a Lamborghini, or even an MG Aston Martin sports car. Instead, I got him a…Fiat Uno. *A sensible motor.*

When Priest arrived in Ibiza, we didn't have a fat lot to do except drink and soak up the sun…because the studio was bare. It had been stripped of every piece of equipment: the desk, microphones, speakers, leads, the lot. There wasn't even a knife or fork in the canteen. *Huh?*

It seemed Fritz, the studio owner, had hit a few cash-flow issues and his creditors had seized his gear, pending payment. As ever, we were on a tight deadline to make the album, so we threw a bit of our recording advance at the problem to make it go away.

A day or two later, a lorry rolled up with the production console on the back. *Hallelujah!* It was a heavy bit of kit, a proper big unit, and we all helped the two delivery guys to maneuver it off the truck and into the street. At which point, those guys got back in their truck…and drove off.

Thanks a lot, lads!

It was too heavy for us to carry into the building, so we had to find an alternative. Spotting some logs by the side of the road, we lay them down like the rollers by the X-ray machines at airport security and slowly, sweatily, *rolled* the console into the studio.

So, three months after being helicoptered in to rock a quarter of a million US metal fans, we were now unpaid manual laborers helping to assemble our recording studio! Lucky we weren't prima donnas! I quietly thought: *You wouldn't catch bloody Kiss doing this…*

The album that was to become *Defenders of the Faith* fell into place very smartly. We knew we had hit on something special when we made *Screaming for Vengeance*, and we were keen to take what we had done there and build on it.

"Jawbreaker" saw me doing my party piece of smuggling gay lyrics onto our albums again. It was a song about a giant cock, about to come, and powerful enough to, well, break the jaw of any guy who tangled with it:

> Deadly as the viper, peering from its coil,
> The poison there is coming to the boil

I didn't tell the band this. I wasn't sure *quite* how well it would go down if I piped up in the studio and said, "That's about a big cock, that is, lads!" I think I figured some things were best kept to myself.*

---

* In recent years, I have told the others what "Jawbreaker" is about. They laughed, and said, "Oh yeah, now that you mention it, we can see that it is!"

Because I take my lyrics very seriously, I always write them when I am sober and focused. I need to be lucid and on top of my game. However, one track on *Defenders of the Faith* was an exception.

We headed down to a local bar one night and staggered back into the studio many sheets to the wind. We had the basic musical plot for one song but I hadn't written the lyrics yet. I drunkenly decided to do the show right here, right now.

As Tom blasted the music through the studio speakers, I chewed my pen and scribbled down a few words. Full of beer and vino, I decided that "Eat Me Alive" should be about the joys of getting a good blow job:

> Wrapped tight around me,
> Like a second flesh hot skin,
> Cling to my body,
> As the ecstasy begins

I had hidden the meanings of a few of our songs from the others, but they had no doubts what *this* one was about! In fact, as I added the fact that the guy getting the blow job had a gun to the giver's head, plus a very lurid metaphor—"The rod of steel injects!"—they were pissing themselves laughing!

That song was to get us into a whole load of grief two years down the line. The moral of the tale? Possibly, stick to writing lyrics when you're sober…

Then again, even worse things than dodgy lyrics can happen to you when you are pissed. One night, we all went down to a club called Jet Circus on a busy street in the heart of Ibiza Town. As we stumbled out in the early hours, we weren't paying much attention to the dark, seemingly deserted road. Which was when a speeding taxi hit Ken bang up the arse.

It sounds funny, but it wasn't. Ken flew ten feet up in the air, came down, and landed on his back on the hood with a sickening thud. It looked horrific.

Shit! Was he dead?

A groan came out of the darkness: "Ow! Bloody 'ell! Me cowin' leg!"

No, Ken was still with us, but he looked in a bad way. At which point, Glenn sprang to the rescue. Ken's guitar partner went straight into full-on *Emergency–Ward 10* mode. "Get him back in the club!" he instructed us. "Gently! We've got to clean the wound! Get me some towels and hot water! Come on—quick! Quick!"

I hadn't known Glenn had secretly undergone years of medical training, but I was impressed! As the others helped a moaning, groggy Ken back into the building, I ran to the club's kitchen, got a bowl of hot water, and carried it to Glenn.

Glenn had, by now, got ahold of a load of washcloths. He plunged them into the bowl, grimaced, yelled, "Argh—my hands are on fire!" and began rolling around on the floor. Which was when we realized that Glenn was in what you might call a bit of an "altered state." Hence his delusions of medical ability.

Ken was taken to the local hospital, where a junior doctor, who may also have been seeing the world strangely, bound his leg up tight in Elastoplast and sent him away. Ken came out in a rash, and went through hell taking the plaster off a few days later. But at least he had no broken bones.

As we wrapped the album up, we all felt satisfied with *Defenders of the Faith*. It seemed like a strong representation of the Priest ethos; a good summary of what we are about. For me, it remains one of our strongest and fiercest records.

Back in Phoenix, I went straight back into the hard-drinking Mason Jar and Rockers bar routine with David and our mates on the Phoenix rock scene. The Surgical Steel guys must have been still wondering about the nature of my relationship with David, because one night, one of them took me to one side.

"Rob, man, you do know that David dates chicks, right?" he said.

I *had* sort of known. Half-known. But I hadn't *known*, properly. Now, I did.

And, now that I did, I had a strange reaction to the news. There was nothing physical between David and me, and there never really had been, but we still did everything together and I felt betrayed.

Superficially, he and I remained as friendly and close as ever. I have never liked confrontation, although as an older bloke, I can deal with it now, when I have to. But in that particular period of my life—for decades, in fact—I was terrified of arguments and would do anything to avoid them.

Did it date back to those painful nights on the Beechdale when Sue and I would lie in our beds as school kids, cowering, listening to Mom and Dad scream at each other, and dreading hearing the sudden SMACK! of fist on face? I think it did.

I loathed those nights, and they had left a profound mark on me. Any time that conflict arose in my life, the memory of Mom and Dad bawling at each other would resurface from the dark depths of my psyche, and I would back down. Because anything, *anything* was better than that.

So, instead of saying anything to David, I bottled it up, and I brooded. Brooded hard. I stayed quiet and drank even harder. I got trashed at the slightest excuse—and, that particular year, Thanksgiving was as good an excuse as any.

I threw a Thanksgiving party for David, the Surgical Steel guys, and other hangers-on from the rock clubs. It was never going to be an episode of *The Waltons*, and it wasn't. I was trashed even before I cooked the turkey, but I took care over it, so I was mildly disappointed to see it get chucked into the swimming pool.

Wine bottles and beer cans followed it in, and then scores of fully clothed, pissed-up local rockers. I took refuge inside the house as shouts, laughter, and the sound of breaking glass filled the Arizona air.

Even when I'd lived with Nick on the Yew Tree, I'd never been a big stoner, but it was another bad habit I had picked up lately. I was crouched over a glass bong jar, like Nick had taught me, puffing away and watching my big-screen TV, when I felt a tap on my shoulder.

Happy and high, I glanced up…to see two City of Phoenix police officers staring down at me. They had walked in the wide-open front door.

"Rob?" asked one of the cops, confident of the answer.

I nodded, earnestly. "Yep."

"We've had calls from your neighbors about the noise. This party has to stop, NOW!"

I staggered outside, where I noticed my garden furniture had now joined the party in the pool. I had to shout to be heard. Luckily, I've always had a loud voice.

"Everybody, fuck off!" I yelled. "The police are here!"

As a guest dispersal technique, it was certainly effective. Everyone jumped out of the pool and scattered in different directions like ants when you pick up a rock. In two minutes, the house and the garden were both empty.

The police gave me a talking-to: "This is *not* the first time we've had complaints about this house. It's *not* the first time we've been here. If it happens again, you're going to jail."

Hmm. Lucky I'm about to go on tour, I thought!

We called the dates to promote *Defenders of the Faith* the *Metal Conqueror* tour, largely because an enormous robot, the Metallian, dominated our stage set. Dave Holland and his drums had to perch on top of it, fifty feet in the air, as we had nowhere else to put them.

The tour kicked off with a handful of UK gigs before Christmas 1983, and we felt slightly wary. We hadn't played British shows on our last tour—would our fans be angry? We needn't have worried. The gigs all sold out and the fans were amazing and right there behind us, 100 percent. They always are.

It was nice to see Mom and Dad on Christmas Day, settled into their bungalow around the corner from the coach house. Then, in the new year, the tour switched to mainland Europe. And my drinking was becoming a problem.

I'd never gone onstage sober. Even in the very earliest days of Priest, I'd liked to have a bit of a buzz going before I got up in front of a crowd. This had been ratcheting up since the band had started getting huge, around *British Steel,* and now it was out of control.

By the time we got to America in the spring of '84, I was necking plastic mugs of vodka and tonic before the shows as if they were orange squash. In the past, I had always drunk water onstage to stay hydrated. Now, it was neat Smirnoff.

I would be close to staggering as I bade the crowd farewell—"THANK YOU! GOOD NIGHT!"—and then I'd run backstage to do some *proper* drinking. My post-gig ritual was two large cans of Budweiser, glugged down in one, followed by a bottle of Dom Pérignon to myself. A bit greedy, but there you go.

I have never been a falling-down drunk, but I was getting so paralytic that Jim Silvia would sometimes have to pour me onto the bus back to the hotel. At which point, I would attempt to hit the bar, or give up and drain the minibar in my room.

I just fucking hated being sober. Hated being how I was—and hated being *who* I was.

The next morning, I would feel dirty and horrible. *Shit, I don't want to feel this bad again tomorrow—I'll take it easy today!* That would last as long as getting to the venue before the show, at which point it was *Groundhog Day:*

I need something to take the edge off before I go on! I think I'll have a vodka and tonic… and another…

I also introduced another element into my ferocious partying: cocaine.

Oddly, I can't remember where we were the first time I took coke, or who gave it to me, but I'll never forget the feeling that seared into my brain the second I sniffed the white, salt-like powder. It was love at first snort.

Oh, my God! This is the perfect fucking drug!

The coke buzz was euphoric and, in an instant, I became extremely powerful and potent. Plus, *incredibly* clever. I knew the answer to every single question, and what everyone should be doing, and it was essential that I shared that knowledge.

Coke felt like a gift from God. Alcohol got me depressed after the twentieth drink or so. Coke took that clean away and lifted my spirits and my confidence. It let me drink more, which let me take more coke. *Perfect!*

Also, it was so more-ish! Once I had had my first line of the night, that was what I needed, nonstop:

More!

More!

More!

One night, I was sitting on my hotel bed with a Priest roadie, shoveling coke up my nose until the sun came up. I was banging on about my dad, and how I never told him that I loved him and I wished that I did.

"Why don't you call him?" asked the roadie. "Tell him now!"

It was a self-evidently stupid idea, but it made total sense at the time. Unfortunately, I was too out of it to work a phone, so our roadie dug out my address book and called my dad's office number.

"Hello! Rob wants to tell you that he loves you!" he said, when Dad picked up. He passed me the phone.

"Hello, Dad! You all right? Yes, I'm in America!" I gabbled at him. "On tour! With Priest, Judas Priest! Yeah! Er, I love you! I know I never tell you, but I do, like! You and Mom! Yeah! You know what I mean?"

"Rob? Rob?" I could hear my dad saying. "What's going on? Are you OK, Rob?" Even off my tits, I could tell that he sounded upset. *Fuck! What am I doing?* I panicked.

"Sorry, I've gorra gew, Dad! I love you!" I blurted, and slammed the phone down. It must have been a horrible call for him to receive. And, like two typical Walsall blokes, neither of us ever mentioned it again.

I didn't want to come offstage and be by myself in my hotel room. I craved company, male company, but it was forbidden: the forbidden fruit I dared not pick.

Everything was catching up with me: everything at once. The years of denying my true self. The sheer torture of being a gay man fronting a straight band in a macho world. The disappointment that my relationship with David, which I had moved across the world for, had turned out to be a mirage. I felt brittle, and jaded, and like it was all too much.

I don't doubt, now, that suicidal thoughts were creeping in on that tour…but I had a rock, an anvil, that held me together. As ever, the music, and Judas Priest, kept me going.

Once I was onstage, I still thought—I *knew*—that this was all that mattered. It was when I got offstage that the problems started…

My sexual frustration was becoming totally unbearable. I knew I would never dare even to *think* of ripping off my mask, of coming out, but I was taking ever-greater chances to satisfy my cravings. And running ever-greater risks of being found out.

We had an overnight drive to Austin after a show in San Antonio, and in the small hours our tour bus stopped for fuel at an all-night truck stop. As usual, I headed straight for the loo. As soon as I walked in, I saw a pair of feet under the door of a middle cubicle. I walked into one next to him and bolted the door.

TAP-TAP-TAP!

I had hardly even sat down when his eager foot started twitching. I tap-tap-tapped my signal back. Within five seconds, we knew that we were on, and our lonely dance began under that Texan night sky.

There was no glory hole, but there was a gap to one side of the toilet partition. The guy squeezed his arm through and gave me a hand job. It had been a while, so let's just say it didn't take him long. Then I put my hand through the gap and did the same for him.

We never said a word. *Obviously.*

Once he had come, I opened the door and went to wash my hands. Etiquette thus required the other guy to wait in his cubicle until I had left…but he didn't.

I heard his door lock click open behind me, but kept my head down as I rinsed my hands. Human nature being what it is, I couldn't help but glance in the mirror to check out his face. He was a young guy and he was staring at me, his gob hanging open in shock.

He was decked out in Judas Priest merchandise from head to toe. *Well, this is awkward! What am I supposed to say?*

As I walked out of the washroom, I winked at him. "See you on the next tour!" I said, climbed back onto the tour bus, and headed off into the night toward Austin.

After years of living my life in the spotlight and my sex life in the shadows, having to cast around furtively for sleazy release, I was coming undone. An excess of booze was loosening my inhibitions. I was out of control.

I was occasionally slipping into gay bars and bathhouses after gigs, despite the risks of being outed. It had not gone unnoticed. Our management took me to one side for a cautionary word about *the sort of places I was going to,* and the damage it could do to Priest if it leaked out.

The conversation was polite, and well intentioned, not to mention tangential—the word "gay" was not even uttered—but its intent and meaning were undeniable. It could basically be summarized thus:

You are gay.

We know you are gay.

But you're also the singer in a world-famous metal band.

It's a macho world.

Metal fans aren't known for their tolerance.

BE CAREFUL.

I understood why I was being told this…and yet, also, I resented it. I knew that they had a point about "protecting" the band's reputation and yet, in my early thirties, I didn't appreciate lectures on where I should and shouldn't go. I wasn't a fucking kid.

So, I largely carried on doing exactly what I wanted to.

When the *Metal Conqueror* tour swung north to Canada, we played a show at the Stampede Corral in Calgary. This was also the venue for the annual Calgary Stampede rodeo event, and a training center for aspiring rodeo riders.

After the gig, as I got wrecked on my own in the bar of the Hyatt hotel, my head was on a swivel and my eyes were on stalks. I was in gay-man heaven.

Cowboys! Everywhere I looked—cowboys!

I made eye contact with a very good-looking, stocky lad, decked out in the full uniform of Stetson, cowboy shirt, jeans, and spurred boots. His huge belt buckle emphasized the even bigger bulge in his jeans. We started chatting: him about rodeo, and me about metal.

We really hit it off, and after the bar closed, we went up to my room to demolish the minibar. He began boasting about shagging groupies on the rodeo circuit, so I followed suit by talking about the willing girls who pursue rock and metal bands.

It's fair to say he was enjoying that conversation more than I was. Which, oddly, worked out to my advantage. The cowboy was getting himself so aroused that he suddenly said, "Man, I am so horny that I would let *you* blow me!"

That was all the invitation I needed. I got to work, but as I got him off and the fireworks were about to explode, he blurted out, "Don't stop—I'm only sixteen!"

Shit! What? He looked a good five years older than that! I was sent reeling. In my head, I could suddenly hear police sirens, the clanging shut of a jail cell door, and…*snoring?* I looked up. The second that my trainee cowboy had come, he had fallen asleep.

Horribly guilt-stricken, I tried to wake him up. For one thing,

I didn't want him to choke on his own puke in the night, possibly adding manslaughter to my imminent rap sheet. He was too far gone, so I gave up, and a minute later I was deep in my own usual bleary, alcoholic stupor.

When I woke up the next morning, John Wayne Jr. had gone. I got up and made my way to the bathroom…at which point, I saw that my wallet, open on a table, had been relieved of hundreds of dollars and my credit cards. My boom box and fifty or so cassettes had gone, too.

So *that* encounter was a load of bull.

We headed back down into America. In Madison, Wisconsin, we had to shelter 10,000 people under the bleachers of the Dane County Coliseum as a tornado approached. Glenn and I snuck a peek out of a back door and boggled at the low black, blue, and vivid green clouds overhead as sirens wailed and the storm raged.

Then, just over a week later, our *own* tornado hit New York City.

A second gig at Madison Square Garden, in a way, meant even more than our first: it hadn't been a one-off! We had become a band who could play the Garden regularly! Or so we thought. Unfortunately, this was to be our last-ever show there.

It was a great, regular gig until the encore. As we came back on and I began wailing "Living After Midnight," I caught sight, out of the corner of my eye, of a flying object. *Huh? What was that?* And here came another one…and another one…

As the song ended, I glanced behind me and saw a pile of foam seat covers from the auditorium cluttering the stage. I looked out into the venue, and the air was black with more seats flying toward us. One or two of them appeared to be alight.

I ran offstage and jumped on my Harley for "Hell Bent for Leather." By the time I rode it onstage, it was like trying to motorbike through a floor-level soft-furnishings jumble sale. There were more seat cushions on the stage than in the arena.

What the fuck? Two thoughts filled my head: a) *This is fantastic! Our own riot!* And b) *They're never gonna let us play this place again!*

Glenn, Ken, and Ian were by now bouncing on foam to play, as there was no bare stage left. Ken later said that it had been like playing guitar on a trampoline. After a quick "You've Got Another Thing Coming," we scarpered offstage and hid.

Madison Square Garden later said, and the press repeated with great relish, that our fans had done $250,000 worth of damage. We didn't do a thing to instigate the riot, but we got a lifetime ban from the venue. They figured we were more trouble than we were worth.

A year or two later, Glenn and Ken went to the Garden to watch a charity tennis match between Jimmy Connors and John McEnroe. Not sure if they'd be let in, they wore baseball caps. Halfway through the match, a steward came up to them:

"Are you guys in Judas Priest?"

"Yeah," they replied, with sinking hearts, expecting to get kicked out.

"Great, thanks for the new seats!" the usher said. "We got the whole place refurbished, thanks to you!"

I hope that, one day, Judas Priest can play Madison Square Garden again. There again, history might repeat itself. So maybe it's best that we don't.

The *Metal Conqueror* tour was exhaustive, and exhausting. After we had rounded off the American dates, including two shows each at the Hollywood Sportatorium and Cow Palace, then played six gigs in Japan, we were spent. We knew we needed a break.

Our new manager, Bill Curbishley, could see this as well. Between us, we decided that, in 1985, Judas Priest would do something that we had not done in more than a decade. We would have a year off from touring.

Yes, we would take twelve months to chill out and relax, enjoy some of the wealth we had earned, and make a mind-blowing new album at our leisure. What a fantastic plan!

Instead, it was to be the most tortured, tumultuous, and terrifying year of my life.

13

This is the one. This is love!

By the end of 1984, I was getting properly pissed off that I couldn't drive. I was living my glamorous dual life in Phoenix and Walsall, yet in both places I had to rely on either taxis or lifts from mates every time I wanted to get anywhere.

By now, it had been more than fifteen years since I had pinballed Brian the Lion's Mini off the parked cars in a side street in Walsall, and I decided it was time to try again. I developed the somewhat simplistic theory that if I bought a car, it would make me learn to drive.

Ian Hill is a big car fanatic, so he came with me to an Aston Martin dealer in Birmingham. I fell in love with a beautiful red Aston Martin DBS, and decided to do the wanky rock star thing of buying a super-expensive car.

"Ooh, look, there's a Jensen Interceptor over there!" said Ian.

"If you buy the DBS, I'll throw the Jensen in for an extra grand," said the salesman, probably already mentally spending his commission.

So, I bought the Aston Martin and a purple Jensen Interceptor and got them both delivered to the coach house in Walsall. They were parked in my double garage, where they stood, untouched, for weeks.

One day, I had the urge to get behind the wheel of the Aston

Martin and try it out. I climbed into the driver's seat, began to reverse it out, my foot slipped off the clutch...and I drove straight into an apple tree. *Yep, you've still got it, Rob!* I thought. I gingerly maneuvered the DBS back into the garage, where it stayed for months.

I decided to try again in Phoenix. Jeff Martin from Surgical Steel was a brave man and took me out in his car a few times. It's quite easy to get a driver's license in America. You answer a few questions about road safety, drive a car through a few cones at a test center, and...*voilà!* I was finally mobile!

So, as soon as I got to Phoenix at the beginning of '85, I went out and got myself a little red Corvette. Prince would have been proud.

David and I still hung out together, got pissed together, and, a few times, bickered as if we were a couple—which a lot of people assumed we *were*. Our strange, sexless partnership was dysfunctional, and yet emotionally we were somehow codependent.

So, it came as a shock to me—and it also didn't—to have it confirmed that the guys from Surgical Steel had been right a few months earlier. David *was* seeing a woman.

Well, fuck you! I thought. But, again, I didn't confront him, or even mention it. I still had my virulent fear of arguments and confrontation. Those scared childhood nights on the Beechdale Estate, as Mom and Dad yelled and fought, kicked in yet again.

In any case, it was soon time for Priest business to start up again. The first element of our relatively leisurely 1985 was for us to reconvene in Marbella, in southern Spain, to begin our writing sessions for the follow-up album to *Defenders of the Faith*. We rented a villa that belonged to a Spanish princess and set about writing and noodling in a local studio.

After a few days, I left to go to England for a weekend for a mate's wedding. Denise, from the Larchwood Road house, and I went up to Newcastle together. I was pissed for the entire weekend. After the wedding reception, Denise and I found a gay bar and I pulled a really hot bloke. I gave him a blow job in the club toilets, and flew back to Marbella with a stinking hangover and a smile on my face.

We picked up writing songs but, a few days in, Glenn stared at me, looking concerned.

"Are you all right, Rob?" he asked me.

"Yeah!" I said. "Why?"

"Because you're…yellow."

"What are you talking about?" I asked, indignantly.

"Yellow. Your skin, and the whites of your eyes. Go and have a look in the mirror."

I did. *Shit!* Glenn was right! My whole face was a horrible jaundiced color. This didn't look good. The princess's villa had a housekeeper who spoke hardly any English, but as soon as I found her and pointed at my face, she winced and called a doctor.

The local medic arrived and took one look at me. He didn't even need to examine me to reach his diagnosis. "You have hepatitis," he said. "It is serious, because you are in the advanced stages, and it has poisoned your body."

What the…?

"How could I have caught it?" I asked him.

He frowned. "It is generally from a sexual encounter."

Bollocks! My mind instantly went back to the hot bloke in the toilet in the Newcastle gay bar. The doctor left, returning an hour later with medicine for chronic hepatitis and a large syringe, with which he proceeded to inject me in the arse. He also gave me a lecture.

"This hepatitis is very bad," he told me. "It has already damaged your liver. I will return every week to give this injection to you, and also you must have no red meat…and no alcohol."

"How long for?" I asked him.

"For six months."

Blimey! So began a long period of living off boiled chicken and steamed vegetables as we worked on the album. It detoxified my body and I felt pretty amazing, which was not a feeling that I was terribly used to at that time.

Weirdly, despite having to go cold turkey, I didn't get any withdrawal symptoms from not drinking. It was as if my body thought, *OK, this is what I've got to do—let's get on with it!* And yet, despite my drinking ban, I had to have a quick, cheeky nip of something before I did my vocals. I simply couldn't imagine attempting them sober.

My newfound, if unwanted, sobriety helped me to concentrate on the early writing sessions for the album. They were… interesting. An instrument company in America had sent Glenn a newfangled synthesizer guitar called a Hamer A7 Phantom. When he kicked his pedal board into life at the start of one song we were working on, a noise like a motorbike roared out.

"Hey, that sounds like a turbo engine revving up!" I said. That moment gave us our album title, and the song turned into "Turbo Lover":

> I'm your turbo lover,
> Tell me there's no other

I'll cut the crap here…"Turbo Lover" was a song about car sex. It was blatant, and fairly graphic. The engine roaring between my thighs was the latest example of me working references to a cock into Judas Priest lyrics. I like to think that it is a noble tradition.

We didn't start to use synth guitars lightly. We knew a lot of Priest fans would regard synthesizers as wimpy and, well, *not metal*, and it would be controversial to adopt them. For years, one of my favorite bands, Queen, used to have a proud boast on their album sleeves:

NO SYNTHESIZERS WERE USED MAKING THIS RECORD

Yet they sounded so powerful, and gave us so many new textures to play with, that we went with them. We didn't see it as "betraying heavy metal," or anything daft like that. Our philosophy was: Priest are a metal band, we do what we want, and the end result is *always* metal. We still think that way today, and we always will.

We were coming up with so much amazing material in Marbella that we resolved to make a double album, called *Twin Turbos*. It was a productive few weeks, and we arranged to meet up with Tom Allom in the Bahamas—*the Bahamas!*—that summer to make the record.

We had a few weeks off, which I split between Phoenix and Walsall, still sober (not through choice, but at least I was no longer yellow!) and proudly developing my driving skills. I also got asked to take part in a very worthy project.

Hideous images of famine in Ethiopia had filled TV news bulletins for months, and Bob Geldof had already corralled big-name British pop stars to make the Band Aid charity single, "Do They Know It's Christmas?" Ronnie James Dio decided the metal world should go one better and record a whole album, called *Hear 'n Aid*.

Getting involved was a no-brainer, and I flew to Los Angeles in May '85. There were some stellar names there. I knew Ted Nugent and the guys from Journey and Iron Maiden, but I'd never met a lot of people: Dio, Mötley Crüe, W.A.S.P., Twisted Sister…

Yet I was most excited that Michael McKean and Harry Shearer, who played David St. Hubbins and Derek Smalls in *This Is Spinal Tap*, were there! Now here was some *proper* fucking rock royalty!

Glenn and I had seen the movie in San Diego the year before. We had read that it was the ultimate satire of a heavy metal band on the road. We had also been told that the director, Rob Reiner, and his cowriters had been to one or two Priest gigs…possibly in search of inspiration? So, we'd snuck into a matinee screening with our collars turned up to avoid detection; we needn't have bothered, as there was hardly anyone there.

As soon as the movie began, we realized it had been miscategorized. This wasn't a satire: *it was a documentary*. Every single scenario of a hapless Brit rock band touring America that Reiner had so brilliantly captured was familiar to us. Getting lost on our way to the stage? Yep, we had done that one. Under-attended record-signing sessions? Tick, in our early days. Issues with backstage catering? Absolutely, even if we *were* just about bright enough to make a sandwich.

And what was this thing with the drummers? John Hinch hadn't spontaneously combusted, and we didn't lose Les Binks to a bizarre gardening accident, but Spinal Tap's rapid turnover of sticksmen felt too close to the bone to be coincidental.

Hey—were these guys talking about us?

We could have had a sense-of-humor failure at *This Is Spinal Tap.* We take our music seriously but not ourselves, and Glenn and I had roared our heads off in that San Diego flick.

A couple of metalheads in the sparse audience, who didn't clock us, were offended by the movie and stormed out: "Fuck this, man, these guys are jerking us around! Fucking assholes!" Of course, that just made us howl all the more.

It felt like the funniest, most accurate film we had ever seen.

At the *Hear 'n Aid* recording, the Spinal Tap guys stayed in character 24/7, whether the cameras were rolling or not. "Hey, man, you're Judas Priest and Iron Maiden, right?" they said to me and Adrian Smith. "*You* wouldn't be here if not for Tap. You owe us everything!" They were hilarious, and I lapped it up.

Rather less amusing, or welcome, was another development in that summer of '85. A pressure group had sprung up in Washington, DC, calling themselves the Parents Music Resource Center, or PMRC. Led by Tipper Gore, the wife of future US vice president Al Gore, the PMRC was started by the wives of four influential Washington men. They were targeting music and songs they felt were so obscene that they might damage public morality (*yeah, right!*).

The PMRC drew up a list of fifteen songs they found particularly disgusting—the "Filthy Fifteen." It was, to say the least, eclectic.

Categorized as "too sexual" (is that possible?!) were Madonna's "Dress You Up," Cyndi Lauper's "She Bop," and the Mary Jane Girls' "In My House." I could see Prince was overtly sexual but…*Sheena Easton? Really?!*

Unsurprisingly, heavy metal charted high on the Filthy Fifteen. Black Sabbath were there, of course, as were Twisted Sister, W.A.S.P., Def Leppard, AC/DC, Venom, Mötley Crüe, Mercyful Fate… and Judas Priest.

It seemed that "Eat Me Alive," the song I had written falling-down drunk and pissing myself laughing in Ibiza, had aroused their ire. Apparently, Tipper and the other Washington Wives didn't feel that violent blow jobs, enforced at gunpoint, are a terribly good thing.

They are quite correct, of course, but…*our song was a joke.* The lyrics were on the level of a graphic comic. When we heard we were in the Filthy Fifteen, we didn't know whether to be angry or to laugh. It was just ridiculous, and part of a political agenda that didn't concern or interest us.

Seeing as they were married to America's decision-makers, the PMRC didn't find it hard to gain traction and coverage. In fact, they managed to cow the US record industry into agreeing to put stickers on any albums that carried profane lyrical content. The stickers read:

PARENTAL ADVISORY: EXPLICIT LYRICS

The irony was, of course, that any self-respecting American teenage rock fan immediately began seeking out the albums that carried that sticker. The PMRC helped metal bands to shift a lot of records!

Early summer rolled around and the time had come for Priest to pack our plectrums and our Speedos and head for the Bahamas to record the *Twin Turbos* album. We flew out in early June and hooked up with Tom Allom at Compass Point Studios in Nassau.

We had settled on that location because we thought, in a residential studio, we'd be working *and* living together and focusing fully on the music. Quite why we imagined a Caribbean hot spot would have no distractions escapes me now. Had we learned *nothing* from Ibiza?

The first thing we learned on arrival was that Columbia had turned down our request to make a double album. We couldn't understand it—surely, we were just giving them extra music, for free? But we had no choice but to accept their ruling. So, goodbye, *Twin Turbos*; hello, *Turbo*.

The Caribbean was as picture-perfect as in the holiday brochures, all white beaches and glittering azure seas, yet I don't remember being all that blown away on arrival. What *really* excited me was that I had finally finished my hepatitis treatment and I could drink again.

And, fuck, did I make up for those six months!

I quickly learned the local art of shotgunning beer. This involved taking an oversize can of mind-blowingly strong Jamaican Red Stripe lager and gouging a hole in the bottom of the tin with a screwdriver. You then tipped the can over your mouth and yanked the ring pull.

WHOOSH! The rush of pressurized air would force the lager out of the bottom of the tin and into your mouth at high speed, meaning you got pissed in no time at all. It was fantastic—*where had it been all my life?*

Just after we arrived, I flew Jeff from Surgical Steel out for a weekend. We held a Shotgun Olympics and spent the entire two days, with a stopwatch, timing our Red Stripe shotgunning contests. I was proud of my personal best: two-and-a-half seconds.

Initially, Priest knuckled down well on *Turbo*. The palaver with the PMRC was fresh in my mind, and I wanted to push back against the self-appointed, puritanical censors. The chorus of "Parental Guidance" was hardly subtle, but left no doubt where we stood:

We don't need no no no parental guidance here!

Priest quickly fell into an easy routine of making the album by day, then spending the nights shotgunning our way around the bars and clubs of Nassau. We had been there a month when Bill Curbishley called from London with major news.

Bob Geldof had upped the ante. He was set to stage a global charity concert in July to raise more money for Ethiopia. The world's biggest pop and rock stars would be playing Live Aid, staged simultaneously in London and Philadelphia—and Geldof wanted us on the US bill.

Bands can get so immersed in their own little worlds, and we were initially disgruntled. "We're on a roll with the album, and this will really get in the way!" we grumbled to one another. "Do we *really* want to go all that way to do three bloody songs?"

Happily, we soon saw sense. The famine in Ethiopia was barbaric. If we could get off our lazy arses and fly from this nirvana to play a few tunes, and thereby do some good, of course we should fucking do it! Plus, a few mates, such as Ozzy, would also be there. It could be a laugh.

Live Aid, on July 13, 1985, was a bit more than a laugh. It was only when we got to the John F. Kennedy Stadium in Philadelphia that we realized the enormity of the event. Half of the most iconic music artists in the world were there—and the other half were at Wembley Stadium, in London.

It was really exciting to be part of something so huge, and Live Aid had a surreal, out-of-body feel from the start. We had to be at the stadium by the time we were normally going to bed in Nassau. At nine in the morning, I was watching Joan Baez sing "Amazing Grace."

Ten minutes later, I got a message backstage: "Miss Baez wants a word with you." Like a naughty schoolkid being caught out, my first reaction was *Oh bollocks!* Did she want to give me a telling-off for Priest's heavy metal duffing up of "Diamonds and Rust"?

But here was Joan, tripping toward me, smiling and waving. "Hey, Rob!" she said. "I just wanted to come over and tell you that the version of 'Diamonds and Rust' that you did…"

Here we go, I thought.

"…is my son's favorite version. He thinks it's great that his mom's song was covered by a metal band!"

"Oh, that's really cool!" I said. And I meant it. Joan was a very sweet and gracious lady.

Judas Priest were on at half past eleven in the morning, after Crosby, Stills & Nash and before Bryan Adams. The crowd looked as humongous as at the US Festival. We knew our three-song set would be over in no time, so we just gave it all we could for those twenty minutes.

Philadelphia has always been a massive rock market, so we got a great reception. "I see we've got a few thousand metal maniacs here today!" I said, and there were chants of "Priest! Priest! Priest!" But the day wasn't remotely about us. It was way bigger than that.

The sole advantage of going onstage so ridiculously early was that I could then start getting hammered straight away. So, I did. The day subsequently took on a dreamlike quality.

I'd already watched Sabbath, who had been on even earlier than we had—*would Ozzy even have been to bed?*—and Zep were fantastic. I remember feeling a daft, pissed pride that Birmingham and the Black Country were so well represented: Sabbath, Planty, Priest… oh, OK, and Duran Duran.

Live Aid went on and on and on. MTV kept banging on about the fact that Phil Collins was playing Wembley, and then getting on a Concorde to do the Philly show as well. That riled me, for some reason. I thought it was all too posey, and he was being a bit of a knob.

Pop tart that I am, I loved seeing Madonna. I've always been a gay metal fanboy for her. But the act that really blew my mind was Mick Jagger and Tina Turner. I'm a sucker for a rock showman and a soul diva, and they certainly ticked both boxes. They were electric, especially when Tina first strode out in her high heels.

I was back onstage for the finale, chirping along as Lionel Richie led the whole ensemble through three thousand bloody choruses of "We Are the World."

It's been an amazing day, I thought, *and it's a fantastic cause, but isn't it time to knock this song on the head now? Surely?*

What—ANOTHER chorus?

Priest were staying at the Four Seasons, where we always crashed in Philadelphia, and there was an after-party for all Live Aid artists and presenters in the penthouse suite of an expensive apartment block across the street. I wandered over on my own.

The first thing I noticed in the party was that it had a sauna, and people were sneaking in, in pairs, fully clothed, and coming out with their clothes disheveled. The second was that, leaning on a wall next to it, in shades, on his own...was Jack Nicholson.

Jack had introduced a few acts at Live Aid and had been wandering around backstage all day, but I'd never have dared to approach him. Now that I had a few gallons of Dutch courage inside of me, it was a different story, and I lurched over.

"All right, Jack?" I asked him.

"Hey, Rob! I saw what you did today—you were great!"

Fucking hell! Jack Nicholson knows my name!!

"Er, cheers! Great day, wasn't...?"

I got no further than that because, at this point, the drunkest man in Philadelphia, and possibly the world, stumbled up to us. I had been drinking all day, and Jack had clearly had a few, but this prick was on another level.

"Jack Nicholsshhon, man!" he drawled, spraying us both with

saliva, and with a trail of drool leaking from one corner of his mouth. "*The Shining,* man! *Cuckoo'sh fucking Nest!* Fucking aweshome!"

The guy wouldn't shut up. I was getting rattled—*Fuck off, pal! You're ruining my conversation with Jack Nicholson!*—but Jack was a model of courteous patience: "Thank you! I really appreciate that!" After five minutes of slur and spittle, the pisshead toppled off to the bar.

"You must get that all the time?" I asked Jack.

He sighed, and raised his eyes to heaven. "Yep. Everywhere I go!"

What. A. Fucking. Day! After being charmed by Joan Baez, saving Africa, entertaining a TV audience of billions, singing backing vocals for Lionel Richie, and boozing with Jack Nicholson, I moseyed back to the Four Seasons. *Might as well have a nightcap,* I thought, and took a seat at the hotel bar.

I saw him straightaway.

He was tall, strong-jawed, good-looking, and very alpha male. *Just my type.* He was sitting opposite me on the other side of the bar and staring at me like I was staring at him. We couldn't take our eyes off each other.

It was a magnetic attraction. It was the most natural thing in the world for me to walk around to the other side of the bar and start talking to him. And when I went to the toilet, a few minutes later, it was the most natural thing in the world for him to come with me.

As soon as we got there, *we were at it.* We were all over each other. We crammed into one of the posh cubicles, and our hands and mouths were devouring all they could touch. It was pure animal lust. Passionate. Uninhibited.

We had to be careful. For some reason, the Four Seasons toilet doors had slats in them, so if anybody came into the washroom, we had to stop and stay totally still so that they wouldn't hear or see us. Then, the second they went out, we were at it again.

The sex was stupidly, mind-bogglingly good. We were in there for ages, getting each other off again and again and again. How long for? I wouldn't have a clue. I lost all track of time. But a soundtrack was running in my head:

Yes! THIS is how it should be!

When we were finally done, and we slunk separately back to the bar, we didn't stay for long. Nor did he come back to my room. His name was Brad, he had just come out of the military, and he was Philadelphia-born and bred. So, he just went off home…after we had arranged to see each other again the next day.

I floated off to bed in a blissed-out haze. I couldn't wait to see him again. And, luckily, I didn't have long to wait.

Brad came over again the next morning. We sat in his car, talking. It could have been awkward, after we had sobered up from the night before, but, again, us sitting chatting felt like the most natural thing on earth.

He was younger than I'd thought: only twenty. But he was big, broad, mature, and seemed a lot older than his age. He was from a working-class Philadelphia family and was living with his parents again after leaving the Army.

What was great was that he had had no idea who I was when we'd met in the hotel. When I told him that I was the singer in Judas Priest, it didn't mean a lot to him. He wasn't a metalhead—in fact, he wasn't a big music fan at all.

"So, where are you going from here, Rob?" he asked me.

"Back home to Phoenix for a week and then to Nassau, in the Bahamas, to finish making a record," I told him.

"Oh, that sounds great."

"Have you ever been to the Bahamas, Brad?"

"No."

"Would you like to come?"

Again, asking him seemed like the only thing I could possibly say, that I *wanted* to say, at that sacred moment in time. And his answer felt equally natural.

"Yes, I'd love to!"

So, that was it. We agreed that he would fly out to Nassau in a week. We had a date. And I had just one other piece of business. I dug out one of my old lines.

"Can you give me a keepsake to remember you by until I see you?" I asked.

"What kind of thing?" asked Brad.

"Anything," I said.

Brad smiled, undid his jeans, and shuffled them down the car seat. I saw that he was wearing a pair of skimpy pants with metal clasps on the side—a regular gay favorite! He undid the clasps, slipped them off, and handed them to me.

"Thanks!" I said. "See you next week!" We had a quick kiss goodbye, I got out of the car, and he drove off.

I was ecstatically, deliriously happy. Meeting Brad was the best thing that had ever happened, and it had shown me exactly what was wrong with my life. It had been intense, passionate, beautiful, and *mutual*.

Now that I had met Brad, everything had changed. From this point, it would all be different. *All of it.*

This was what I had been waiting for.

This was the one.

This was it.

This was love!

14

In the court of the King of Philadelphia

I felt like a completely new person. I was excited and energized by meeting Brad.

Back in Phoenix, I caught up with everyone, including David—and, to my delight, found that my feelings about him had changed overnight. Put simply: *I no longer had any*. I didn't say a word to him about me meeting Brad because, frankly, it was none of his business.

Compared to the volcanic feelings Brad had awakened in me—and he'd given me a few eruptions already!—my thing, or rather non-thing, with David suddenly felt trivial and irrelevant. *He fancies women? So fucking what? Good!* I no longer felt a flicker of interest, or jealousy.

I didn't start to hate David. I felt sure we'd stay drinking buddies. He probably never even noticed anything different about me: he certainly never knew that I was in love. But I *was*. My first thought when I woke up, and my last one before I went to sleep, was...*Brad*. I couldn't wait to see him again in Nassau, and a couple of warm, friendly late-night phone calls stoked my anticipation.

Only six days to go now! Five! Four!...

That Saturday night, to kill some waiting time, I drove my little red Corvette down to Rockers to meet the Surgical Steel guys. The brothers who ran it had my usual pitcher of beer waiting as I walked in, and I had a proper buzz on when I left after midnight.

I got into my Corvette without a thought to how much I'd drunk. I'm not proud of that…but, let's face it, I wasn't alone in my shit behavior. It was the eighties, when anything went, and it wasn't the first time I'd driven home pissed. It would, however, be the last.

I had hardly pulled down the ramp and onto the freeway when I saw the blue lights flashing behind me. For some reason, when the police pulled me over, I wasn't all that bothered: *Ah, it'll be fine!* I suppose I thought I was invincible.

When I wound down the window, the fumes from my four hours of downing pitchers must have blasted the cop as he saw my leather pants, leather vest, and studded bracelets. He examined my driver's license and registration, then asked, "Do you have any weapons?"

I did. I usually carried a small loaded revolver with me—it's standard practice in Arizona. It was in the middle console, next to me, and I gestured toward it.

"Don't reach for that!" barked the cop. "Now, get out of the car!"

He Breathalyzed me. My bizarre feeling that it was all going to be OK ended when the Breathalyzer showed I was well over the limit. "I'm arresting you for driving under the influence," said the cop, and slipped handcuffs on me (to be fair, this was not a new experience!).

He led me to the squad car, where a female officer was waiting, and stuck me in the back seat. I was always quite a lucid, chatty drunk, and my verbal diarrhea kicked in. I didn't *quite* say "Don't you know who I am?" but I wasn't too far away.

"Oh, this is such a shame!" I told them. "I'm just back from playing Live Aid with my band, Judas Priest! I was out celebrating…"

I heard the words as they came out of my mouth and I cringed for myself. *You fucking dickhead!* I thought. *You DESERVE to be in this police car!*

It was two in the morning when we got to a downtown cop shop. A couple of officers recognized me and greeted me: "Hey, Rob, what's up? We love Priest, man!" Cool—so maybe they might let me off? No chance. They booked me, and took my mug shot.*

The cops Breathalyzed me again. Yep. Still over. Not unrelated to the fact that I had so much beer inside me, I was by now desperate for a piss. "I'm sorry, but I have to urinate," I told them.

"You'll have to hold it in," one of them answered.

"I can't! If I don't go to a bathroom, I'll have to do it right here!"

"You can't go to the bathroom by yourself!" a cop brusquely told me. "And I'm not taking your handcuffs off."

"Well, *this* will be interesting, then!" I replied.

The cop relented and came to the washroom with me. He took one cuff off me and fastened it to his own wrist, like he was Andy Warhol or something. Like most blokes, I can't pee if someone is watching. "You'll have to turn around!" I told him. He sighed, and did.

The police told me I'd be locked up for the night and go before a judge the next day. I was allowed a phone call, so I rang David. "I'm in jail!" I told him. "Call Jim Silvia!" I had a pathetic hope that my ex-cop tour manager would be able to make it all go away.

The cops locked me in a big cell on my own. At first, anyway. Then they tipped another drunk in, then another, then another. Some were so paralytic they just fell on the floor. Two wasted Native Americans stumbled in and clocked me in my rocker's garb.

"Hey, Rob, we love Judas Priest!" they said. "Give us a hug, man!" They instigated a lengthy, repetitive debate on the comparative merits of Priest and Mötley Crüe. By six the next morning, there were fifteen or twenty of us sorry drunkards in that cell.

The cops brought breakfast: a baloney sandwich, a cardboard cup of weak orange juice, and…a pouch of tobacco, with rolling

---

* I feel lucky that photo has never seeped out and appeared in any of those "celebrity mug-shot" features. Although now I've told this story in this book, I guess there's a good chance it will surface.

papers. It seemed smoking was not just permitted but *compulsory* in that jail, which struck me as odd. Fierce trading ensued. A Native American swapped his baloney roll for my tobacco.

An hour later, a cop came to the cell and pointed at me. "You! You're free to go! You'll hear from us about your charges!" I later found out that Jim Silvia *had* called the station and asked them to release me…but not straight away.

"Keep him in the cells for the night first!" Jim had told them. "Teach the stupid fucker a lesson!"

Walking out of the station, I found myself in downtown Phoenix on a Sunday morning. My leathers stank, the thermometer was already pushing 110°F, and my Corvette was locked, five miles away, on the freeway. It took me twenty minutes to hail a taxi and slink home.

Jim Silvia managed to keep me out of a courtroom but took me to see a judge. She gave me a stern lecture, fined me $500, put me on probation, and banned me from driving for eighteen months. "If I ever see you again, it will be a *lot* worse!" was her parting shot.

Fair enough, really.

I couldn't wait to get out of Phoenix and back to the Bahamas, and it was a relief to be on the plane to Nassau. We picked up where we had left off on the record but, really, my heart wasn't in it. I was just aching to see Brad.

When he flew in that weekend, it was fantastic to see him. I felt just as passionate about him as I had at Live Aid, and the sex was just as good. He seemed to feel the same. We got down to enjoying each other's company again.

I had done things backward with Brad. I had fallen in love with him, and now I had to get to know him. The great—and very fortuitous—thing was that the more I saw of and learned about this handsome Philadelphia guy, the more I liked him.

The military had made him mature beyond his years, sure, but he'd also kept a really irresistible, exuberant sense of humor. He was easy-going and fun, and loved a laugh. I totally fell for his cheeky chuckle that always led to a full-on belly laugh.

Brad laughed a lot because he was an incorrigible practical joker and a masterful piss-taker. He was a real force of nature. And he had his own specialty line of humor: water jokes.

Within a day on Nassau, I realized that Brad was a water prankster par excellence. I was a bit nonplussed the first time he chucked a glass of water over me. Also, the first time I walked through a door and a water-filled balloon fell on my noggin. But I soon got used to it.

I've never been a practical jokes sort of bloke. Had anybody else done that shit to me, I'd have ignored them, or asked Jim Silvia to sort them out. But I was so infatuated with Brad that I found it all hilarious. He made me laugh and I loved being with him.

So, yes, Brad and I got down to enjoying each other's company— in *and* out of bed—and to finding out about each other. But the main thing we got down to was drinking.

Brad was as much of a pisshead as me. He had a prodigious capacity for alcohol and proved to be a natural at shotgunning. Our local in Nassau was the Duke of Wellington pub. One night I got so pissed that I couldn't walk, and Brad threw me over his manly ex-Army shoulder and carried me home to bed.

Yes, please! Now THIS was more like it!

I had been besotted with Brad on first meeting him, and in a few days of fun in the Bahamas, my infatuation had multiplied tenfold. When he flew back to Philadelphia, I realized how much I would miss him until he came back in two weeks' time.

A cloud descended on me. I began pining for him. He was on my mind in the studio; in the bars; everywhere. I'd find any excuse to call him in Philadelphia and plot our next madcap adventures.

And when he did fly out for his second visit, I loved it as much as his first.

I was getting so obsessed with Brad, and my time with him was so precious, that I didn't want to share him with anyone else. I wanted him all to myself. So, I flew the two of us to Cabo San Lucas in Mexico. We had an amazing few days hanging out, and when it was over, it felt too soon. I arranged for him to fly back to Nassau from Philly three weeks later and planned out an even more exotic adventure for us.

I flew us to Bermuda for three days and rented a beautiful suite in a luxury hotel right by the beach. I said we should stay in and get some "us" time, but Brad wanted to do what any sane person would if they were dropped into a Caribbean paradise: go out, explore, and see the island.

Indifferent to how needy I was, Brad told me, "You do what you want, Rob, but *I'm* going out!" He hit the beach and soaked up the local life and atmosphere while I skulked in our room and drank myself into a stupor like a proper mardy-arse, as we say in Walsall.

Well done, Rob. Very mature. Very clever.

When Brad and I flew back to Nassau, I hugged him goodbye at the airport before he went on through security for his flight to Philly. I watched as he vanished through passport control, down a corridor, and around a corner.

Each time Brad had left Nassau, a hateful emptiness had seemed to descend over me. A black cloud. And here it came again. I couldn't bear it. Suddenly, I knew that I had to see him again. *Urgently. Right now.*

I ran up to the passport control. "Hey, I need to go through for two minutes, just to talk to somebody!" I said.

"Excuse me, sir?" the guy replied. "Do you have a ticket?"

"No! I'm not flying! I just need to…"

"Then, I'm sorry. You can't come through."

"I just need to speak to somebody to tell him something important! Look, I'm Rob Halford from Judas Priest…"

I heard those wheedling words fall out of my mouth and I felt the same self-hate that I had in the police car in Phoenix.

"…and I just have to see my friend! I promise, I'll be two minutes. *Please* let me in!"

"Well, this is most unorthodox, but…" The guy could sense my need and panic. "OK. You will be back here in two minutes or I'm calling airport security!"

"Thanks so much!" I brushed past him and ran down the corridor and around the corner. I don't know quite what I was expecting when I saw Brad again. A classic, cinematic, passionate parting? Our *Casablanca* moment? *We'll always have Bermuda?*

When I ran into the departure lounge, Brad was sitting with a gang of guys and women he had just met. He was talking, and everybody was laughing. It was typical Brad: he made instant friends everywhere he went. He glanced up, saw me, and looked surprised.

"Hey, Rob! What are *you* doing here?" He didn't get up.

"I just needed to see you again, before you got the plane," I said. "I wanted to say goodbye again!"

Brad smiled, like it was no big deal. "OK, sure! Well, give me a call in Philly! See you soon!"

As I left the lounge, I turned around and saw him talking to his new friends again. He wasn't watching me go.

The incident triggered a paranoid line of thought in me:

Does he not like me as much as I like him? If not, why not? Does he want the same thing from our relationship? I love him—does he love me?

Those questions pinballed around my head for the next few days in Nassau, in the studio and out. I tried to shut them up in my usual way, by drowning in lakes of alcohol. I'd sit alone, in my room, knocking back Red Stripe or rum, and wondering what Brad was doing in Philadelphia:

Is he thinking about me like I'm thinking about him? Is he on his own? Is he…with someone else?

I was thirty-three years old, and behaving like a lovesick teenager.

While this was all going on, of course, I had an album to make. I was showing up to the studio, and trying to show willing and do my bit…but my mind just wasn't on *Turbo*. I had never felt so remote and detached from a Judas Priest record.

The lads were on great form and the music was coming together, but I just couldn't get into it. In the studio, I seemed to be always pissed or hungover, or usually both. I could still perform my vocals OK, but when it came to songwriting, I was on autopilot.

I knew I was in a bad way. I felt brittle and jaded from the non-stop drinking, and angry and frustrated at having to be away from Brad. And then I became something I had never been before—*violent*.

It happened on a glorious Caribbean summer afternoon. The band decided to take a few hours away from the studio. We would hang out at the beautiful bay just down the road, hire motorboats, take a few cans with us, and do a bit of fishing. *Sound!*

When we picked up the boats, the guy who ran the hiring company gave us a safety lecture. "Please be very careful with my boats!" he cautioned, pointing to one area of the bay. "Over there is coral reef. If you hit it, and damage the propellers, you will have to pay!"

Yeah, yeah! Whatever! We weren't really listening, and as soon as we were out in the bay, and I cracked open my first beer, I forgot every word the bloke had said. I gunned the throttle and powered my boat into a load of coral. I heard the propeller crunch: *CRACK!*

Oops! Oh, well! Another beer?

Glenn's little daughter, Karina, was with him, and he also smashed into the coral in their boat. We didn't catch a fish between us, the scorching sun was unbearable, and by the time we called it a day, I was pissed, pissed off, and irritable.

We returned the boats. The guy looked underneath to check the propellers, and was outraged at what he saw. "That's it!" he yelled. "You are never renting from me again! You've got to pay for this. I want money, now!"

It was impossible for us to deny that we had damaged them, so we paid up, but the guy's attitude, the absence of fish, and—primarily—the fact I was now absolutely arseholed left me riled and spoiling for a fight. I didn't have to look far to find it.

As we walked along the dock to our hire cars, an open-top Jeep came speeding toward us, full of shouting, partying locals. The laughing driver wasn't looking at the road and I had to quickly yank Karina to safety. As they passed, I screamed abuse at them.

The dreadlocked Bahamian driver slammed his brakes on, and fast-reversed back to us. He jumped out of the Jeep, got right up in my face, and started shouting at me in thick local patois. Fuck knows what he was on, but his wild eyes looked intense.

"What's your fucking problem, eh?" he asked. "Eh? Fucking clart!"

"You need to bloody look where you're going!" I told him. "You nearly hit this little girl!"

"Shit! I wish I *had* fucking hit her!" he yelled.

What?!

Fuck. This. Guy! I peeled my fist back and punched him, hard, in the mouth. He reeled back, grabbed me, and suddenly we were rolling around on the ground, in the dirt, beating the shit out of each other.

Right! I'll fucking kill him!

"Stop! Stop! Rob, stop!" yelled Glenn, and pulled me up and off the guy. He was lying in the dust with a bloody lip. His mates from the Jeep were trying to help him up, and more locals came running up and surrounded us. Suddenly, the numbers weren't looking good.

"We've got to get out of here!" said Glenn. "There's too many of them. Come on, run! Run!"

We sprinted to our cars and screeched away. The Bahamians yelled after us, jumped back in their Jeep, and chased us. They tailed us for five minutes, shouting and flashing their lights, as we sped toward our base, then they gave up and turned off.

It had been totally out of my usual placid character, but as we held our postmortem on the fight back at the studio, I was too livid to feel any shame. *Bollocks to that! He was asking for it! I'd bloody do it again!*

I think we had all gone a bit stir-crazy in Nassau and it felt like time to get off the island. Tom Allom called a halt to our sessions at Compass Point, and we arranged to meet up again in Los Angeles at the year's end to wrap up the album.

That gave me the next three months off. Mentally, I rubbed my hands. I intended to spend every single minute of them with Brad.

The first thing I wanted to do was take Brad to Phoenix.

We had a great time there. He loved my house by the mountain, and my swimming pool gave him infinite fresh scope for yet more water-related pranks (I mean, anybody would love having a carrier bag of chlorinated water dumped over their head, right?).

I loved staying home with Brad, and when we went out, he fit into the Rockers and Mason Jar scene like a hand in a glove. The guys from Surgical Steel loved him, partly because he drank even more than they did. One of them even took me to one side and told me he'd never seen me so happy.

However, one thing that I was rapidly learning about Brad was that he had a very short attention span. After a week or so of laid-back, alcohol-fueled shenanigans in Phoenix, he decided that he was bored and fancied a change of scenery.

"I'm going back to Philly," he told me. "Why don't you fly over and stay with me in a few days?"

I knew Brad had recently got his own place, so I agreed. I was

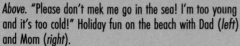

Above. "Please don't mek me go in the sea! I'm too young and it's too cold!" Holiday fun on the beach with Dad (*left*) and Mom (*right*).

Right. A Beechdale bab on a bike, not long after we'd moved into our brand new council house in Walsall.

Below. Me, Mom, Dad, and Sue in my grandparents' garden in Birchills, Walsall. I used to love going to stay with them at weekends.

Below, right. "Yeah, I'm meeting the Queen here in five years!": showing off to Sue and her friend in Walsall Arboretum.

Above. Playing a king (fourth from right) in the infants' nativity. "Uneasy lies the head that wears a crown"? Too bloody right if it's digging into your skull!

Below, left. In junior school. Smart little bugger, wasn't I?

Below, right. Me and Sue getting ready to brave the walk across the cut through the choking fumes from the G. & R. Thomas Ltd. pig iron factory.

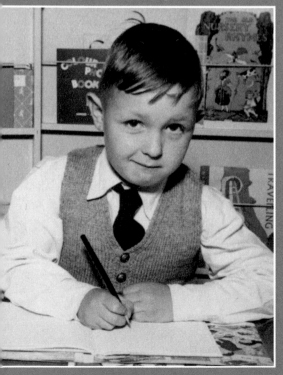

My family never caught planes but at least we could look at 'em. Sue and me at Heathrow to gawk at the planes with friends from the estate.

I used to perfect my Gay Gordon in my secondary school's old-time dancing class. I'm third from the left on the back row.

In the back garden at Kelvin Road, with a surprise late arrival to the family: my brother Nigel.

This wasn't to be the last time that I caught crabs at the seaside.

Above, left. Going through a corduroy phase. Thankfully, it didn't last.

Above. My sister Sue and her mane man, Brian the Lion, who probably still has nightmares about my disastrous driving lesson. That poor Mini!

Left. Indulging my teenage passion for acting at Walsall Grange Playhouse. "Watch this kid!" advised the *Express & Star*.

Giving it some vocal welly in an early band. I wasn't a big star, but my shirt was.

Above. Me (second left) in the short-lived, hat-loving Lord Lucifer.

Left. A rare train trip to a Priest gig, sporting Mungo Jerry sideburns and a Harry Fenton tank top. Nice!

Below. The legend that is former Priest manager Dave "Corky" Corke, with his girlfriend, Lynn (left), and my sort-of girlfriend, Margie (center).

Right. By a lake, trying to look deep on a very early Judas Priest tour.

Below. Unloading our Mercedes tour van before an early working men's club gig. Pretty glamorous, huh?

An early press picture: Ken, John Hinch, me, and Ian at a local beauty spot. We had no cash for a photographer, so Corky took it. You can tell.

In LA, on our first trip to the US in 1977: "Bloody hell, Les! Not the cowboy shirt again!"

Supporting Led Zep in Oakland in front of 80,000 people in July 1977. My head wants to explode.

I still can't believe
Rob "The Queen" Halford
never caught on!

Below. Image rethink time:
getting kitted out in our
leather gear at a fetish shop
in Wandsworth.

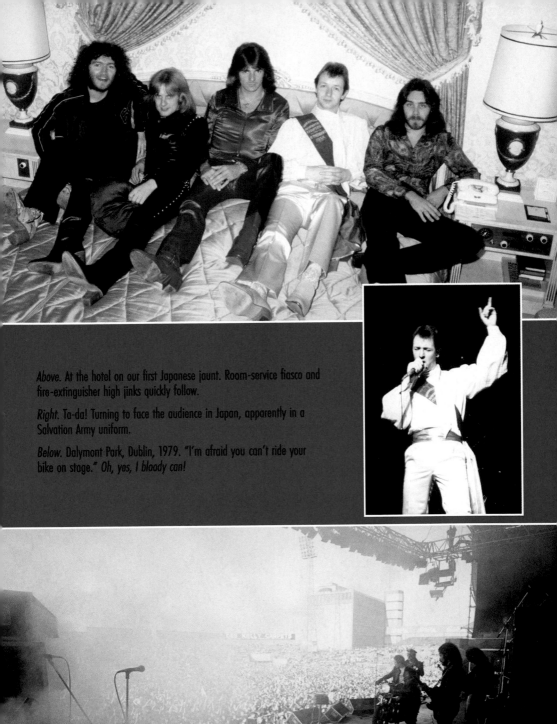

Above. At the hotel on our first Japanese jaunt. Room-service fiasco and fire-extinguisher high jinks quickly follow.

Right. Ta-da! Turning to face the audience in Japan, apparently in a Salvation Army uniform.

Below. Dalymont Park, Dublin, 1979. "I'm afraid you can't ride your bike on stage." Oh, yes, I bloody can!

Left. "Bloody hell . . . *how many?*"
Gazing out at a quarter of a million
metalheads at the US Festival in
California, May 1983.

Below, left. The metal world
assembles in LA for Hear 'n Aid.
Ronnie James Dio is on my left,
I still miss him and play his
music every day.

Below. Rocking Live Aid in
Philadelphia, July 13, 1985.
That was a . . . busy day.

Above. Ardith, the rehab counselor who helped to save my life, gave me this book of meditations. I have read it every night for the last thirty-four years.

Right. 1986: Fuel for Life, my first sober Priest tour. I look happy, and I felt it.

Below. Human tragedy leads to a stupid circus: Priest in court, being accused of hiding messages in our songs telling our fans to kill themselves. Reno, July 1990.

Above, left. If you are lucky, you find The One. An early photo with Thomas, my rock and soulmate.

Above, right. Getting reacquainted with intimate venues with Fight, my first solo project after I accidentally quit Priest: London Astoria, 1993.

Left. 1998: Going through that awkward electro-goth Dr. Fu Manchu phase in 2wo.

Below. The Metal God when he didn't need a bus pass.

THE METAL GOD IS BACK! HALFORD

RES URRECTION

Back in Priest—thank God!—and on the road for Ozzfest, 2004.

"Ladies, ladies!" With Gaga and Starlight, Phoenix, 2014.

A rare selfie with Lemmy, Chile, May 2015. Sadly, he was dead within the year.

Happy golden jubilee to Judas Priest: a band, and a life, forged in the Black Country.

looking forward to it. But when I got to Philadelphia, I was horrified. He was in a squalid little bedsit over a convenience store in the sort of neighborhood where you took a baseball bat when you went to buy milk. The secondhand furniture had seen better decades, and the rat droppings in the kitchen showed he wasn't the sole occupant.

It was a shithole, but Brad said it was all he could afford. In any case, he had other things on his mind. We sat in his grotty dump for a couple of hours, drinking in front of an old movie on his tiny black-and-white TV, then he made a suggestion.

"Hey! Shall we do some coke?" he asked me. "I have a little!"

Brad had told me in Nassau that he was partial to Charlie, and I was always happy to dive nose-first into a pile of gak, so it struck me as an excellent notion. His thin wrap had barely two lines each… and then we started fiending for more.

It began a long afternoon, evening, and night of what Lou Reed once called *waiting for my man*. Brad told me that he had the number of a local drug dealer called King. "Yeah, I've got a few hundred dollars on me!" I said. "Get him over!"

Brad dialed the number. A guy picked up. "Is King there?"

"No—call back in five minutes!"

"OK."

Five minutes later: "Is King there?"

"No. Ring back in five."

"OK."

We must have called twenty times before we got King. He sent one of his runners over—a nervy, damaged-looking, pallid guy— with $200 worth of coke. It lasted us maybe an hour. Tops.

"Hey, is King there?"

"No. Call back in five minutes…"

It went on for hours. Through the afternoon, into the evening— we didn't bother with dinner—and all night. When the sun came up the next morning, we were still sitting there, sweaty, red-eyed, and our lips chewed scarlet, and King was a thousand dollars better off. At least.

When I flew back to Phoenix a few days later, and reflected, I was horrified by how Brad was living. *He couldn't stay in that dive—and was he always on the phone to King?* I figured the apartment was dragging him down. If he had a nicer place, it might give him a boost.

I called Brad and asked him for his bank details. "I'll drop money in your account," I told him. "Find yourself a nice place to live. It doesn't matter how much it costs—just do it!"

Brad was grateful. The next time I visited, a week later, he was in a smart two-bedroomed town house in the heart of Philadelphia. He seemed happy. "Thanks so much, Rob," he told me. "This place is so cool. Just what I needed. Hey, shall we get some coke?"

I should have known. Brad wasn't doing coke because he lived in a shitty apartment—he was doing it because he loved doing coke. As, to be fair, did I. With my Priest earnings meaning that money was no object, we quickly developed an insatiable appetite.

Brad and I had a strange dynamic. I was the older guy, and the one with the money, but his alpha-male energy and charisma meant he took the lead in our relationship. He'd say what we were doing, I'd go along with it—and nine times out of ten, what we were doing was cocaine.

Not every trip to Philly was so sordid. We'd go to his folks' house for dinner. His parents were kind and welcoming. Brad had two sisters, and from intercepting one or two glances, I'm pretty sure they'd sussed that Brad and I were lovers. His mom and dad were oblivious.

Mostly, though, Brad and I sat in his new Philly town house, drank like hobos, and paid hundreds—no, thousands—of dollars to King and other scumbags like him. We were morphing into a gay Pennsylvania take on *Sid and Nancy.* By the end of that summer, we were total coke fiends.

Then it was time to go to Los Angeles, to wrap up the work on *Turbo.* Brad came with me. We met up with Priest and moved into a set of executive apartments in Burbank. It was a short drive from there to Record Plant Recording Studios in Hollywood, where we were to finish off and mix the album with Tom Allom.

It's never been hard to procure narcotics in LA. Brad and I carried on doing exactly what we had been doing in Philadelphia—only more so. Our drinking, and cocaine use, was by now so insidious that it was all we wanted to do. It was our *raison d'être*.

The two of us had spent the summer and autumn in isolation. Our insane existence made sense in our little bubble, but it wasn't until I met up with Priest again that I realized what a hideous state I was in.

Fuck! How had I got like this? How had this happened?

An average day in Burbank would start when Brad and I fell out of bed at six in the evening. We'd start drinking straight away—beer, vodka, whatever we'd spared from the fridge the night before. Then the Charlie would come out and it was *Scarface* time.

Superhuman drinking and cocaine-snorting exploits are not known for encouraging harmonious relations, and tensions were creeping in between me and Brad. The days of water pranks and balloons were gone. We would bicker over stupid, trivial shit:

"Hey, Rob, shall we go to a bar after the studio tonight?"

"Nah, I can't be arsed. Let's just come back here and drink."

"Well, fuck you, *I'm* going!"

"Good! Fuck *you!*"

Normally, we rubbed along OK. But our arguments, when they did happen, were vicious.

When I got into the studio, I was in a horrible mess. If I'd felt distant from *Turbo* in Nassau, now I had no connection to the album at all. I had to record my vocals in short bursts because I was too wasted to sing for long. Most days, it was hard to stand up.

Nor had I packed my trusty thesaurus. When it came to writing lyrics, I had stopped trying and was just churning out any old crap. I might as well have asked the band, "Will this do?" When I read some of my words on *Turbo* today, I absolutely cringe.

Even my song titles were rubbish. "Rock You All Around the World," "Wild Nights, Hot & Crazy Days," "Hot for Love"—the music that the guys were coming up with deserved better than that shit. They were just clichés. They certainly weren't metal.

I can hardly remember making this section of the *Turbo* album. My attendance and performance in the studio worsened even further when I got hold of a coke grinder. It looked like a funky pepper mill, and it shaped my existence every day.

When Brad and I woke up in the late afternoon, we'd sit in our room drinking as I turned the grinder's handle to break big rocks of cocaine into powder. After doing a few wake-up lines, I'd tip the coke into a neat little bottle (with a spoon) to take to the studio.

That bottle saw a lot of action in the Record Plant toilets.* I'd sneak off with it between vocal takes to do some serious snorting in a cubicle. I'd return to the studio cocky yet also sweaty and nervy, eyes fixed on the clock to see how soon I could get out of there.

I was barely holding it together. In fact, I wasn't. I was a basket case, a walking disaster zone, an accident waiting to happen. And under my fear and confusion bubbled a ferocious, volcanic rage. When it erupted, it was spectacular.

One day, I had to call somebody from the record label from a phone on the wall of the Record Plant reception. It didn't go well. God knows what we were arguing about, but in no time I was yelling at them, incoherent in my coke-addled rage. As I slammed the phone down, I punched the nearest door, swore at nobody… and tore the phone off the wall with my bare hands.

I heard a noise behind me. I spun around to see that Dee Snider from Twisted Sister was nervously tiptoeing past.

"Oh, hey, Rob!" he said, brightly.

"Hey, Dee!" I replied, the wall phone still cradled in my hands.

---

* When I come to think about it, it really is amazing how many fucking ways I've found in my life to break the law in a toilet cubicle.

Nobody from the band said anything to me as I went mental. It's not Priest's way. But they could see I was miserable, out of control, and sinking fast. It couldn't go on. And it didn't.

Shortly afterward, Brad and I were wired in our room in Burbank. Empty beer and vodka bottles lay around us on the bed and floor. My coke grinder had been in use for hours. As was our wont now, when we were wankered, we began squabbling.

Who knows what it was about? Who should make the phone call for the next drug run? Which TV channel to watch? It could have been anything, but it escalated, and we were bawling at each other at the tops of our voices. We only stopped when we heard the knock at the door.

"Open up! Police!"

I ran around hiding the grinder and empty coke wraps before Brad opened the door. Two uniformed LAPD cops came in. "We've had a complaint from other guests," they informed us. "You guys need to keep it down. If we have to come back, we'll arrest you."

The police left. Brad and I were subdued for a while. We snorted the last of the coke and, when we had run out, went to bed. We started bickering again…and then I snapped. I lost it. *Enough!*

"Right, you fucking stupid prick! Fucking loser!"

I was kneeling on Brad's chest, on the bed, raining blow after blow down on his face. I couldn't stop, and I didn't want to. His face was turning into a bloody pulp, and that was just how I wanted it. My flailing fists were soaked in his blood. *Good!*

Ex-Army guys don't take that kind of shit lying down and Brad was fighting back. He was punching me as hard as he could, which was bloody hard, and wrenching out big clumps of my hair. It was a full-on, animalistic, no-holds-barred fight.

I think one of us would have killed the other had Brad not suddenly jumped up and stormed out of the apartment. I watched him go. He looked like he had been in a car wreck, or a horror film. His entire face was covered in blood. He didn't come back that night. I had no idea where he had gone. I fell back onto the bed and blacked out.

When I woke up the next day, I was on my own. I got up, still in the stinking clothes I had been drinking and taking drugs in for hours the night before, and jumped in a taxi to the airport to get a flight to Phoenix. I didn't even bother to shower or look in a mirror.

When I walked through the door at home, I saw myself in the hallway mirror. I looked as if I had been in a ring with Mike Tyson and the bout had not gone well. I looked even worse than Brad had. But I didn't see a doctor—I lay on my bed, and passed out. When I woke up, more clumps of my hair lay around me on the pillow.

I phoned Brad's place in Philadelphia and he picked up. He sounded as sorry as me. We made up, sort of. But I couldn't face going back to LA and Priest. I couldn't face going anywhere, or doing anything. I called the Record Plant and told Tom I was feeling sick, had flown to Phoenix, and needed a time-out.

"I'll be back in a few days," I promised. I don't think I meant it.

This was the worst. The nadir. I could not have felt sorrier for myself. I stayed at home and lay low for a week, drinking alone, until my face looked halfway-decent enough for me to go out. Then, feeling lonely, I called David and suggested a night out. What harm could it do, right?

David drove over to my place and we got a cab down to Rockers. He pretty soon wished that he hadn't. Wallowing in self-pity, I rapidly got moronically, pathetically drunk.

Here we were again. Six barley wines and a Mogadon: the Phoenix remix.

We were in the bar until kicking-out time, then got a cab back to my place. David had had a bit too much to drive home, so he crashed out in my spare room. I lurched to my bedroom with a bottle of Jack Daniels—*because why stop the party now?*—and my eyes fixed on the box by my bedside.

My coke and drink binges had rendered my insomnia even worse in recent weeks, and a helpful LA doctor had prescribed me a month's worth of sleeping pills. And there they were, on my bedside table. Smiling and winking at me. Invitingly.

I made a decision. It was surprisingly easy.

Sure. Let's do it! Why not?

If I went, who would fucking miss me?

Nobody loves me!

I slouched on the side of the bed, unscrewed the JD, and opened the box of medicine. I popped open the foil pocket on a sheet of tablets and swallowed one.

I look a slug of JD.

Nobody loves me.

Tablet.

Slug of JD.

Nobody loves me.

Tablet.

Slug of JD.

Nobody loves me.

Tablet.

Slug of JD.

Nobody loves me.

God knows how many times I did it. Twenty? Twenty-five? I had lost count. Yet all the while it was going on, there was another voice in my head, low but insistent, talking to me. I recognized it. It was my own voice:

What are you DOING, Rob, you fucking idiot?!

I came to my senses. *Just.* I was already feeling drowsy as I got up from my bed and stumbled to the spare room. I banged on the door. David was half-asleep when he opened it.

"What?"

"I think I've OD'd," I said.

"Oh, Jesus!" David ran to my room and saw the empty pills box and JD bottle. "Get in my car, quick!" he said, running to get dressed. "Now!"

He drove me to John C. Lincoln Medical Center in downtown Phoenix. They rushed me to the emergency room, pumped my stomach, and gave me some black liquid that made me vomit all the poison out. I wasn't scared. It felt like it was happening to someone else, or in a movie.

When they declared me out of danger, a doctor sat me down to talk to me. I was still drunk, but I felt together and rational.

"We think you need to speak to someone," he said. "You shouldn't be doing this. You need to talk to someone and figure out what's wrong."

I knew that he was right. I felt grateful for his kindness. I'd just nearly killed myself—of course I needed to talk to someone! But I wasn't ready. Not quite yet. I thanked him and said I'd think about it.

David drove me home. He was afraid I might try to do it again, as was I, so he offered to stay with me for a few days. He threw away all of the medicines in the house, but I could still drink, and I did, every night, until the blackouts got me.

My anger consumed me: my vivid, inchoate anger that had built up over twenty-five years of living a lie about my sexuality. I had been struggling to control that anger, and now I was too tired. I gave up. It had won. It took over.

The end came a week later. It was January 5, 1986. I was drinking in my room, then suddenly I was crying, howling, and punching the wall like a sad, crazed beast. SMACK! SMACK! SMACK! The shallow imprints of my fists stared back at me from the wall. My knuckles were red-raw and bleeding.

SMACK!

SMACK!

SMACK!

Please, God, make it stop!

I was curled up in a sobbing heap on the floor when David burst into my room. He ran over and stood looking down at me.

"Rob, we need to get you fixed!" he said. "Or you're going to die!"

I stared up at him.

"You need to go to rehab. Now!"

I nodded.

"Yes," I agreed. "Yes, I know. Let's go."

15

The smell of cordite

David drove me back to the John C. Lincoln Medical Center and they checked me into the rehabilitation unit. The nurses took me to the alcoholic recovery ward and put me on an IV drip. I lay in bed, looked around me, and took stock.

So, here I am. I was now officially an alcoholic and a drug addict. No doubt I was going to be in this hospital for quite some time.

How did I feel about this?

My overwhelming reaction was…relief. I felt very calm. I knew I had gone to the bottom of the shitpit and there was no way I could have fallen any further. I had been in free fall, and the next step down would have been death. Doing this wasn't a choice. It was a necessity.

I don't want to lapse too far into therapy-speak—I know how boring that can be—but my suicide attempt was a cry for help. A subconscious cry for help. My life had been spiraling out of control for too long, and I'd been clinging on and hoping for the best.

Well, the best hadn't come. From my depths of rage and despair, I had finally admitted that I had a problem, I was powerless to solve it, and I needed help. It was a fucking profound moment.

Many addicts get intense withdrawal symptoms when they go cold turkey in rehab, which was why they had put me on the IV drip, but I didn't have any of that. It was strange: I didn't crave booze or drugs the entire time I was in John C. Lincoln.

The smell of cordite

It's just the way I am. Even at points in my life when I was drinking super-heavily (all of it, bar six months, up until this point!), I'd always been able to put the brakes on for a few days if I had to. That ability had always let me kid myself that I wasn't really an alcoholic. Now, I had found out this just wasn't true.

The rehab unit had a very kind, gentle routine. The hardest part was having to get up early in the morning. I've always hated that, even today, because of my insomnia. But we'd get up early and sit in a circle for their internal AA meetings.

My fellow patients were regular people: businessmen, bus drivers, teachers. A lot of the women were homemakers. A few knew who I was. Most didn't. Nobody cared. We all sat together and, for the first time, I publicly recited those famous words:

"Hi, everybody! I'm Rob, and I'm an alcoholic."

I felt fine saying them...because I knew it was true. And it had been true ever since I was getting wankered every night down at the Dirty Duck in Walsall.

I gave David the number, and he called the studio in LA for me and told them I was in rehab and would be out of action for a while. Priest were shocked—they hadn't seen this coming, any more than I had. The band flew straight to Phoenix to see me.

I was still on the IV drip and they all sat around my hospital bed. We tried to chat as normal, but it was a bit awkward for them, and they didn't really know quite what to say, so I told them: "I'm in here because I'm an alcoholic."

"*You're* not an alcoholic, Rob!" said Glenn.

"Yes, I am, Glenn."

"You're not, mate! You just like a drink, like we all do!"

Glenn was doing his best to make me feel better, but he couldn't have been more wrong. *I was an alcoholic*. I knew it now. Before they left, Priest told me to take as long as I needed to recover, and said they were there for me. I knew it already, but it was great to hear.

The daily therapy sessions could get intense. The counselor would bring a baseball bat into the room, put an object on a chair in the middle of our circle, and encourage us to beat the shit out of it. The idea was that it represented a person, or an incident, that had damaged you. Violently destroying it would be cathartic.

The women in the group took to this better than the men. I'd sit in the circle and watch demure ladies go crazy, smashing the hell out of a teddy bear, then collapse on the floor in a heap, their grief and angst pouring out of them. "Wow, that feels better!" they'd say. The men were more reticent.

I never once took the baseball bat. Ardith, my counselor, a lovely lady a few years older than me, would say, "You're suppressing, Rob!" She was probably right. But I just didn't want to do it.

Rehab was a bubble, but they let us make occasional phone calls. I rang Mom and Dad to tell them where I was. Ardith talked to them as well. They were relieved. Mom sounded delighted. I guess they'd been watching me go downhill for a while.

I also phoned Brad. It was good to hear his voice, and even better when he said he was glad I was getting treatment, he was missing me, and he was about to do the same thing: he was going into rehab, too. My heart leapt.

Brilliant! I thought. *Maybe we can make this relationship work, after all!* Because I knew I still wanted to. I knew I still loved him.

I stayed thirty days in John C. Lincoln, and when I came out, I knew my life had changed. I made a commitment that I would never drink or take drugs again. *It was time.* I hated feeling sick all the while. I hadn't felt physically healthy in years. That had to change.

The other, biggest stimulus was that I wanted to be a better musician again. I wanted to reconnect with Priest, and with our music. It was—*it is*—the most important thing in my life, and my alcoholism and addiction had knocked me so low that I had lost touch with it. Lost touch with my life force.

Rehab changed my life. *It saved it.* After I left, I kept in touch with Ardith. She was such a kind soul. She even went to Walsall to talk my mom through the process of my illness and recovery. They became firm friends, and went off on holiday to Scotland together!

I haven't had a drink or touched a narcotic in thirty-four years— and counting. I can't say that I never will, but I hope to God that I don't. The cliché of recovery is true: you take one day at a time. I know I am sober today. I hope I will be sober tomorrow.

I have never been to an AA meeting since I left rehab. I just stopped drinking, and I stayed stopped. I'm not saying that would work for everyone, but it has for me. I guess it's that Walsall thing again:

If you've got to do something, you just get on with it.

I went back to LA to finish making *Turbo.* My return to the studio was the most low-key, Black Country affair imaginable. I just mooched into the Record Plant one afternoon. The rest of the band were hard at work.

"All right, lads?" I asked.

"Sound! You all right, Rob?"

And that was it. They didn't grill me on my rehab or what I had been through. They gave me my full privacy. They were just glad that I was back, recovered, and ready to crack on with the album.

I was more than ready. I was fighting fit. It was the first time I had ever recorded vocals sober for Priest, but when I came to sing "Out in the Cold" and "Reckless," I really let rip. It felt great. Maybe it was easier to sing when you're not off your tits, after all! *Who knew?*

Having had to deal with my knackered, substandard efforts in Nassau and earlier in LA, Tom Allom was absolutely delighted with his new, improved vocalist. "Bloody hell, Rob, you sound so much better! It's terrific!" our patrician Old Carthusian* producer rhapsodized.

I've never been good at taking compliments, for my voice or anything else, but I accepted that one gladly. Because, without being cocky, I knew Tom was right. I was sounding far better. My new sobriety in the band had started off well.

As we finished *Turbo*, a movie company got in touch asking to use "Reckless" in a new Tom Cruise film called *Top Gun*. It would have meant leaving the track off the album, which we didn't want to do, and we didn't think the film sounded like it would be very good, so we turned them down. *Good move, huh?*

I had been AWOL, or at least not *compos mentis*, for many months, so I caught up on band business. A piece of news from London was that Bill Curbishley had asked one of his team, Jayne Andrews, to be Priest's full-time manager.

Bill would still be involved strategically, but Jayne would handle our day-to-day management. I'd liked Jayne from the day I met her and thought it was a great idea. She was driven and efficient, and I knew she'd be excellent for the band. She was…and she still is today.

Once I got home, I felt I needed a new start, away from the Mummy Mountain house where I had partied so hard. I found a new place in no time. Five minutes away in Paradise Valley, it was wonderful. As I viewed it, I kept saying, "This is amazing!" It was airy and spacious, and had jaw-dropping views of Arizona's natural splendor.

From the pool deck, I could see the planes landing in the distance at Phoenix Airport. "Dad will love *that*!" I thought. I fell in love with the house and paid $500,000 cash for it on the spot. Just like

---

* Tom's accent is so cut-glass that I had always assumed he had gone to Eton, until he informed me that he was a Charterhouse alumnus. "But we're just as posh!" he added, proudly.

my Walsall coach house, it was money well spent: I am still there, more than thirty years later.

Then I flew to Philadelphia to reunite with Brad. I had spoken on the phone to one of his sisters first and she said that he was doing OK. I hadn't seen him since our vicious fight in LA, so I was nervous, but we quickly put it behind us. It was water under the bridge.

Brad had said he was going into rehab...but he never did. When we reunited in Philly, he went out on an errand or two and came back stinking of beer. I didn't say anything—that hatred of confrontation again!—but it troubled me.

I was worried for Brad, but also for myself. After becoming sober, I knew I couldn't run the risk of relapsing. It was great to see him, but he was still the same wild, impetuous, fun-loving Brad. He was a loose cannon where I needed stability.

I flew home feeling wary.

After its long gestation, *Turbo* came out in April '86. It got a strong reception, even if a few metalheads bridled at the addition of those pesky synth guitars. Having felt detached from it, by now I loved it—and it was to give us two big US hits in "Turbo Lover" and "Locked In."

We did a week of rehearsals for our first tour in nearly two years. They went great, and I loved not having to pause every few minutes for a refreshing beverage of half-vodka-half-tonic. There again, I could see I would *need* to be aware and alert for this show.

Fuel for Life would be the most ambitious tour we had ever staged. We were to roam between multiple metal platforms, as if we were in an alien machine. Giant robot hands would lift me high into the air. No, this was not a set to be necking neat Smirnoff on!

It was to last nearly a year. Our label was still fixated on America, so there were no British shows—*again*—but scores of US arenas and coliseums, a four-week European leg, and finally, a trip to Japan. By now, I was a veteran of such itineraries, but this time there would be one major difference.

I had never performed sober in my fucking life.

In the nights leading up to the tour, my insomnia kicked in and I lay panicking and freaking out in the small hours. The same questions ran around my head: *How can I get up and sing in front of thousands of people without a drink inside me? Will I crack? How will I cope?*

I had no answers, just fear and blind hope, and on the first night, I was on my nerve ends. *Oh, fuck!* Standing in the wings of the sold-out Tingley Coliseum, in Albuquerque, I was shitting myself. Ten thousand fans were screaming for Priest…and I would rather have been anywhere else but there.

The auditorium lights went down. The crowd roared. I walked to the mic. And something happened. Something precious and real.

As soon as I opened my mouth and started to sing, I felt something I had never felt onstage before. I had nothing getting in the way of my expression: no alcohol, no chemicals. I felt that most intense, sacred natural high: the great joy and sensation of the human voice.

I luxuriated in the sheer animal delight of opening my throat and letting rip. I could have been singing in the shower. I could have been belting out "The Skye Boat Song," aged eight, in junior school again. It felt great. It felt transcendent.

I got in touch with a thing in my body, my mind, my soul, wherever it was, that had been closed off to me for so long. For the whole show, I felt as if I was floating on air. I was so euphoric. And a new, blissed-out internal narrative had replaced my stressed neurosis:

Wow! I have been missing out on this feeling for my entire career as a performer! But thank God I have it now!

I felt just as happy after the show. Previously, I would have dived headfirst into a pile of coke or a bottle of JD. Now, I sat quietly, on my own, and enjoyed a warm sense of pride and achievement. They were sensations I hadn't felt for far too long.

As the tour wended through California and the Midwest, I felt the same every single night. There were occasional difficult moments backstage. The rest of the band hadn't stopped drinking or partying, and neither would I expect or want them to.

There was always alcohol in the dressing room. We'd go out for a post-show meal most nights, and while the others tried to rein it in a bit, which I appreciated, they'd always end up drinking. I would sneak a look at Ken or Ian, knocking back a glass of wine and laughing their heads off, and think, *That looks fun!*

But I was never really tempted. *Not really.* I think what saved me was that old Black Country stubbornness. If I've said I'll do something, I do it. I see it through. I felt secure—plus, the memories of my recent nightmares were too vivid for me to contemplate giving in.

Instead, I called Brad in Philadelphia every night as soon as I came offstage. A strange, lovely ritual developed. I would tell him how the gig had gone, and any news…and then, he would ask me to sing him "Swing Low, Sweet Chariot." He said it helped him fall asleep.

So, every night, mere minutes after I'd been yowling "Turbo Lover" or "Freewheel Burning" to 10,000 headbanging metal maniacs, I would be backstage, in a quiet room, crooning an exquisite old gospel tune to a drowsy young man in bed in Philly:

> I looked over Jordan, and what did I see?
> Coming for to carry me home

I always looked forward to doing it. It was a sweet, tender, and very intimate moment.

Our Dallas show saw a mishap. Ken's guitar tech had restrung his guitar but forgotten to trim the string ends. I flung out my arms during one of my more exuberant onstage moves, and inadvertently smacked the neck of Ken's guitar.

It got knocked upward, and one of the stray strings penetrated deep into Ken's right eyeball. *OUCH!* Blood came pouring out and it looked grotesque. A real trouper, Ken finished the show, but he had to grab a pair of sunglasses—especially as Wayne Isham was there to film "Parental Guidance" for a live video later in the set.

The funny thing is that everyone who ever sees that video thinks that Ken was just being a total poseur! Thankfully, the injury did no lasting damage, but poor Ken was in absolute agony. As he told me many, many times.

Bon Jovi joined us as our support act on the Canadian leg. They were cool guys, but our more hard-core fans found them too light-weight and didn't take to their pop-metal shtick. One night, they bottled them off. Credit to Jovi, they stuck it out and did every show.

Well, Priest fans know what they like and what they don't… and at least the Jovi lads took their bad medicine well.

Singing a nightly lullaby to Brad was one thing. Having him out on the tour would be another. My recovery was going well, but I knew what a bad influence on me he could be. He was a rogue element: Could my new stability cope with him?

But I missed him, and our late-night chats were great, so I invited him back out. As ever, he fit in well. He gave us his smiles and energy again and I remembered just why I had fallen in love with him. Not that I had ever forgotten.

Brad wasn't sober, but nor was he a pissed-up, coked-up mess. He was trying to be better: I could see that. Yet now I was sober, I saw a side to him that I hadn't noticed before—or, probably, had ignored because I didn't *want* to notice it.

He could be edgy and irritable. After he had a drink, he would pick fights over the most trivial thing. He would kick off for no reason. Six months earlier, I would have been drunk and kicking off back. Now, I stayed calm, withdrew…and worried about him.

I could see the same alcohol- and cocaine-induced signs of decline and anger in Brad that I had just come out of. I longed to ask him to go to rehab, and to offer to pay, but I knew he would just explode and go crazy at me. The easiest thing was to do nothing. So, I did.

I care for him, but I don't know how much longer this relationship is going to last, I thought. *And I don't know how it is going to end.*

But Brad had plenty of good days and we had some fun on the road. The water pranks made a comeback (*oh, great!*) and 90 percent of the time he was great company. When *Fuel for Life* transferred to Europe that autumn, I invited him to come with me.

We had a few days in the Walsall coach house first. As soon as we got in and dropped our bags, Brad started doing what he routinely did in Philly: announcing what we were going to do next, and where we were going to go. Making plans for both of us.

"Hang on!" I told him, half-jokingly. "We're on *my* turf now. We'll do things *my* way!"

Big mistake.

Brad went ballistic. Suddenly, cups and plates from my kitchen table were flying at my head and smashing on the wall behind me. "Shut your fucking mouth!" he yelled. "Asshole! Nobody fucking talks to me like that!"

I was cowering. It took me totally by surprise. *Where the fuck had that come from?* And then I thought: *Was he always like this, and I was just too wasted to notice?* Either way, it was seriously disturbing and upsetting.

A year earlier, I'd have screamed abuse back at Brad. Maybe there'd have been a fistfight. Maybe another run-in with the police. Now, I just apologized and made light of it: "Sorry, I was only joking! Tell you what—I'll make us a nice cup of tea!" It took a while, but I calmed him down.

And yet, under all the anger, Brad still had his boyish sense of fun. For some reason, he got into model trains in Walsall. We'd go to the local toy shop, and he constructed a lengthy railway network in my living room. Locomotives, stations, sidings, the lot.

I introduced him to my family. I didn't define our relationship to them, but I didn't really need to by now. I imagine they could see it just by looking at us. Brad was an utter charmer and Mom and Dad adored him from the start. Sue really took to him, too.

Being sober with me 24/7 didn't suit him, though. He got antsy and restless in Walsall. He discovered an all-night snooker club and bar five minutes from my house, and I'd lie awake in the early hours and wonder when he'd be coming back—and what state he'd be in.

Another thought also began eating at me. We were having a lot less sex than we'd once had, and his sister had recently inadvertently let slip to me on the phone that Brad had a close female friend in Philadelphia. It triggered my inevitable paranoia.

Could it be that Brad was actually straight? Like David? Had I made the same stupid mistake again?

Surely not, I would think. And, at last, I would hear Brad drunkenly fiddling his key in the front door, and I'd drift off to sleep, relieved.

After the European leg of *Fuel for Life*, Brad went back to the US as we finished off in Japan. I also had a casual but meaningful chat with the rest of the band about a subject that had been on my mind for a while.

Newly sober, I was happier in Priest than I had ever been, but I had also been thinking of undertaking a solo side project. I just wanted to see what it would be like.

I didn't know how the band would feel, but when I floated the notion backstage after a Japanese gig, they seemed totally unfazed. "Yeah, why not?" they said. "Go for it! Just make sure it's when we are on a break, and it's not too much like Priest, and it'll be great!" It was a relief to get their all clear as we went our separate ways at the end of the tour.

Brad came back to Walsall in December and we had a lovely Christmas Day at Mom and Dad's bungalow. To mark my first year of sobriety, on January 6, Sue made me a cake in the shape of a Perrier bottle. I was really touched.

The smell of cordite

Then I flew back to Phoenix and Brad headed home to Philadelphia. We arranged that I'd visit the following weekend. Yul Vazquez and Gigi Fredy had moved to New York, then split, amicably, but I still saw both of them. Gigi and I were due a catch-up, and Brad liked her a lot, so we decided to ask her to come along. Should be fun, right?

This terrible trip will haunt me for the rest of my days.

It was January 19, 1987. Gigi and I flew in and went straight from the airport to Brad's town house. It had two bedrooms, so we were both planning to stay there. When we arrived, we went in, carried Gigi's bags up to her room... and Brad went off.

I've racked my brains forever and I still can't remember what it was about. *It was nothing.* Something innocuous would trigger Brad and he would start screaming and trashing the place. That was what he was doing right now.

I had seen this film before. *Brad's Demons.* It never ended well.

"I think we'd better get out of here and get a hotel," I said to Gigi. "Can you go and call a taxi?"

Gigi ran downstairs, which made Brad even more mad. He was still wild-eyed and smashing the room up. I tried to calm him down but it was making things worse. So, I made a decision.

"Brad, I'm leaving," I said. "I'm going because there's nothing I can do. You've got to get this out of your system. I'm going to a hotel. I'll call you later."

I went downstairs. Gigi had already got a taxi and was waiting in it by the front door. I was about to climb into the cab when Brad came running out of the house and into the street.

He ran up to me and gave me a hug.

"I love you," he said.

"I love you too, Brad," I told him.

As he turned around, I noticed the handgun poking from the waist of his trousers.

I got into the taxi.

"Fuck me," I said to Gigi as we pulled away. "Did you see that gun?"

"What gun?"

"Brad has got a handgun in his pants. I didn't even know he owned a gun!"

We asked the driver to take us to the Embassy Suites hotel by the airport. The first thing I did when Gigi and I got to our room was call Brad. He didn't pick up. I knew something was wrong: Brad *always* picked up. I called again. No answer.

"I don't like this," I told Gigi. "It doesn't feel right. I'm going to call his uncle."

Brad had an uncle who lived five minutes away and had a key to the house. I phoned him and said that I was worried. "OK, thanks for letting me know, Rob," the uncle said. "I'll go straight over now."

When the uncle let himself into the house, the smell of cordite was still heavy in the air.

I didn't know for two hours, until the uncle phoned me back. Brad had blown his brains out in his bedroom. He shot himself in the head just minutes before his uncle got there. The poor guy was beating himself up for not getting there sooner.

He wasn't the only person blaming himself.

Fuck. I had seen the gun. I knew the state he was in. Why didn't I say something? Why didn't I do something?

WHY?

I felt…how did I feel? I didn't know. Numb. Cold. No, I felt dead too, dead inside, because I had lost the person that I had loved more than anybody I had ever met. Somebody I felt so, so much for.

I had been to heaven and hell with Brad. Sometimes, within the same day; often, within the same five minutes. I didn't know what to do. I didn't know what to say. I *did* know that nothing would ever be the same again.

Brad's uncle said that his body had been taken to the hospital. He was on life support, because his family wanted to donate his organs. And as soon as I heard that, I knew that I had to see him again. One final time.

I didn't dare call his parents, or his sister, to ask permission: Would they want to hear from me ever again? *Would they blame me?*

Gigi saw the state that I was in. She took over, and called his family for me. Yes, they said, it was fine if I went to see him one last time.

It was three in the morning as the taxi pulled through Philly's dark, deserted city streets. They were full of memories of Brad: the bars we had hung out at, and fought and loved in. The clubs we had been to. The restaurants we had eaten at.

The hotel where we had met.

When I got to the hospital reception, I explained who I was, and why I was there. The night receptionist nodded and called an orderly, who took me up a flight of stairs to a darkened ward. He showed me into a side room and left me there.

Brad was lying on the bed. He had tubes down his throat to keep his body breathing until the doctors could remove his organs. His eyes had filled with blood, and yet he looked peaceful: at peace, at last. I went over, leaned down, and gave him a kiss on the forehead.

And then I left.

The next morning, I got a flight back to Phoenix on my own. I felt completely empty. I couldn't face being in my house, alone, so when I picked up my Corvette from the airport, I drove it straight to David's place and told him what had happened.

David may never have become my partner—but, when the chips were down, and I was at my lowest ebb, he turned out to be a good friend. "I'm sorry, Rob," he said. "Stay here, for as long as you need to."

I hunkered down in his spare room for a week, still feeling cold and numb. I spent my time doing nothing, staring into space. Then Gigi called me to tell me the details of Brad's funeral.

"Do you want to go?" she asked me.

I couldn't. I felt too raw, too desperate, and I didn't want to cause any more grief to his poor family. They had been kind to me, but I didn't know if they'd want me there. My presence at the graveside might be a distraction. I decided to mourn on my own.

At the exact time of Brad's funeral, I drove to a local Paradise Valley beauty spot that he and I used to hike to. I sat on the hillside, stared into the valley, and tried to make a spiritual connection with events in Philadelphia, more than two thousand miles away.

I've still never been to Brad's grave. I want to, and I don't. I've told Jim Silvia so many times that I need to go there. "Rob, whenever you want to go, we will go," Jim always says. "Just tell me when."

I will do it one day.

16

We should be so lucky!
(Lucky, lucky, lucky...)

If I were ever going to start drinking again, it would have been after Brad's suicide. Nothing is more traumatic than the sudden death of a loved one, especially in such a brutal manner. You need comfort, and solace. It's often found, temporarily, in a bottle.

I had had my own long, dark night of the soul and tried to kill myself just a year earlier, but somehow that had been...different. Even as I swallowed the pills, a voice in my head had been telling me not to do it. It was a cry for help. I had an escape route.

This was something else. To put a gun to your head, and pull the trigger...what depth of emotional torment must you be in to do that? I lay wide awake, night after night, wondering what might have driven Brad to it. And then I got a clue.

Gigi talked to one of his sisters, who said she thought Brad had gotten a girl pregnant in Philadelphia. *So! He was straight after all!* I thought of him trying to cope with that stress, plus our joint life, on top of his drink and drug intake, and it made a little more sense. *A little.*

I'm sure people reading *Confess* will think, "Oh, he was bisexual!" But gut instinct tells me Brad was a straight guy who made an exception for me. I suppose I could have felt hurt that he cheated on me, but I didn't. *What's the point? It's too late for that.* Instead, I felt a sad wash of relief that he was out of his misery.

It would have killed *me* if I was still drinking…but being sober was a blessing. A miracle. It gave me a clarity of thought that allowed me to process my emotions in a way I could never have done while wasted. It helped me come to terms with Brad's death. And I was grateful.

1987 was to be largely a year off for Priest, and that was lucky. It gave me a chance to recover and to ensure this hideous tragedy did not knock me off the wagon. I lay low in Phoenix, didn't go to any bars or clubs, and severely limited the friends that I saw.

The sole Priest activity in the first half of the year was to meet up in Florida with Tom Allom to mix a live album. *Priest…Live!* was a set of tracks from two gigs on the *Fuel for Life* tour: Atlanta and Dallas, where I had turned Ken's eyeball into a pincushion.

Unlike *Unleashed in the East*, the mixing was straightforward, with no need for me to rerecord any vocals in a panic. It was a very relaxed process, which gave me plenty of chances to hit the beach.

Ian and I shared a beautiful villa right on the waterfront. Now that I had stopped drinking, I was getting into decent physical shape, which let me spend my afternoons strolling up and down the sand, in a miniscule white thong, ogling the talent.

I got into the habit of eating an apple a day, which I was doing when Tom's wife, Louie, spotted me, in my tiny posing pouch, trying to chat up a lifeguard. "Honestly, Rob, you're like a heavy metal Eve in the Garden of Eden!" she sighed. And I guess, in a way, I was.

With Priest on hiatus until autumn, I went to Walsall in early summer and had a few weeks at the coach house. Mom and Dad told me how sorry they were to hear about Brad. On the plus side, I could see the joy it gave them to see me still sober and lucid.

New York has always been one of my favorite cities in the world. In those days, whenever I flew back to Phoenix from the UK,

I liked to stop off there for a few days. That summer of '87, I did so and stayed with Gigi in her apartment in Manhattan.

We went to the Limelight, an unspeakably trendy NYC club in a former Gothic church. Billy Idol was wandering around. The thumping house music was crazy loud, so Gigi and I meandered into a tiny side room, where a big Jamaican woman was sitting on her own.

The woman introduced herself as Pearl, and said she was a psychic. A medium. *Oh, it's just one of the club's gimmicks,* I thought. I wasn't interested. But Pearl asked me: "Is there any particular person you would like to speak to?"

I was just about to say no, and make some kind of skeptical remark, when Pearl said, "Well, there's somebody here who wants to talk to *you.*"

I looked at her, blankly. *Huh?*

"He wants to know if you have kept the underwear that he gave you, with the clasps on the sides?"

My mouth ran dry. My heart stopped. I felt like *the world* had stopped. *What the...?* I had never told a single soul about Brad giving me his pants with the clasps when I met him. And now here was a jolly Jamaican woman, in a nightclub, talking about them.

"This person who is asking you," continued Pearl. "He has got a really infectious laugh, yeah? He was a really naughty guy?"

Yes, I found myself telling her. Yes, he was.

"He must have been! He was always doing practical jokes with you, with water!"

My. God. What was happening here? There was no way this woman I had never met before could have known any of these things about Brad. They were private, special, intimate. *Our things.* After that, she—or he—didn't really have much more to say.

But that was Brad for you. He always was a tease.

It was the most extraordinary encounter of my life and, in an instant, it shaped and solidified my whole attitude toward death, and spirituality, and an afterlife. Now, suddenly, I *knew* that we go somewhere when we die. I *knew* that Brad's body was no longer alive, but *he* was, and he was keeping an eye on me.

And, best of all, I knew that he still had that big, beautiful laugh.

Toward the end of 1987, Priest spent a couple of weeks at a house that Glenn now had in southern Spain, writing songs for the follow-up album to *Turbo*. And then, before Christmas, we shifted to Puk Studios in Denmark, with Tom Allom, to record what would become *Ram It Down*.

In stark contrast to the debauched distractions of Ibiza and Nassau, Puk was slap-bang in the middle of nowhere. We started the sessions with a few songs left over from when *Twin Turbos* got cut down to a single *Turbo*. It was also my first full album of recording sober, and I enjoyed the clarity that let me give full commitment to my lyrics and vocals.

I've always found it difficult to listen to myself sing, but when I hear the tracks that came from those Puk sessions, I can tell I was singing without alcohol or chemicals. I just sound *different*, and sharper, than on earlier albums. I sound like I was in a better place—which I was. It felt great to be a fully contributing member again.

I was enjoying working in Puk…but Dave Holland wasn't. Dave's simplicity and directness on drums, which we had appreciated when he first replaced Les Binks, were now being viewed as a limitation.

Bands, eh? They can never make their bloody minds up!

The decision was made to get a drum machine. All you had to do was hit a drum, or a snare, a couple of times, and then you could literally create the drum beats electronically in the studio. It meant that our poor drummer hardly drummed.

Dave was pretty annoyed by this, and I don't blame him—*I'd* have been pissed off if the band had drafted in a robot to do most of the singing! And, if I am honest, I *do* think the drumming on this album sounds artificial.

Halfway through the recording, Bill Curbishley flew out to see us. He told us that we had been offered the chance to contribute a song to the soundtrack of an upcoming comedy movie, *Johnny Be Good,* starring Anthony Michael Hall, Robert Downey Jr., and a young Uma Thurman.

After the *Top Gun* debacle, we didn't want to miss out again, so we did a cover of Chuck Berry's "Johnny B. Goode" for the movie and also stuck it on the album. When I saw the film, I was disappointed by how short our soundtrack bit was…and, let's face it, it was no *Top Gun.*

Ozzy came to Puk while we were working, arriving with a bevy of model-like chicks. He'd come to check the place out, to see if he wanted to record there. He quickly decided the studio was too remote for his liking, but the Viking owner was bending over backward to persuade him otherwise.

"Well, I'd need a helipad!" declared Ozzy, assuming his crazy demand would end the discussion.

"Sure, no problem!" said the Viking, nodding earnestly. "I'll build you a helipad!"

Ozzy never did record at Puk but, while he was there, he and Glenn hit it off. They vanished for a swim in the studio's Olympic-length pool. When I wandered in later, in my Speedo, they were sitting getting pissed in the Jacuzzi with Ozzy's bevy of chicks.

As we were wrapping up the album, we also took a remarkable leap into the unknown…or some of our fans might call it a dance with the devil.

As I've said, I may be a metal god, but I've also long been a pop tart. I always keep an eye on the charts and, back then, I loved some of the manufactured dance-pop—Kylie Minogue, Rick Astley, Bananarama—that was coming off the conveyor belt of Stock Aitken Waterman.

That trio of producers ruled the British singles chart in the late eighties. Priest have always been an albums band but, at the same time, we hadn't had a Top 20 single since "United" in 1980, and I began to wonder if SAW might be able to rectify that.

Judas Priest and Stock Aitken Waterman?! It sounded ridiculous… but I've always held the view that if you don't take chances in life, you don't know what you're missing. Don't be scared of shit! If you try something and it doesn't work, at least you've had a go.

I broached the idea with the band. I had no idea how they would react but, after the initial double take—"*What?!*"—they were all open to the idea. They trusted my instincts. I think the general opinion was: *This is so daft that it just might work.*

Jayne Andrews approached SAW, who were also quite taken by the idea. I guess the novelty appealed to them as much as it did to us. *A heavy metal band? Sure, why not?* So, that springtime, we flew to Paris and joined them in a studio.

I liked SAW straightaway. I particularly warmed to Pete Waterman,* who was a no-nonsense West Midlander like us. But what absolutely blew my mind was the speed and efficiency with which the three of them went about their work.

We were going to record three songs. One was a cover of "You Are Everything" by the Stylistics, an old soul tune from the seventies that I had always loved. SAW were also going to write two songs for us…and they did it in about the time it would take most people to make a sandwich.

The three of them went into a creative huddle:

"OK, we'll do *this* for the chorus."

"Yeah, let's put this note here—actually, no, it works better *there*."

"Agreed. How about this *here*? It will lift the verse."

---

* Although Coventry born and bred, Pete is a big follower of Walsall F. C. I'm no football fan, but I reckon he must be the only bloke not from Walsall ever to *choose* to support the Saddlers!

"Now for the hook…and the bridge…yeah, that works great!"

"OK, Rob, we're ready for you!"

It was absolutely staggering. When the red light went on, we did "You Are Everything" and the two songs that SAW had knocked up for us: "I Will Return" and "Runaround." It was certainly a different way of working! We were in and out of that Paris studio in an afternoon.

We went away and listened to the results. I had enjoyed the session, and thought that we sounded great with a dance beat. At the same time, we knew releasing them would be controversial— and might even be the kiss of death for our career. A serious band discussion ensued.

We knew a lot of our fans would view Stock Aitken Waterman as musical Antichrists; purveyors of empty, worthless pop pap for kids. I didn't agree, but I could already imagine the hostility we would face:

What is this disco shit, Priest? Have you gone fucking mad? This isn't heavy metal! YOU TRAITORS!

With "Johnny B. Goode" already on the album and outside our normal remit, we decided that putting our bubbly new SAW ditties on it as well would be a step too far away from what we do: *metal.* Caution prevailed, and we shelved the tracks.

If I ever bump into Pete Waterman, he tells me he's still got the recordings in his vault in his house somewhere. Snippets have leaked onto YouTube over the years. Will we ever put the full session out? I honestly don't know. But I still love what we did, and that we did it.

While I was in Europe, I caught up with Michael from the Yew Tree house, who was now living in London and working at the London Lighthouse hospice for men suffering from AIDS.* He knew Princess Diana, who would turn up unannounced in the middle of the night to comfort patients.

---

* Tragically, Michael himself was later to die from AIDS.

Michael told me he was going on a big Pride march that day to protest against the Thatcher government's hostility toward gay people. On a whim, I decided to go with him.

I have never been a political animal, but even I saw that Margaret Thatcher's government was doing some nasty shit. They brought in Section 28 legislation, which banned councils from "intentionally promoting homosexuality" and forbade schools from talking to pupils about it. It dismissed gay people as freaks and perverts.

Marching through central London with thousands of other gay men, whistles peeping, rainbow flags fluttering, was exhilarating: *these are my people!* There was a real buzz and energy. Oh, yeah, and plenty of eye candy!

As we passed the end of Downing Street, I joined in with the mass chant: "Maggie! Maggie! Maggie! Out! Out! Out!" Mentally, I pictured her having a cup of tea, listening, and shaking her head in dismay at this mass display of queer defiance.

It was a spontaneous and empowering decision by me…but also, of course, a very high-risk one. I was a gay man but I was still very much in the closet, and my fears of being outed and it destroying the band were as stark as ever. It only took a fan or, worse, a *journalist* to see me…and then what?

But I passed unnoticed. I got lucky. In that respect, at least, I always seemed to.

Ram It Down emerged to a decent reception and, after a week of rehearsals in Sweden, we kicked off the *Mercenaries of Metal* tour to promote it. This six-month affair was to roar through mainland Europe and Britain, then finish up in North America.

Priest had by now been touring for fifteen years, each outing bigger and better than the one before. We knew what we were doing on the road. We were a ferocious, well-oiled metal machine on this outing…until we hit the States, and a wheel fell off.

The curse of the Judas Priest drummers struck again. Dave Holland was still brooding about being sidelined on *Ram It Down*.

He was not a happy bunny, and when we got to the Nassau Veterans Memorial Coliseum in New York, it came to a head.

Dave was so fed up that he declared he wouldn't go on. His back was hurting, he said, so he couldn't play. I sat by him for two hours, commiserating and trying to sweet-talk him into changing his mind. By the time he relented and we went on, we were an hour late.

The gig was solid but, back in the dressing room, Dave threw another strop. He hurled a few insults at Glenn, whom he saw as the prime instigator of our embrace of a drum machine, and said he was fed up of life on the road. At the end of the tour, he would quit the band.

That negative feeling continued to bubble in the background—or, specifically, behind the drums—as the tour progressed, but the dates were still going great. And then, in August, we hit Minneapolis.

It was now eighteen months since Brad had died. With the exception of the odd one-night stand, or cruising fumble, I had been solitary and celibate. It was a lonely existence, and it had dawned on me that I was ready for another relationship.

At our show at Minneapolis's Met Center, I couldn't help but notice a good-looking young guy, headbanging and going crazy for the band in the front row. He was seriously hot, and as I hurled myself into my performance, a thought formed: *I want to meet that guy*.

Before the encore, I grabbed a crew member and asked him to give the guy a backstage pass and invite him to hang out after the show. I did that every now and then, if I clocked a fit bloke in the crowd. Some of the band did it with women; *why shouldn't I?*

The guy came backstage, looking excited. His name was Josh and he was at the gig with his brother, Ted. Josh was in his early twenties, he and Ted shared an apartment in a little town in South Dakota, and he was a big Priest fan and metalhead in general.

It was nothing like meeting Brad, where the atmosphere was electric and we were doing each other in the bog within ten minutes.

But Josh seemed a sweet guy, and we chatted amiably and did a few devils-horn photos together. As he left, I got his phone number.

I'll give him a ring, I figured. *Who knows? I might even get lucky…*

Throughout the tour there had been a dark cloud hanging over us. We knew two young guys had shot themselves dead three years earlier while listening to our album *Stained Class*. We were horrified and saddened to hear this—what a terrible, pointless waste of their lives.

Now, word reached us from management that their parents intended to sue us, claiming that our music was responsible for their sons' deaths. Immediately, we thought of Ozzy up in court three years earlier, after a fan had killed himself while listening to Ozzy's song "Suicide Solution."

Ozzy's case had been dismissed, and we figured that it was pretty unlikely we'd end up in court—it just seemed too ridiculous. Yet as we pulled up to the Starplex Arena in Dallas in September, Jim Silvia had a word with us.

"When you get off the bus, the sheriff is going to serve you with subpoenas," our tour manager said. "Don't say anything to him. Just take them."

We did exactly that. The papers said we would have to give evidence in the event of the case going to trial. It was a concern—but it seemed so far-fetched that we didn't worry too much about it. We passed the summonses to our lawyers and half forgot about them.

I phoned Josh a few times from the road, and when the *Mercenaries of Metal* tour wrapped up, I went to visit him in South Dakota. He lived in a sleepy little town, where he worked in a local gym, and his parents were straitlaced but very gentle and lovely.

I was growing fond of Josh…but we had no romance or intimacy for weeks. When we *did* finally get physical, it seemed experimental for him, as if it was his first time with a man (although not the first time he'd grappled with one: he had been the quarterback for his school's American football team).

I had met him at a good time. 1989 was another down year for Priest, so I focused on getting to know Josh. Slowly but surely, I fell in love with him. He came to visit me two or three times, and in the spring of that year he moved to Phoenix to live with me.

Compared to the roller coaster of Brad, life with Josh was chill and sedate, but I figured that was exactly what I needed. We ate well, took health supplements, lifted a load of weights (I developed my first-ever six-pack!), hung out at home, and watched TV.

I took Josh to Walsall with me, and my family all liked him. He and I watched countless episodes of *Cheers*—he was obsessed with that program! I didn't quite get the humor, and the pub seemed nothing like the Dirty Duck (where were the Mogadon and the go-go dancers?), but I enjoyed how much *he* enjoyed it.

Josh used to have trouble with the bones in his hands, so I'd massage them as we sat watching Sam, Carla, and Woody's wise-cracking japes in the bar. It was all very domestic—it reminded me a bit of my first-ever boyfriend, Jason, on the Yew Tree.

At the end of '89, it was time to crank the Priest machine up again. As was now a habit, we decamped to Glenn's place in Spain for the initial writing sessions for the album that was to become *Painkiller*. Our first job was to find ourselves a new drummer.

We didn't fancy the whole kerfuffle of auditioning scores of hopeful drummers. Luckily, I had an alternative suggestion.

Back in Phoenix, Surgical Steel had finally given up and called it a day. Jeff Martin had moved to LA and gotten himself a cool new metal band, Racer X. Their drummer was an enthusiastic and very talented young Judas Priest fanatic named Scott Travis.

When I say "fanatic"…I am not kidding. When we'd played Hampton Coliseum, in his home state of Virginia, on the *Fuel for Life* tour, Scott had planned to set up his drum kit in the parking lot to play as our tour bus pulled in. He hoped we'd spot him, and offer him a job!

In the end, he'd settled for handing a demo tape of his drumming to one of our road crew at the stage door. I don't think we ever listened to it—we already had a drummer at the time! But when I told him the seat was now vacant, he could not have been more excited.

I told the guys about Scott and we flew him to Spain. He had never left the US before, and when he arrived in our remote corner of Marbella, his first questions were "Where's the nearest 7-Eleven? Circle K? McDonald's?" Horrified that we had none of those amenities, he nicknamed the place Death Camp One.

As soon as Scott got behind the kit for a knock, it was clear to all of us that he was a fucking amazing drummer. He knew all of our songs and he was perfect for the band. Well, perfect in all but one respect…he was American.

It sounds daft now, but this was the subject of some very serious band discussions at the time. *We're a British heavy metal band—will it work to bring a Yank into the mix?* Happily, we soon saw sense. Musically, Scott was ideal for us. His passport color didn't matter.

We made *Painkiller* in Studio Miraval in southern France, at the start of 1990. Having made six studio albums and two live records with "Colonel" Tom Allom, we fancied a change, and drafted in Chris Tsangarides to coproduce the record with us.

It was no reflection on Tom. We knew the sound we wanted and we aimed to produce a lot of the album ourselves. Chris had worked with us as an engineer back on *Sad Wings of Destiny*, since when he had produced Thin Lizzy, Magnum, Gary Moore…and Samantha Fox. But nobody's perfect.

Studio Miraval was set in picturesque countryside and was as remote as Puk had been (a dismayed Scott christened it Death Camp Two). It didn't even have a TV. That suited us, because we went into making *Painkiller* with a determined agenda.

We should be so lucky! (Lucky, lucky, lucky…)

It was a new decade and the music world was changing. A whole new generation, and genre, of rock was coming out of Seattle, where the grunge movement was kicking off and Nirvana, Pearl Jam, and Alice in Chains had all emerged. Metal was shifting into a new cycle.

It made us feel that this would be an important, pivotal album for Judas Priest. So, we decided to go for it and endeavor to make the strongest, most intense, and most powerful album of our career. We felt it was the record that would dictate the future of the band.

We went into the recording sessions with maximum discipline and purpose…and it worked. Scott's titanic drumming gave us a fresh lease on life, all of the components fell into place, and I still think that *Painkiller* is Priest's *Sgt. Pepper*. It's our musical high benchmark that everything else is measured against.

Painkiller was relentless. Aside from the symphonic "Touch of Evil," it didn't let up from start to finish. It was the special album we knew we had to make, and its music strove to equal the brutal intensity of the title track's uncompromising lyrics:

Faster than a laser bullet, louder than an atom bomb
Chromium-plated boiling metal, brighter than a thousand suns

We were all delighted with *Painkiller*. From Miraval, we moved to Amsterdam to finish off and mix the album. I flew Josh out to join me…and I bought an apartment.

I have always liked Amsterdam and appreciated the Dutch people's down-to-earth openness. There is a real chill freedom about the place…and most of all, let's face it, I love the fact that Amsterdam is a gay mecca! So, I got a cool little place near the Rijksmuseum and Josh and I hung out for a few weeks. We had a fantastic summer…but my pleasure ended the day before we flew back to Phoenix.

I had—*mostly*—been faithful to Josh. Being faithful in the gay world is not the same as for straights: gay men are more promiscuous, but we often tell our partners about our little dalliances. Sometimes they join in, in a good old threesome! But Josh and I didn't do that.

I was happy with him, but the day before we left Amsterdam, I got the urge for a little hanky-panky. Ten minutes from my flat was a gay club called Drake's Cruising. As well as selling porn, whips, and gimp masks, it had anything-goes rooms, and cubicles with glory holes.

My sap was rising. I had to go there. *Now!*

"I'm just going out to...do something," I told Josh.

Everybody in Amsterdam has a bicycle and I jumped on mine and started peddling furiously to Drake's. I was in Doc Marten boots, a green bomber jacket, a wooly hat, and the tightest jeans I could squeeze into. I needed to show my bulge to its best effect.

Amsterdam is famous for its sex shops, its bikes, and its trams... and I was about to combine all three. I was so keen to get to Drake's that I wasn't looking where I was going, and my front wheel got snagged in a tram track. I went flying over the handlebars.

Oh, shit! I arced through the afternoon air in slow motion. I distinctly remember thinking: *This isn't going to end well!* It didn't. I stuck out my right arm to try to break my fall, hit the tarmac with a resounding thud, and dislocated my elbow.

CRACK! I heard the bone go. The pain was so excruciating I thought I was going to faint. I *wanted to faint*. People ran up and stood over me, trying to comfort me. They could see I was in agony and called me an ambulance, which arrived quickly.

In the back of the vehicle, I was in so much pain I could hardly speak. "I'm going to give you some gas and air," the paramedic said, noting my discomfort, and passed me a tube and a face mask. I clamped it on and sucked greedily.

WHOOSH! I had been sober for four years now, and at my first gulp of anesthetic, I was as high as a kite. It was fucking fantastic!

We should be so lucky! (Lucky, lucky, lucky…)

God, I've missed this feeling! I thought. *Right, that's it! When this is over, I'm going back to booze, and coke…maybe try a bit of heroin…*

The medic gently slipped my jacket off. I looked at my elbow and was surprised to see my bone poking out through my skin. By now, I was so wasted that I didn't care. We got to the hospital, they put me into a bed, and a doctor came to examine me.

He gave me an injection, sat on the bed, and started chatting to me. I was enjoying the small talk…until, without warning, the doc grabbed my arm and wrenched it. It felt as if he was trying to pull it off, but instead he snapped my elbow right back into place. It was masterful.

Josh and I flew back to Phoenix the next day with my arm in a half cast. It hurt for weeks, and when I was home, I had to have a full cast. So, that was where trying to cheat on Josh and get a quick hand job had got me! As Lennon once said, it was instant karma.

In America, we got some very bad news. *Painkiller* was done, dusted, and ready to roll…but suddenly, the album we were so proud of, and excited about, had been put on hold. The subsequent live tour to promote it had been put on hold. In fact, our entire career had been put on hold.

The thing that was so ridiculous that it couldn't possibly happen… was happening.

Judas Priest were going to court.

17

I – I – I asked her for a peppermint!

The boys' names were James Vance and Raymond Belknap, and they were from Sparks, Nevada. Vance was twenty; Belknap was just eighteen. On December 23, 1985, they had spent the day in Belknap's bedroom drinking, getting stoned, and listening to our *Stained Class* album on repeat, before agreeing to a suicide pact.

They had taken a sawn-off shotgun to a local kids' playground and attempted to kill themselves. Belknap had shot himself in the head and died straightaway. Vance only managed to shoot off the bottom half of his face and survived, hideously maimed.

It was a horrible story: but what came next was bizarre. Vance had written to Belknap's parents, claiming it was our music that had made them decide to top themselves: "I believe that alcohol and heavy metal music such as Judas Priest led us to be mesmerized." Vance and the parents had then decided to…*sue us.*

Vance had since died of a methadone overdose, but the boys' parents had pressed ahead with their lawsuit. Initially, they had claimed that our song "Heroes End" incited suicide, until Jayne Andrews sent them the lyric, pointing out that it said the exact opposite: *"Why do you have to die to be a hero?"* Then, the parents changed tack.

Their attorneys hired audio engineers, who claimed to have found "masked lyrics" secreted on *Stained Class*. They reported that, within our music, we had hidden subliminal messages exhorting anybody who listened to kill themselves.

The crux of their argument concerned our cover of Spooky Tooth's "Better by You, Better than Me." Their so-called audio experts said they had detected seven separate examples of me rasping "Do it!" during the song's choruses: a clear exhortation toward suicide!

That wasn't all. We had apparently also gone to the considerable trouble of concealing what they called "backmasked" lyrics on other tracks on the album. When they were played backward, I could supposedly be heard saying, "Try suicide," "Sing my evil spirit,"* and "Fuck the Lord, fuck all of you." *Among other things.*

When the band and I first heard that this was what we were charged with, we could not believe it. What was this bullshit? It was so far-fetched that we were baffled: Why the hell would we ever do that? Surely nobody in the world could take this rubbish seriously?

Well, it appeared that they could…and they were. The band were summoned to appear at Washoe County Courthouse in Reno on July 16, 1990. Vance's family were suing us and our record label, CBS, for $5 million. Belknap's would be satisfied with $1.6 million.

Before the trial, we hired condominiums a fair way outside of Reno and hunkered down with our lawyers. We were with them for hours…days…*weeks.* They wanted to know everything about *Stained Class,* and about Priest, in order to be prepared for whatever might be thrown at us in court.

We went along with it all, but there was still a general air of disbelief among us. We didn't want to belittle the tragedy of two lives that had been ended far too soon, but…*this was all fucking stupid.*

In Britain, defendants are not allowed to discuss their cases in public before their trial…but this was not Britain. *This was America,*

---

* "Sing my evil spirit!" I would *never* sing anything so ungrammatical!

where they do things very differently. In the run-up to the trial, our team fixed up media appearances for us to put across our side of the story.

I did a radio interview with Howard Stern. I wasn't sure it was a good idea, as he was a notorious "shock jock"—would it *really* help our cause? Our attorneys assured me it would, and it went well. He thought the case was ridiculous, and tore it to shreds on the air.

Less successful was an invitation to go on Geraldo Rivera's TV talk show. We found out in advance that it was an ambush: the lads' parents would also be there. So we pulled out. Rivera, a Republican fond of exposing "satanic abuse," put empty chairs on the TV set and called us "heavy metal chickens."

It all felt like being part of a stupid circus, and the trial itself didn't alleviate that feeling. As we nervously walked up the court-house steps on the first day, and press cameras clicked, local metalheads had gathered to support us. We signed a few autographs and they chanted "Priest! Priest! Priest!" They were to turn up day in, day out.

Once we got inside the court, I saw Vance's and Belknap's parents. They were the ones bringing the case, yet I didn't feel a flicker of anger toward them. They were misguided, but they had lost their young sons. They had been to hell. I wanted to go over and give them a hug.

I didn't feel the same sympathy toward their lawyers. As soon as the case began, it became evident that, where British courts are all about soberly finding the truth, American trials are essentially an adjunct of showbiz. It was clear from their lead attorney's opening statement.

"Your honor, this case is all about these poor families scream-ing for vengeance!" he told the trial judge. "They have come here to defend their faith! They don't want to be left in the sad wings of destiny…"

Sitting in a line, in our sensible suits and ties, Glenn, Ken, Ian, and I stared at each other, gobsmacked by this verbal diarrhea. *Was this bloke taking the piss? Was this case all one big joke?*

There was no jury. The case was to be heard by a judge—a middle-aged, conservative-looking Mormon called Judge Jerry Carr Whitehead. He remained virtually inscrutable for the entire trial.

Judge Whitehead had already dealt us a body blow before the case opened. Ozzy's "Suicide Solution" case had been thrown out as song lyrics were covered by the US First Amendment, guaranteeing and protecting freedom of speech. We had hoped for the same outcome.

It was not to be. The judge passed a pre-court ruling that, as we were charged with "backmasking" lyrics in our songs, and the amendment did not apply to such subliminal, implanted messages, the trial would proceed. Our case had been made doubly difficult…by something we hadn't done in the first place. *Great.*

When the trial began, the parents' lawyers unveiled their parade of audio "experts" who swore they had detected maleficent misdoings beneath the surface of *Stained Class*. They played clips of our tracks backward, supposedly to demonstrate the evil messages buried beneath them.

It was gibberish. The supposed message, "Sing my evil spirit" sounded more like *"Seeg mowevo sparee!"* "White Hot, Red Heat" backward *didn't* sound like "Fuck the Lord, fuck all of you!" but, as a *Village Voice* journalist covering the case wrote, "like an evil dolphin, chanting."

The parents' attorneys' Exhibit A was a different matter. When they played "Better by You, Better than Me" to the court, you could *just* make out a short, sharp, glottal noise after I sang the main chorus line. If you squinted, and tried hard, it could even sound a little bit like "Do it!"

The parents' lawyers played that clip to death in the court. As they did, I was watching Judge Whitehead closely and, in a rare display of emotion, I suddenly saw a flicker of recognition cross his face.

Shit! I thought. *He believes that it is there!* Yet even if it was—what did "Do it!" mean, anyway? *Mow the lawn? Have a cup of tea?* Why did it have to mean "Kill yourself"?! It was absurd beyond belief.

The parents' lawyers were showboating and hamming it up like bad actors throughout. Their lead attorney explained to the judge that, while we were respectably dressed in his court, that was not our usual attire.

"Onstage, they wear leather, chains, and handcuffs, and wave whips!" he said, as if that proved our satanic intent. As the bemused judge peered at us, my heart sank again. What would a sedate, reactionary US justice know of heavy metal bands, and how they dressed?

A female lawyer depicted our whole career as an exercise in mass hypnosis. "They are experts at creating illusions and images," she said, ominously. "They make their living by these illusions; by making things appear to be what they are not."

Fuck me! We had gone WELL through the looking glass here!

In contrast to the fantastical speculation of the parents' attorneys, our defense case sounded to me like pure hard-headed common sense. Our own sound engineers pointed out that the supposed "Do it!" injunctions were mere audio accidents.

They were a chance combination, on the twenty-four-track recording, of three elements: me exhaling as I sang; a quirky guitar sound; and a drum downbeat. It was a sonic glitch; a total coincidence. Well, it seemed bloody obvious to me—but would the judge believe it?

Our lawyers focused, correctly, on the backgrounds of the poor lads who had killed themselves. Both were from families with histories of abuse and domestic violence, and had dropped out of high school. They were drinkers and drug users, and already had criminal records.

I – I – I asked her for a peppermint!

As our attorney chronicled their "sad and miserable lives," an awful thought struck me: these troubled boys had a wretched existence, and their favorite band, Judas Priest, may have meant more to them than anything else. It made it all even more of a tragedy.

It *was* a tragedy, and my heart bled for them and for their parents, *but it wasn't our fault.* On purely logical grounds, our trial seemed to me to be an open-and-shut case…but I had no idea how it was going to pan out. It felt like all bets were off.

The boys' parents were devastated, their attorneys were slick and articulate, and the poker-faced Judge Whitehead was giving nothing away. It felt as if we were fighting not just for our lives as a band, but for heavy metal, for *music*, as a whole.

If we lost the case, the ramifications would be huge. And I wasn't feeling optimistic. Every day, as we left the courthouse, CNN and the other TV news channels' cameras and reporters would converge on us: *Had we urged our fans to kill themselves? Did we bury subliminal messages on our albums?*

"If we were going to put subliminals on our albums," I sighed to one journalist, "we wouldn't say, 'Kill yourself!' We'd say, 'Buy more of our records!'" Such black humor was just about keeping us sane.

We knew one of Priest would be required to give evidence and, in a meeting with our lawyers, we decided that I would do it. I was fine with that. I was the singer, the lyricist, the guy who loves words. Plus, I *wanted* to get up there, cut the crap, and tell the truth.

Finally, I was called to take the witness stand. As I walked across the court, I heard a message of encouragement that was maybe a little louder than its perpetrator had meant it to be. It was in a Brummie accent, and coming from the direction of Glenn:

"Go on! Gerrim, Rob!"

I was confident about giving evidence, although I knew I had to face hostile questioning. The families' lawyer had called a youth counselor who had argued that heavy metal *per se* was invidious and damaging to impressionable young people. I completely refuted her argument.

Priest only send out positive messages, I explained. When we have songs that are good versus evil, good always triumphs. If we ever do have bleak messages, we turn them into something bright. This was true…and it always has been.

Our lawyer asked me to sing the chorus of "Better by You, Better than Me" to show my singing style, and my exhalation that could be mistaken for "Do it!" I sang it a cappella from the witness stand, precisely as I would do in a studio. It was a dramatic and, I think, convincing moment.

And I had a secret weapon up my sleeve. I had spent the morning in a local recording studio, listening to other tracks from *Stained Class* played backward, in search of any other gobbledygook "subliminal messages." I had struck gold.

On the boom box that I had brought into court with me, I played the song "Invader" backward. One lyric runs: *"They won't take our love away."*

"I think you'll find, your honor," I said, addressing Judge Whitehead, "that, backward, it seems to say, 'Look, Ma, my chair is broken!'" I played it, and there it was, that ridiculous phrase, way clearer than any of the so-called "backmasking" the court had previously heard.

I hadn't finished. I then pointed out, politely, that "Exciter" backward yielded the even more nonsensical, "I – I – I asked her for a peppermint! I – I – I asked her to get one!" The words rang out, as clear as day. There was even some laughter in the court.

"If you play any song backward, whether it is Judas Priest or Frank Sinatra, you will hear messages," I told the judge. "It is just the way that humans hear." Looking at him, I got the impression that my point had hit home. I certainly hoped so.

And that was it. The case was concluded, and all we could do was await the judge's deliberations and written verdict. As we left the building for the last time, one of our fans, whom I had spotted nearly every day, ran up to me.

He handed me a huge Stars and Stripes flag, covered with signatures and best wishes from the many fans who had gathered outside the courthouse. "We're sorry our country has put you through all this!" he said. It was so lovely. I still have that flag in my house in Phoenix.

Now the trial was done, I didn't want to hang around Reno waiting for the judge's verdict. I vanished on my own to Puerto Vallarta in Mexico and had a few days in a lovely villa with a lap pool—that I filled with a local muscle boy I picked up in town. Well, I got lonely!

I was in Mexico when Jayne Andrews phoned me with the verdict. Judge Whitehead had largely found in our favor. He said he *could* hear a phrase similar to "Do it!" on the chorus of "Better by You, Better than Me," but he believed it was a "chance combination of sounds" we had not put there intentionally.

Well, you don't say!

The judge also found "no proof" of "backmasking." He fined our record label, CBS, $40,000 for being slow in providing the court with our master tapes,* but Judas Priest were in the clear.

Yet I was dissatisfied with the verdict. I still am. The judge's summary, to me, merely stated that their lawyers hadn't proved their case adequately. It wasn't the total vindication we needed, and deserved.

I had wanted the judge to say: *"Judas Priest had nothing at all to do with these poor young people losing their lives. These charges were entirely false. One hundred percent!"* But he didn't, and it rankled with me.

Despite the mealy-mouthed nature of the judge's statement, I was so relieved that the verdict had gone our way. And it made it all

---

* The judge said that, had CBS been speedier in supplying the tapes, the case would probably never even have come to court. THAT would have been nice.

so much sweeter that, when *Painkiller* finally emerged, it did so to a fantastic reception.

The wrist merchants were wanking themselves silly over this one. We got some of the best reviews of our career. The critics seemed to recognize our mission—to make the hardest, truest metal album we could—and that we had succeeded in it.

I grabbed a few days of downtime with Josh in Phoenix and then it was time to go again. The *Painkiller* tour was kicking off in Canada in October, so we headed to a freezing-cold sports hall near Lake Placid for ten days of rehearsals.

I had one of my light-bulb moments there. Rollerblading was making a bit of a comeback, and I headed into the nearest town and bought a pair. Soon, I was rollerblading around the stage, and singing, as we got the tour production and set list together.

"Hey, wouldn't it be a great idea if I rollerbladed during the shows?" I suggested. "You know, all in leather?"

Some of my ideas get waved through—but on this one, the reaction from the rest of the band was unanimous: "No, it would bloody NOT be a good idea for you to rollerblade on tour, Rob!" So, that was that. I didn't rollerblade on tour.

The rehearsals went well, and one evening I was in my hotel watching MuchMusic, a Canadian equivalent of MTV. They were talking to a guy called Dimebag Darrell about his band, Pantera. I had never heard of Pantera, but Dimebag was wearing a *British Steel* T-shirt, so I cocked an ear.

He said nice things about Priest, and then they played the video for Pantera's "Cowboys from Hell." *Fucking hell! They were phenomenal!* I knew a guy at the TV channel, which was near my hotel, so I called him and asked him to ask Dimebag to stick around.

I walked down to the studio to meet him. Dimebag was a lovely guy—within minutes, I felt like I'd known him for years. That night, Pantera were playing a gig in Toronto. I went, and was blown away. *What a band!* And what cool, easy-going Texan guys!

It was heavy metal and it sounded brutal, and original, and fresh. The next day, I told the rest of Priest all about Pantera. "Let's take them on tour in Europe!" I suggested. Nobody quibbled. Done deal. Cool!

The *Painkiller* outing was to be one of the most successful tours in Priest's history. Like the album, it really set a high benchmark. The fans were eager for us, after we'd had to postpone the tour for the court case, and the new tracks sounded ferocious live.

The whole tour was a release of the frustrations and tensions that had built up in us in Reno. I found singing "Painkiller," with its sheer metal overkill and Scott's seismic drumming, incredibly cathartic:

> Faster than a bullet, terrifying scream,
> Enraged and full of anger, he is half man and half machine

While we were still in Canada, Jim Silvia fixed me up a little treat. I had become quite a connoisseur of preshow massages, and Jim told me, as a late birthday treat, he had arranged a local guy for me in Winnipeg. Into the dressing room walked…a super-hot bodybuilder.

Well, hello!

The guy gave me a fucking great massage and we chatted while he did it. He told me that his other line of work was as a male stripper and he was doing a late show that night, an hour or so after the Priest gig finished. Did I want to come down and see him?

Well, I had certainly had worse offers than that!

After I got offstage that night, Jim Silvia and I bowled down to the male strip club. We were the only blokes in the audience. A couple of the women were Priest fans, and made a fuss of me… until the male strippers came on, at which point I was completely forgotten.

"Get 'em off! Show us your pecker! Hey, over here, big boy!"

It was absolute bedlam. I hadn't seen quiet, polite women

transform into rabid animals so quickly since…well, since Mom at the wrestling in Walsall. There again, it was a cracking strip show, and I must admit I was just as excited as they were. Or, maybe, more so.

When the show was over, and I was vigorously fanning myself to cool myself down, my masseur came over to me. "Hey, Rob, what are you doing now?" he asked.

"Oh, probably just going back to my hotel," I said.

"Great! We'll come with you! We want to give you our blue-light special!"

I had no idea what this was, but I was very eager to find out. The masseur and an equally hunky second stripper came up to my room with me and put a boom box on my desk. They pushed the "play" button and loud house music started pumping out.

"Get on the bed!" they ordered me.

Oh, OK then…

It was heaven. Two off-the-chart buff bodybuilders did an erotic striptease just for me. They felt each other up and then, as I was really getting into it, they climbed on the bed, and on top of me, and started fondling me and feeling me up. And then…

That was it. No happy ending for Rob. Well, it was probably for the best. After all, I had a boyfriend back in Phoenix (ahem)…*

The US dates were sleek, sheer, and magnificent. Scott's drumming gave us a new dimension, and definitely helped us to reproduce the power and ferocity of the *Painkiller* album. But this didn't mean we didn't have our usual comedy moments.

My hair had been thinning in recent years (always a tragic loss for a metalhead!) and, around *Painkiller*, I had finally taken the plunge and shaved my head. I hadn't yet embraced tattoos and covered myself with body art…but I took my first, baby step.

---

* It transpired that it was called the blue-light special because, at the time, Walmart was running "blue-light special offers" where you got two for one. And that was what I had just got. Two for one.

I – I – I asked her for a peppermint!

One early evening, somewhere in the Midwest, I spent more than an hour on my own, in front of a dressing-room mirror, drawing a huge "JP" logo on the side of my head with a Sharpie pen. I made it into quite a work of art. It looked fantastic.

Jim Silvia came in to give me my ten-minutes-to-stage call.

"How does it look?" I asked him.

Jim looked at me. "It looks great…in a mirror."

What? Oh, fuck! Like a dickhead, I had drawn it so it read "JP" in the mirror. On my bonce, in real life, it said "ЯL." *Shit!*

"What do I do now?" I asked Jim as we stood in the wings.

He shrugged. "Just do a lot of headbanging! Nobody will notice!" So I did. It took me two or three days to scrub that bloody ЯL off my bonce, after which I started going to tattoo parlors. I figured I'd leave it to the professionals.

After one *Painkiller* show, I was flicking through a magazine and I saw a personal ad in the guys-looking-for-guys section. It leapt out at me:

YOUNG, ACTIVE-DUTY GAY MARINE SEEKS SIMILAR

Well, I was neither an active-duty Marine nor particularly young, but this was too good an opportunity to miss! I scribbled down a letter on hotel notepaper, posted it to the guy's PO box number, and forgot about it. *For now.*

The *Painkiller* tour ran right up to Christmas, and then the start of '91 brought another major landmark in Priest's long globe-trotting career: our first trip to South America.

The Rock in Rio festival was a huge deal. Held over ten days in the Macaranã football stadium, in front of 80,000 people a day, its lineup was as random as *Top of the Pops*. Prince, INXS, and Santana were there, but so were A-Ha, George Michael, and New Kids on the Block.

It was our first taste of fanatical South American fans. I'd have loved to have a gander at exotic Rio de Janeiro, but we couldn't take even a step outside of our hotel without hordes of hyperventilating metalheads descending on us: *"Please, sign! Please, photo!"* Jim Silvia earned his dosh.

We were second headliners on the metal day to Guns N' Roses, who were then the biggest band in the world. I loved their music, and Axl Rose's presence and charisma. To me, they were a heavy metal Rolling Stones. But I'd also heard that Axl could be... difficult.

This was confirmed on the day of the show, when we got a message from the Guns N' Roses camp that I couldn't ride my Harley onstage for "Hell Bent for Leather." *Axl didn't want me to,* I was told. It was Dublin all over again... and I felt totally the same as I had then. "Well, the show is off, then," I said.

There was some dissent in our camp—"Oh, come on, Rob, we've come all this way!"—but I held firm. *No. Fucking. Way.* The bike is part of our show. The fans will expect it. And it's a point of principle— *what's it got to do with Axl fucking Rose if we use it or not?*

A standoff ensued, with harassed organizers running between our dressing room and Guns', until finally a factotum materialized with a message from The Great Man himself.

"Axl wants you to know that this whole thing about your motorbike is nothing to do with him!" he claimed. "He never said you can't use the bike. You can use the bike!"

So, had it been an officious tour manager getting above himself, or had Axl backed down and was now trying to save face? Who knew? Who cared? All I was bothered about was that I was riding onstage on the bike. Whether Axl bloody Rose liked it or not.

Our set was broadcast live across South America and, like Zep at Oakland, or the US Festival, or Live Aid, it was a huge adrenaline buzz to play in front of such an enormous, seemingly never-ending crowd. We knew we had to pull out all of the stops, and we did. We killed it.

As the *Painkiller* tour switched to Europe, Pantera joined us. They had never left America before but they were absolutely fearless. It is not easy to be a Priest support band. Priest fans know what they like, and can be brutal.

Pantera went out there and blew them away. It was the same as us supporting Kiss. Our fans had never heard anything like them before, so the first song would be greeted by a stunned silence, but by the end of the set, they had always won them over. It was great to see.

I flew Josh out for some European dates. He loved being on the road with us, it was nice to see him, and our easy, no-drama relationship ambled on at its low-key, comforting level. It's amazing how many different countries you can watch *Cheers* in.

The European dates were great, but I was beginning to flag. One issue was in-band friction. Our twin guitar heroes, Glenn and Ken, bickered like an old married couple, and it got worse as our tours neared their end. You could set your watch by it.

It was always the same. Ken would moan about something, and Glenn would pass a sarcastic comment, then forget about it. *He* would forget, but Ken wouldn't. He'd brood over it for days. It could be funny… but I had seen that film *so* many times. I was bored of it.

It strengthened my desire to step away from the band and do a solo project for a short time, away from those tensions. Plenty of artists do it. I'd do my own thing, away from the band, and then come back to Priest when the band's calendar required it.

This tour is over by spring, I thought. *I'll do something on my own, get it out of my system, and be ready to go again when Priest come to record our next album next year. I'll prove that I can do it, and it will be good for all of us.*

So, it was deeply unfortunate that when Priest finished up this particular outing… we went right back out on tour again.

While we were touring *Painkiller*, the Gulf War had kicked off in the Middle East. Iraq had invaded Kuwait, and American, British, and coalition forces mounted Operation Desert Storm to go in, drive them out, and protect the world's oil supplies.

One theme that developed during the tour was friends of mine in the military, and Priest fans, sending us videos of themselves in their barracks, preparing for action. They would be getting psyched up for war by playing *Painkiller* at full blast.

It spoke to me on a gut level. These guys were about to go into battle knowing they might get killed, or maimed, as might their mate next to them. It had to be the most terrifying moment of their lives…and they were turning to us for inspiration. *For heavy metal motivation.*

We got asked to play a multi-artist tour called *Operation Rock & Roll* to honor the victorious US forces. It was to tour the States for six weeks that summer, with a cool lineup: Alice Cooper, Motör-head, Dangerous Toys, and Metal Church.

Should we join it? It wasn't an easy decision. Oddly enough, we never sat down as a band and discussed the political aspect: *What are we putting our name to here?* It feels strange now that we never talked about it.

Our minds were focused more on the timing. We were just coming off a major tour. I wasn't the only person in the band feeling bushed and in need of a break. We'd just played the US, extensively: Would fans want to come out and see the same show again?

Priest had never repeated ourselves. We went on tour when we had new music, and a new stage show, for the fans. This time, we would have neither. I felt uneasy about it, and I know Ken wasn't keen. Yet, somehow, we ended up agreeing to do it.

I headed home to Phoenix to hook up with Josh again. He had some news. Like a lot of small-town guys, he had been missing his family since he had moved away. He and his brother, Ted, were particularly close, so Ted and his fiancée had just moved to live in Phoenix.

Good! I was glad Josh would see more of Ted, and figured he would have company while I was away touring. Josh started going over to visit Ted and sometimes stay the night. He would return the next day rubbing his lower back and complaining of soreness.

I – I – I asked her for a peppermint!

"Ted hasn't got much furniture yet, so I have to sleep on the couch!" he complained. "I wish they had a spare bed over there!"

That seemed easily remedied, so Josh and I went bed shopping in Phoenix. I bought one and arranged for it to be delivered straight to Ted's place. Josh then came with me as I headed back out on the road—the last place I wanted to be.

The *Operation Rock & Roll* tour was an anticlimax. After our great *Painkiller* outing, where we were on top form and masters of our own metal domain, joining what was basically a traveling festival felt diluted. In fact, it felt like a mistake.

I'd been a fan of Alice Cooper since I was blasting out "School's Out" in Harry Fenton's in 1972, but Alice wasn't happy on this tour. He was going on before us, and he wanted to headline. I wasn't fussed, and I'd have been happy to swap slots, finish early, and watch telly in the hotel. The promoters weren't so laissez-faire. They wanted the lineup to stay as it was, with Priest going on last, and they wouldn't budge. As a sop to Alice, they let him headline two dates: his home-town of Detroit and the last night of the tour, in Toronto.

Commercially, the tour did OK…but no more. Where we had had packed arenas of Priest nutters for *Painkiller*, a lot of *Operation Rock & Roll* dates didn't sell out. Staring out at rows of empty seats made this jaunt feel even more superfluous and underwhelming.

I felt as if I desperately needed time off as we arrived at the last date of the tour, at the CNE Stadium in Toronto, on August 19, 1991. It was an utter disaster from the start.

We arrived to discover that the show was in a baseball stadium. The stage was in the middle of the field, with fans both on the pitch and up in the bleachers. It was an unusual setup, and not what we were used to.

We were starting our set with "Hell Bent for Leather." The routine was that our intro tape would start up, the hydraulics would lift up a section of raised platform at the back of the stage, I'd roar under it on my bike, and we'd power into the song.

Something went wrong. Somebody fucked up. I was being driven from our dressing room to the stage in a golf cart when I realized that I could already hear our intro tape. *Shit! I should be on the bike by now!*

"You'll have to go faster, mate!" I told the laid-back Canuck driver.

"Dude, it's a golf cart, eh?" he said. "They don't go any faster!"

"*Make* it go faster!"

By the time we put-putted up to my bike, I should already have been onstage—the stage in front of me that was by now, as ever, a thick fog of dry ice and smoke. I jumped onto the Harley, opened its throttle, and vroomed off at quite a lick.

I didn't know that the stage guys had been told that we weren't in place yet, and so had only just begun to raise the upper stage. I couldn't see a thing through the smoke and the dry ice. I just sped onto my ramp, into the fog, and…

CRACK! The bridge of my nose smashed against the solid metal section of stage that was only just being raised. I felt my neck SNAP! all the way back, as if I'd been hit with a sledgehammer. I crashed off the bike, hit the stage hard…and I was gone.

BLACKOUT!

When I came to, a minute or so later, I didn't know where I was. I was lying on something hard…in a cloud of smoke…it was incredibly loud…I was in agony…and somebody was… kicking me?

I looked up to see Glenn stumbling around, playing his guitar. He hadn't seen me, and booted me in the ribs again.

"*OW!*"

Glenn looked down. "Rob? Is that you? What you doing? Gerrup!"

I couldn't. I was in agony. A couple of roadies ran on, helped me offstage…and put a plaster on my nose. Meanwhile, the band riffed on and did "Hell Bent for Leather" as an instrumental. The fans had no idea what was going on. Nor did I.

I – I – I asked her for a peppermint!

I was groggy as fuck and my neck was in agony. What I should have done, what any sane rock singer *would* have done, was to fall into an ambulance and go straight to the local ER. But you don't do that when you're from Walsall.

You don't do that when you've seen the blokes grafting and making pig iron at G. & R. Thomas Ltd.

If you've got a job to do, you just *gerronwithit.*

I limped back onstage and I played the show. God knows how. My nose and my neck felt about to snap. I was in excruciating pain. I could have burst into tears at any point during the set. *Fuck, it was grim.*

Somehow, I got through it and made it back to the dressing room. Jim Silvia had dialed 911 and he and Josh sat with me, comforting me, as we awaited the ambulance. Then, from the other side of the room, there came a noise. A horrible, high-pitched, whining noise.

"I day! I day! I day do it!"

It was a harsh, irritable sound. The sound of a pissed-off bloke from the Black Country. *An angry yam-yam.*

Glenn and Ken had kicked off yet again. Who knows what it was about? Who cares? But Glenn had that usual beatific half smile on his face, as if it were all a bit beneath him. And, as for Ken…

Ken was so livid that he had jumped up on a coffee table, shirtless, still dripping with sweat from the gig. He was red in the face and he was bawling his head off. He had gone full nuclear yam-yam.

"I day! I day fuckin' do it! I day!"

Fucking hell! Right now, right at this moment…I. Did. Not. Need. This.

The paramedics arrived. They strapped me up in a neck brace. I couldn't move. Jim came with me in the ambulance, and as I was driven through the Toronto traffic, still in agony, my mind was racing:

I've had enough. I've had enough of the rows. Enough of the touring.

ENOUGH OF THE BAND. I've got to get away for a bit and do my own thing. Now!

They X-rayed me at the hospital and told me I had broken my nose and severely sprained my neck. I would have to wear a neck brace for the next few weeks. I flew back to Phoenix with Josh, shattered, miserable, and, in my hefty neck brace, very sorry for myself.

Josh said he was going to his brother's place for a day or two, and vanished. He called me a couple of days later.

"Hey, Rob!"

"Hey! How's it going? When are you coming back?"

"I don't think I am."

"What?"

"I think I'm going to live with Ted now. I miss him and I'm happy here. But it's been great, and thanks for everything! Bye!"

And that was that. The end of Josh. I had bought his bed, and he was going to lie in it.

He had never been a once-in-a-lifetime, stars-exploding passion like Brad, but I was hurt and I missed him. For all of my odd dalliances along the way, I had thought Josh and I were doing well together. Clearly, I was wrong.

I was on my own again and I went into an emotional tailspin. I guess sobriety helped me cope with the breakup but, even so, I just felt…*spent*. Gone. So much tension had been building up in me, and now I felt like a husk, a hollow man.

I was just turning forty, a difficult age, and I was not in a good place or state to do it. Too much bad shit had happened too fast. Reno, the bike accident, the band friction, Josh dumping me out of the blue…one of those things would have been hard to cope with.

All of them? I had no chance!

I shut down. I slipped into a withdrawn, empty, flat semiexistence. I felt as if I had no feelings at all, and nothing was important to me. For a few weeks, I mooched around the house on my own. I never went out and I hardly bothered to eat.

I – I – I asked her for a peppermint!

I remembered Mom, after she had Nigel, sinking into a deep depression and never talking, until she took her happy pills. I hadn't understood back then how she felt. Well, now I did.

I also allowed myself to recognize something I had been ignoring, and in denial about, for months: *Josh had been straight.* He was straight all along. I think he was overawed at being with his favorite rock star, and initially liked living with me…but then it had worn off.

Yes, Josh had been straight. Just like Brad. Just like David.

Why did I keep fucking up and going after straight men? What the hell was wrong with me?

There is this theory that some gay men pursue straight men without even knowing they are doing it. They have been told by society for years that they are inferior, *damaged goods*, and they end up believing, on a subconscious level, that straight blokes are "better" than them.

So, they go after them. Although, even if they get one of them, they have no chance of holding on to them. It's a damaging, futile, and stupidly masochistic mindset…but *there they go*, hoping for a miracle, chasing straight guys. Sometimes, they do it again and again and again.

Fuck. Was I REALLY one of those guys? WAS I?

Newly forty years old—*forty!*—I looked hard at myself, and what I was, and I didn't like what I saw. But I didn't see any way of changing. I felt as trapped by my sexuality, *by myself*, as I had done ever since I knew that I was gay. Ever since school.

I was halfway through my life, and being gay, *being gay in a heavy metal band*, still felt like the shitty, sordid little secret I'd always have to keep. I saw no way out. I saw no hope.

So, I sat, on my own, in Phoenix, and I stewed. It was fucking shit.

18

Loose lips sink ships

I had known John Baxter since not long after I had moved to Phoenix. He was part of the Mason Jar and Rockers drinking scene with Surgical Steel and the other guys. He had always seemed a nice guy, and we got on well.

John and I had kept in touch when he got himself a place in Los Angeles and began spending a lot of his time out there. I knew that I needed a break from the lethargic self-pity that I was wallowing in in Phoenix, so when he invited me to stay, I accepted.

John proved to be a good listener as I told him all about my recent travails. He offered me emotional support, and one evening I found myself telling him about my current disenchantment with Priest, and that I wanted to do a solo project in the band's downtime. He could not have been more encouraging.

"Yeah, Rob, you should definitely do that!" he said. "You could be a huge solo star. Look at Ozzy, when he left Sabbath! You could be as big as that!"

I doubted very much whether *that* was true, but at a time when I was feeling very low, John's enthusiasm and encouragement gave me a lift. He told me that he had recently taken and passed a couple of courses in music business management, and asked me if he could be my manager for my solo, extra-Priest activities.

In truth, I wasn't that bothered either way. My solo career was going to be a fresh start, in a way, so…*sure, why not? Let's give it a go!*

Glenn, Ken, and Ian had already given me their OK to do a solo side project. However, I felt that I also needed to tell Bill Curbishley and Jayne Andrews about my plans. John agreed and watched me bash out a fax to send them.

It took me five minutes. I didn't give it too much thought at the time but, nearly thirty years on, to the best of my memory, here is roughly what it said:

Dear Bill and Jayne,

I think the band and I need to take a break from each other. I am going to step away and do a solo musical project. It's something I have wanted to do for a long time—and it's something that I NEED to do. My friend, John Baxter, will be managing this project for me.

Thanks, Rob

That was it. It didn't say a word about me leaving Priest—because I didn't want to. John and I faxed the letter to Bill and Jayne and I forgot about it until the next day—when Bill replied.

He sent a very aggressive fax, saying I was stupid to want to quit the band when we were at our peak, and telling me I must need my head looked at. You certainly wouldn't call it him giving me his blessing and wishing me well! I was astonished. *Where had that come from?*

Maybe my fax had been too ambiguous, and Bill had thought I was quitting? I should probably have picked up the phone and talked to him, but I felt quite hurt, and his tone was so hostile that I didn't want to. *That fear of confrontation again!*

In the meantime, John set up a press conference to announce my solo sideline. It was at this point that I realized that journalists, and therefore fans, had two main expectations, or fears, about this mysterious press conference. Their first worry was that I would use it to announce that I was quitting Priest.

They could relax. I was absolutely categorical on this point. Time and again, both in the press call and in a handful of follow-up interviews, I stressed that my as-yet-unnamed solo band would be *in addition to* Priest, and one hundred percent not *instead of* Priest.

"It's important for everyone to know that in no way have Judas Priest broken up," I said. "We're still very much together and we still have a great relationship. When the time is right, we'll be back."

The other speculation going on was far more lurid and personal. I had heard that there were stories flying around that I had called the press conference to break the news that I had AIDS.

It was a fecund, toxic time for gossip like that. Freddie Mercury had recently told the world he was HIV-positive just days before he died, and the scandal sheets were on alert for the next high-profile victim. Tongues had been wagging that it might be me.

In a way, it wasn't a surprise. I was still in the closet, very much so, and I had no plans to come dramatically bursting out of it anytime soon. At the same time, on a personal level, some of the unbearable pressure on me to keep my sexual orientation secret had relaxed.

The first reason was my sobriety. Since I had stopped drinking six years earlier, I was less paranoid about being found out. I was happier in my own skin. I was less bothered about people's perceptions of me—going on Pride marches was hardly a way to keep a low profile!

The other reason I was more relaxed was that I was temporarily away from Priest. Ever since those early days rehearsing at Holy Joe's, I'd been paranoid about my sexuality becoming public knowledge and destroying the band. Now I was on my own for a while, I guess I felt less stressed about that.

Innuendo had swirled around me for ages. I'd got used to journalists dropping sly questions about my views on gays into rock interviews. I always took the same approach as Freddie had: "That's nothing to do with the band." I just figured it was nobody's business.

So, when it came up in the press conference, I just answered it as matter-of-factly as possible: "No. No, I don't have AIDS, thanks. Next question, please?"

One cool thing that happened around this time was that I got a letter back from the US Marine whose small ad I had answered on the *Painkiller* tour. He said his name was Thomas Pence, and he sounded like an interesting guy.

Thomas wrote that he had grown up in a tiny hamlet of three hundred people in eastern Alabama with no traffic lights, a single general store…and a branch of the Ku Klux Klan. Boys there grew up and went into the military. Girls waited for the boys to come home and marry them.

He said it was a hard place to grow up gay and he had never had a relationship or sexual experience. In fact, he'd never even met another gay man before! However, he had decided to place a small ad to dip a nervous toe into the water.

Thomas explained that he'd just served in Kuwait, and when he came back, he had opened a PO box and placed his ad. That box had been crammed every day. He hadn't realized that Marines are a hot commodity in the gay world.

Wow! This guy really WAS innocent!

In his letter, Thomas wrote that 95 percent of the replies he'd received had begun, "I'm not a Marine, BUT…" and the person would then claim to be "really hot" or "really rich." He'd had letters from people claiming to be Hollywood actors and millionaires.

So, it was quite reasonable that he had a question for me: "You say you are the singer in Judas Priest—is that true?"

I wrote back to him eagerly. "Yes," I told him. "Yes, I am."

Over the following weeks, Thomas and I wrote to each other a lot. He was keen to ask me loads of questions about heavy metal, Slayer, and Ozzy. I was more interested in talking to him about… well, sex.

We progressed to chatting on the phone, and while I think he still found my lewd innuendos (*I just can't help myself, sometimes!*) a bit off-putting, we got on really well. But then, all of a sudden, the calls just stopped. He simply wasn't there anymore.

I had no idea where he had gone. But I really missed our talks.

Now that my solo venture was public knowledge, I threw myself into the songwriting process. Because that was my huge motivation: to prove to myself, and everybody else, that I—*me, me, me!*—could write songs all by myself. That was what mattered most.

Bands are all about compromise. There were many times in Priest I'd had an idea on how a song should progress, and been overruled. It was a frustration…every group has it. Well, here was my chance to take a break, scratch this itch, and return to the band refreshed.

Having always written songs in a close-knit team, it could have been intimidating—but it wasn't. It was liberating, empowering. I wrote, and I wrote, and I wrote, as if I had opened a floodgate. The songs came together really quickly. I played the guitar and the bass myself, which I found I was surprisingly OK at, and I programmed the drums. It sounded just like it had in my head. My *me, me, me!* moment was coming together.

Mainly as an investment, I had bought a house in Marina del Ray, in LA. It was a gorgeous place, so I started splitting my time between there and writing music in Phoenix, where I had all my gear.

I worked very, very hard. But I also made plenty of time to play.

Thomas was still absent from the scene. I guessed that I had been too lewd in our letters and phone chats, and had scared him off. Shame, because he seemed a nice guy—but, *Ah, well! There were plenty more fish in the sea!*

In a bar in Marina del Ray, I got talking to another US Marine: a tall, handsome, very masculine guy called Hank. He made a lot of smiling eye contact, and invited me to visit the Marine Corps Base Camp at Pendleton. I got there so fast I could have been the Road Runner.

Beep beep!

For a gay guy, Pendleton was an Aladdin's cave. There were just *so* many amazing male specimens there: young, buff guys at the height of their physical powers! With my thing for men in uniform, my eyes were on stalks.

Hank was a married man but, like a lot of Marines, he got bored and sexually frustrated on base, and would hook up with fellow squaddies and other guys. I soon became a regular visitor to Pendleton, and he and I would fool around.

Given our circumstances, and the fact that he was married, we were never going to be any more than *wham-bam-thank-you-man* fun, but I could live with that! At a time when I was free and single, and when even my work was now solitary, Hank was exactly what I needed.

It came to a very sad end. Hank used to ride big, powerful motorbikes and quad bikes around the base. Like all Marines, he loved to showboat, and one day he was sitting, revving his bike up loud, when it suddenly went into gear and flipped up into the air.

Hank landed on his stomach and the bike came down *BANG!* on top of him. It landed on his back and broke his spine. It was what they call a life-changing injury: he lost the use of both of his legs in that instant, and he never walked again.

When he was in a wheelchair, Hank and I kept in touch and I

would still see him sometimes, just as a friend. I heard that when he died, a few years later, his wife went through his possessions, found letters from me…and realized we had been having an affair.

I felt awful, and guilty, about that. It made me realize that the sexually free-and-easy way I had gone about my life sometimes had consequences, and victims. I never contacted her: I just wouldn't have known what to say. *That poor woman.*

There again, another military wife at Pendleton didn't at all mind me having an affair with her husband. Because *she* was in the bed with us.

Through Hank, I met a bisexual Marine sergeant on the base called Steve. He was just as ultra-masculine as Hank, but his big thing was threesomes—with his wife, Dawn. Marines were allowed family visits, so I would go along at the same time as she was there. Once the door was shut, we would go at it for hours. I'd leave there more exhausted than if I'd been for a gym workout.

In fact—world exclusive!—Dawn is the only woman that I have ever had full sex with. She was a lovely, beautiful woman, with a perfect body. I know most men would have killed to be in bed with her and there I was, banging away, with her husband encouraging us!

I did it…but *my heart wasn't in it*. It was canoodling with Margie on Ken's sofa in Bloxwich all over again: *I could do it, but I didn't really want to.* I was far more interested in Steve, and my blow jobs and hand jobs with him felt like a reward for persevering with Dawn.

While I was regularly slipping in and out of Pendleton, the camp got caught up in a big sex scandal. A sleazy local Mexican guy who went by Bobby Vasquez was picking up horny young Marines in straight bars in nearby Oceanside and inviting them home.

Vasquez would give them a few beers and cigarettes, and maybe $20, put on a straight porn film and encourage the soldiers to have a wank. He would film them doing it and make the footage into compilation DVDs, which he'd then sell to gay guys. He was making a fortune.

Vasquez got busted and I think my name may also have been going before me at Pendleton because, one day, as I was walking onto the base with Steve, the security guy on the main gate stopped me.

"Sorry, sir," he said. "But I'm afraid you can't come in here anymore."

And that was the end of that. *Banned from a US Marine camp for lewd behavior!* I guess that is some kind of achievement…

Pendleton wasn't the only site of my sexual prowling. When I was in Phoenix, I would drive around Papago Park by the old Phoenix Zoo, cruising for cock. These were mostly sad, fruitless excursions, and I'd go home frustrated.* But I still carried on going.

I don't know particularly why I became so sexually rampant just as I turned forty. Was it because I was coming out of a long, fairly vanilla relationship with Josh? Was it a textbook midlife crisis? Was it because I had time on my hands? Was it *just because I could?*

I think it was probably a combination of all of those…and it was to lead to another of my occasional, very embarrassing pratfalls.

When I was staying in Marina del Rey, part of my daily routine was to go for a ride on my mountain bike. I would ride along the cycle path all the way up the coast to Malibu and back. It was a beautiful route, and I would look forward to soaking up the sun on two wheels.

I was in shorts, T-shirt, and a baseball cap when I set off on my usual circuit one glorious sunny Californian afternoon. One of the first places I came to on my route was Venice Beach, which had a notorious men's washroom. I decided to stop off and try my luck.

That toilet didn't even have doors on the cubicles, to deter cruising and drug users. There were four or five guys lurking in the

---

* Thank God that Grindr came along!

dingy, murky loo, so I leaned my bike against the wall, went into one of the stalls…and waited.

I'd been in there ten minutes when a good-looking, muscular guy came in, walked past, and glanced in my cubicle. He smiled, and gave me a nod. *Wa-hey! I'm in here!* I thought. I slipped my hand inside my cycling shorts and began fondling myself. *Getting ready.*

The guy stood in front of my stall, his back to me, at a sink, looking in the mirror—or, rather, into the polished stainless steel: there were no mirrors, as the druggies always smashed them. He smiled at me in the reflection. My hand between my legs, I smiled back.

He turned around to face me, reached into his shirt—and pulled out a badge.

"You're under arrest for public indecency," the cop said.

Oh, fuck! A million thoughts raced through my mind. *This is it! I've fucked up! It's going to be in the papers! I've lost everything!* And yet, at the same time, I felt oddly calm.

I nodded. He unfastened his handcuffs from his waist and slipped them on my wrists (this was getting to be a routine).

"What shall I do about me bike?" I asked, for some reason sounding very yam-yam.

"We'll take care of that," he said. "Follow me."

The cop led me around the back of the loo, to a small building that looked like a storeroom. We went in to find five or six other guys in there, heads bowed, all in cuffs. He put my bike in with me, went out, and closed the door without a word.

I sat down. The other blokes and I didn't have a lot to say to each other. It didn't feel like a time for small talk. We all sat there for what felt like an eternity until two other officers arrived, put us in a white van, and drove us away.

We drove inland for miles and miles. I had no idea where we were, or where we were going. Eventually, we arrived at a police station and got led in through a back door. They took us to a holding room and left us sitting there, still handcuffed.

Ten minutes later, I was staring forlornly at the floor when a pair of police feet appeared in front of me. The cop leaned down, pulled my baseball cap off, and stared at me. I saw a flicker of recognition. He put my cap back on, leaned down, and undid my cuffs.

"Follow me."

We went into a little cell and he closed the door behind us.

"I *thought* it was you," he said. "What the hell are you doing here, Rob Halford?"

"I'm a fucking idiot," I admitted.

He shook his head. "I can't believe that you're here. Let me see what I can do."

Was he going to let me off? "Thank you so much," I mumbled. He went out and locked the door behind him.

I sat on the tiny, hard bench. Over the next two hours, every single officer in the station came up to the cell, one by one, looked at me through the glass strip in the door, and flashed devil horns at me. I did the same back, and stuck my tongue out. It passed the time.

Eventually, the first cop came back in. He sat beside me on the bench.

"We're going to keep this out of the press," he told me.

"Thank you!"

"But that's *all* we can do." He took me into another room, took my mug shot—*another one for the collection!*—and fingerprinted me. I didn't have to pay bail. "We'll be in touch," he said. "You're free to go."

I had been lucky. *Again.*

"Where am I?" I asked the cop. He told me.

"Cowing hell, that's miles away! How am I going to get home?"

"That's *your* problem, Rob."

I found a pay phone, and John Baxter came to pick me up. I didn't have to go to court, but I pleaded guilty, paid a fine, and got put on probation. And had another federal offense to add to my record.

How did I feel? Stupid, and ashamed, but also angry—that, this late in the century, gay men still had to live in fear like this. I always call this arrest my "George Michael moment," after he did the same thing in Beverly Hills six years later. The only difference was that George wasn't so lucky with the newspapers.

I had time for such dumb sexual shenanigans because, career-wise, I was in limbo. I didn't have a solo record deal but, as I had a whole album written, I began recruiting band members. Finding a drummer was easy. I'd asked Scott Travis during the *Painkiller* tour if he wanted to play on my solo project and he was up for it. With Priest on hiatus, he was available immediately.

From local Phoenix bands, I recruited Brian Tilse on guitar and Jay Jay Brown on bass. They were both mates, and Jay Jay was doubling as my tattooist, turning me into a walking tapestry. Russ Parrish, also on guitar, was a friend of Scott's.

I told them that I had already written the album, but they were way, way more than hired hands paid to play it. I valued their input, their talents, their ideas. We'd be very much a band, not just a vehicle for me. We were no vanity project.

I decided to call the band Fight and the album *War of Words*. I liked the air of both aggression and literacy that those names conjured up. Scott, Brian, Russ, and Jay Jay loved the demos I played them. Now, we needed that record deal.

Columbia, Priest's label, had an option on the next music I recorded, but they didn't seem keen on the Fight project, so I needed to hawk the demos around other record companies. I was advised that I would have to write Columbia a letter "resigning" from Priest. I was told that it was purely a legal technicality, and no big deal.

This sort of made sense to me, and so I wrote to the label. Somehow, my letter got leaked…and suddenly—who'd have thought it?—everybody thought I really was resigning from Priest. The next week's music press headlines were unambiguous:

HALFORD QUITS PRIEST!

What. The. Fuck? This was not remotely what I wanted. I felt like saying, like *shouting*, "No! No! Hang on! This is wrong!" But I didn't know how to do it.

If I couldn't face speaking to Bill, I should have called Ian, or Glenn, or Ken. We'd been mates, heavy metal brothers-in-arms, *family*, forever. We could have cut the crap and talked it out.

But I didn't. I didn't know what to say, or do. So, instead, I did what I used to do a lot back then. I hid my head in the sand. I ran away. *I did nothing.* And then, in September 1992, it became official.

I was no longer the singer of Judas Priest.

I felt like there had been a mistake, a miscommunication. Somebody had misread a memo. I'd never wanted things to come to this. *How the hell had it come to this?* It felt like being kicked out of my own family. It was a shitstorm, an utter fuck-up, and I knew I had to take most of the blame...for standing by and doing nothing.

The ultimate irony was that I hadn't even needed to write that dumb letter. It wasn't true that CBS, Columbia's parent company, weren't interested in Fight. I went to see David Glew, the president of CBS imprint Epic Records, in his New York office (for some reason, I wore my suit and tie). I played him the demos I'd recorded on my own. Four tracks in, he'd heard enough. "OK!" he nodded. "Let's make a deal!"

The best way to avoid brooding over the grim Priest situation was to keep busy, so John and I immediately began to arrange for Fight to record *War of Words*. First, though, I had a very surprising guest appearance to make.

The phone call in Phoenix came completely out of the blue:

"All right, Rob? It's Tony Iommi!" Black Sabbath's guitarist was getting in touch with a proposition regarding a slightly delicate matter.

Ozzy was playing his farewell tour (*yeah, right!*), No More Tours,* and his two last-ever live shows were scheduled to be at the Pacific Amphitheatre in Costa Mesa, California, on November 14 and 15, 1992. To mark this momentous occasion, Sabbath were to be the support act.

There was some friction between Ozzy and Sabbath's then-singer, Ronnie James Dio. I can't remember now exactly who couldn't bear to be onstage with whom, but Ronnie wasn't going to do the shows, and Tony wanted to know if I would stand in.

Singing with Sabbath! Bloody hell! I was never going to say no! I told Tony I'd need to rehearse with them first, and so Sabbath came to Phoenix for a day and we did a few hours running through songs that I knew off-by-heart already. It was *such* a fucking thrill.

We rehearsed everything except…how Sabbath actually opened their shows. On the first night in Costa Mesa, I was standing behind the drapes at the side of the stage. The stage was pitch-black, dry ice was swirling, and the intro tape was playing.

Tony was behind me. Or so I thought.

"When do we go on, Tone?" I asked him. Silence. "Tone?" I looked around. No sign of him. *Bloody hell! They must all be on already!*

I couldn't see a thing. I walked onto the stage, a light went on, the fans roared, and I looked behind me to see…nobody else onstage whatsoever.

Bollocks! I've buggered this up! I wondered if I should walk off again, but that would have looked too ridiculous. I stood on my Jack Jones for a very long minute before Sabbath wandered on…and, despite my Norman Wisdom–style entrance, the show was a blast.

---

* Nearly thirty years later, as I write this book, Ozzy is scheduled to play another farewell tour, No More Tours II—and Priest are scheduled to support him!

I got to be Ozzy for the night—and how many people in the world can say that?!

I started 1993 out of Priest but with an album to make. I decamped with Fight to Amsterdam to record *War of Words* with Attie Bauw, a Dutch producer who had been an engineer on *Painkiller*. We had got on well and he seemed like a good fit.

Attie was just what we needed and, while I had written the songs, the band were all equals in the studio. Everybody was free to pitch in with ideas, and they did. I stayed in my apartment there, and even managed to get to Drake's Cruising without smashing any bones.

The sessions were exhilarating. *War of Words* was a lot more primal and thrashier than Priest, even heading into death metal territory. When I flew from the Netherlands to spend a few weeks in Walsall, I could not have been more pleased with the record we'd made.

That autumn, *War of Words* came out and got excellent reviews. The reviewers gave it a thumbs-up, saying that Priest fans should like it, but there was a lot there for younger metalheads, too. Which was exactly what I had intended.

I hadn't honestly expected the album to chart, but it squeezed into the Billboard 200 and was to go on to sell more than 250,000 copies around the world. *That would do for me, mate!* And now, it was time to take it on tour.

My old threesome squeeze from Pendleton, Steve, was no longer a Marine. He was at a loose end, so I took him on tour as a personal assistant, security man...and company.

We still had our thing going on, but he was a married, bisexual bloke more interested in women. *Yeah, just my type!* It was only ever a stopgap. So, it was great when, out of the blue, Thomas wrote to me again. He was on a ship off the coast of Africa!

It turned out he had been posted to Somalia. The Marines have a saying: "Loose lips sink ships." Originally a Second World War slogan, it means they should not tell civilians what they are up to.

A-ha! That explained the radio silence from him!

Thomas gave me his military address in Somalia but stressed I had to be discreet as there was very little privacy on his ship. I'm afraid I kind of ignored that instruction and sent him my usual stream of horny letters.

"*You're* the reason they don't allow gays in the military!" he wrote back, horrified. "*You have zero self-control!*"

Thomas's African posting ended soon afterward and he came back to the US—to my old stomping ground of Marine Corps Base Camp Pendleton! I was desperate to meet him face-to-face. He seemed wary about this but, eventually, he acquiesced.

We arranged to have lunch at a restaurant in Oceanside. Thomas suggested to me that we both bring a friend along—I suppose as chaperones?—but I was having none of that. I did, however, take along my enormous sex drive.

Thomas had sent me a photo of himself before we met. I fancied him at first sight, but he was even hotter in the flesh. An athletic, drop-dead gorgeous redhead, he was just as smart and funny in person as on the phone. As a bonus, his mate was buff, too!

I flirted manically with them both all through the lunch—ignoring the fact that Thomas seemed pretty uncomfortable with it. As soon as we'd eaten, I suggested that we get a room, and marched them to a hotel down the promenade.

We got to the room and I made a play for both of them. Well, the mate turned out to be straight, and Thomas *definitely* wasn't up for it! He made some excuse about having to go and they scarpered. "That's a shame!" I told their departing backs. "We could have had a threesome!"

Driving home, I felt stupid. *Bollocks!* The cock has no conscience— or at least, *mine* had never had one—and it had fucked things up for me yet again. I didn't hear from Thomas again after that debacle. It was a shame. Because I really liked him.

But now…it was time to take Fight out on the road.

We did a couple of warm-up gigs at the Mason Jar in Phoenix and the Whisky a Go Go on Sunset Strip, but we began our first tour proper in Europe in October '93. And as we crisscrossed the continent, I realized how much the rules of the game had changed for me.

In countries where Priest routinely filled 10,000-capacity arenas, we were playing clubs to 500 people. Priest always sold out the Olympiahalle in Munich: now, I was half filling rock bars like the Rockfabrik in Ludwigsburg, which looked like a German Walsall.

In the UK, I could forget multiple nights in Birmingham and Hammersmith Odeons. We did two dates: Rock City, a medium-sized club in Nottingham, and London's Astoria, a hip venue but the kind of place that Priest might have used for an after-show party after an arena gig.

I was getting flashbacks to Corky, Transit vans, and gigs in St. Albans pubs. *No more golf carts to the stage for you, pal!* I was starting from scratch, in a brand-new band that had to prove itself, and I had to pay my dues all over again.

It was nice to see new, younger metal fans among the older guys in their Priest T-shirts. There were tons of shouts for "Breaking the Law" and "Hell Bent for Leather," but I wasn't listening. I was determined only to play Fight songs. Whether they liked it or not!

It was fun but hard work, and it was obvious that if we were to get Fight across to a wider audience, we'd have to do something *else* I hadn't done in more than a decade: play support tours. Luckily, we were able to start right at the top.

Metallica were then the biggest heavy metal band in the world, and Lars Ulrich called me up and invited us on their epic *Shit Hits the Sheds* traipse around the world's enormo-domes. We joined a gaggle of other support acts: Danzig, Suicidal Tendencies, and Candlebox.

We didn't do the whole tour, but the dates we played were ace.

I reacquainted myself with vast crowds (great!) and going onstage just after teatime (not so great!). Metallica were big Priest fans, and in Miami I sang "Rapid Fire" from *British Steel* with them. That was cool.

I also made an unexpected new acquaintance. I had got matey with Candlebox, who were signed to Madonna's record company, Maverick. Their singer, Kevin Martin, told me that their label boss was coming down to check them out in Miami.

That afternoon, I saw her walk past my trailer—or, rather, I saw a flash of peroxide hair atop a tiny woman surrounded by an army of security gorillas. She vanished into Candlebox's trailer. A while later, Kevin came out and wandered across.

"Hey, Rob! You want to come over and say hi to Madonna?" he asked.

Did I just! What kind of gay metal pop tart *wouldn't* want to say hi to Madonna?! Eagerly, I walked over to the trailer…and into what appeared to be some kind of tableau from a Renaissance painting.

Madonna was reclining regally across a chaise longue like Cleopatra on her gilded barge floating down the Nile. A cluster of worshipping chicks were sprawled on the floor around her feet. It reeked, in a very nice way, of Chanel and Christian Dior.

As I walked toward her, she regarded me, quizzically.

"This is Rob, from Judas Priest and the Fight band," said Kevin.

"Oh, hey, Rob, great to meet you!" Madonna said, without getting up. She looked me up and down. "*You* have a lot of tattoos!"

I did, by then. "Yes," I said.

"Do you have them everywhere?" she asked me.

I pulled up my shirt to show her the designs on my torso.

"And how far *down* do they go?" asked Madonna, coquettishly.

I pulled the waist of my shorts down to the top of my pubes. She leaned forward and peered at my crotch. Her nose was virtually touching my stomach.

Bloody hell, Rob! I thought to myself. *You only met Madonna two minutes ago, and you've already nearly got your cock in her gob!*

"Oh, wow!" she marveled. "And do they go *further* than that?"

"Yeah, but I think we'd better stop there," I said.

"Yes," agreed Madonna, nodding. "I suppose that's probably a good idea."

And that was the end of my very short backstage encounter with the Queen of Pop. I hope that she remembers it as fondly as I do.

After the Metallica tour was over, it was time to work out my next musical move. In my heart, I knew exactly what I wanted that to be. I wanted to go back to Judas Priest.

I had gotten the desire to make a solo record out of my system. *War of Words* had done well, the tour had gone OK, and, most importantly, I had proved—to myself—that I could do it. My solo work had given me intense personal satisfaction...but now what?

What I wanted to do now was to run back to Priest and say, "Guys, is there a way we can work this out? Because I really want— *I really need*—to be in the band."

But I couldn't see a way to bridge the chasm between me and the Priest camp. I couldn't see a way to get back to where I needed to be. I couldn't see a route home.

Somehow, my side project had become my sole project. I seemed to have driven my professional career into a cul-de-sac. It was hugely frustrating...but at least there was one great thing about this deeply difficult time.

My personal life was about to receive a major, major boost.

19

Knocking on Sharon Tate's door

It upset me that I had fucked things up so badly with Thomas. He was clearly a sweet, funny guy, but he also seemed like he had led quite a sheltered life. I could see now how a heavy metal maniac obsessed with getting into his pants on a first date had probably terrified him.

Well done, Rob! Your relationship golden touch strikes again!

The only action I was getting now was occasional bouts with Steve, who had just left Dawn. But he swung far more the other way and was basically after another woman. We were good friends, though, and he was one of the few people I could properly talk to.

I would sometimes pour my heart out to him. He knew my history of moving to America for David, falling in love with Brad, and living with Josh, only to find they were all straight. I bent his ear so often that he was quite an expert in the tragedy of my love life.

One night, I was wallowing in self-pity about Thomas when he gave me some very cogent and straight-talking (as it were) advice.

"For God's sake, Rob, get in touch with him again, then!" he said. "Get yourself a genuine gay dude in your life, for once!"

Well, when he put it like that…

I wrote to Thomas again, and he replied. It turned out that he had finished his military service and decided not to reenlist. The

Marines forwarded my letter to him in Alabama, where he'd moved back home with his mom and was now doing dreary manual labor in a local factory. Thomas was miserable and hating his dull existence after his life of adventure in the Marines.

It was great to be in touch again, and our communications seemed to have a kinder, gentler feel, maybe because I'd stopped trying to turn the conversation to sex every ten seconds. I suggested we should start talking on the phone again.

Thomas agreed to this, but there was one problem—his mom didn't have a phone. There was only one telephone he could use—a public pay phone in his town's one store.

So began a regular routine whereby Thomas would call me, reverse charge, from that general store and we would talk for hours. Now, our chats weren't just "carnal," as Thomas put it: we'd talk about anything and everything, and discuss every aspect of our lives.

And…it was strange. This guy was thousands of miles away, living in Buttfuck, Alabama, and yet he felt more like a partner than anybody I'd ever been with before.

From being so far apart, we grew closer together. And I knew that I wanted to see him again.

In the absence of any opportunity to reunite with Priest, I set about making a second Fight album. After the first record had done well, Epic basically wanted me to do *War of Words II*…but I have never worked like that.

I had proved to myself that I could write a whole album on my own and I had no desire, or need, to do it again. For Fight's follow-up, *A Small Deadly Space*, I wanted to return to the kind of collective songwriting style that Glenn, Ken, and I had always had in Priest.

We had a lineup change. Russ Parrish had amicably left the group, and somebody recommended Mark Chaussee as a replacement guitarist. He was a lovely, solid guy and fit right into the band.

We became a creative team and started writing material together. It meant that Fight's second album was a lot more diverse than our debut, which had just been my own, singular vision, but I was cool with that and I thought it worked.

We had gone to Attie Bauw to make the first album and this time he came to us. Our Dutch producer flew to Phoenix to record *A Small Deadly Space*, which had a completely different texture from *War of Words*, and ended up having a far grungier feel.

It was a relaxed, easy process. I'd enjoy spending the day in the studio, putting down tracks like "Mouthpiece" and "Beneath the Violence," yet I was also looking forward to finishing at teatime, so I could drive home and spend three hours talking to an ex-Marine on a pay phone in a general store in Alabama.

When it came out, in April '95, *A Small Deadly Space* sold less than a third as many copies as *War of Words*. I think fans had wanted more of the same, and that wasn't what we gave them. I guess that's the reason most bands just repeat themselves again and again and again!

When we did a six-month US tour, it was the same story of having a "more selective appeal," as Spinal Tap put it. Where Priest used to headline Madison Square Garden (well, until they banned us) when we went to New York, Fight played CBGB's. At least I got to tick off another iconic venue.

I was forty-three years old, and living like a teenage, tyro musician: doing small club shows, seven nights a week. Fight songs also required a different style of singing from Priest, so I was blowing my voice out a lot. It was a real slog.

While we were on the road, I wrote to, and spoke to, Thomas as often as I could. I couldn't wait to get back to Phoenix so we could reestablish daily contact. And when I was home, I did what I'd been wanting to do for ages. I invited him to come and stay with me.

Thomas flew out to Phoenix for ten days. We had the best, most relaxed time. During those hours of conversation on the phone, we had grown very open and sincere with one another. We had got to properly know each other.

Thomas was less shockable by now as he'd been to a few gay bars and got a little more experience, and we just *clicked*. I didn't want him to go back to Alabama at the end of his stay, and nor did he. Within a few days of him being back working at the factory in the middle of nowhere, I had asked him to come and live with me. And he had agreed.

I don't want to get too soppy here, because that isn't the point of *Confess*, but when Thomas and I settled down together, I realized that he was different from anybody I had thought I had been in love with before. And it was a very profound difference.

Let me put that difference in the simplest fucking terms possible: *THOMAS WAS ACTUALLY A GAY MAN!*

It made me realize that all my previous relationships, with straight guys, had been doomed to fail. They had started with infatuation and lust, but basically all those guys would rather have been with a woman.

Well, there was no danger of that this time!

Thomas moved in at the end of the cycle of the unsuccessful second Fight album and so I had a lot of downtime for us to get used to each other. We hung out with friends, went to the local Phoenix rock and metal clubs, and took trips to LA and San Diego.

It was a relaxed, blissful, happy time. When it came to my love life, these were really *not* emotions that I was used to experiencing.

It turned out we had a lot in common. We were both coming out of environments where we'd had to hide our sexuality: Judas

Priest and the Marines. We were both recovering alcoholics. Although we had seemed worlds apart at first, we discovered we had a lot in common.

I hate to use the cliché, but it was yin and yang. Our different personalities balanced each other out…and they still do.

Work-wise, I was still casting my mind around for ways to reconnect with Priest. I missed Glenn, and Ken, and Ian every day. Could I find a way to reach out directly to the lads?

I was mulling over how to do it…when it suddenly became clear that any route back to the band had been completely cut off. Because Judas Priest had got themselves a new singer.

Horrified, I read all about him. His name was Tim "Ripper" Owens and he had been singing in a Priest tribute band in Ohio, which meant he could do a pretty precise impersonation of me. He'd sent a tape in to the band, they'd flown him over, and he was in.

I didn't blame him. He had seen an opportunity and taken it. And, let's face it…going from a tribute rock group to fronting the actual band must be the dictionary definition of a dream job!

Nor did I blame Priest. It had been three years now since I had announced my solo plans, and while the band had never reached out to me, nor had I made any moves toward them. I'd *wanted* to, many times, but I'd ended up doing my usual trick of prevaricating and doing nothing.

No, the main thing that I felt when I heard that Priest had gotten a new singer was incredibly *sad*. I'd been through so much with that band, over nearly twenty years, and I'd always assumed that, at some point, we'd put all the crap behind us and get together again.

Now, I knew that would never happen. I'd never be able to go back.

So, what should I do now?

There was talk of a third Fight album, and we even got together to begin writing it, but my heart wasn't in it. *A Small Deadly Space* had flopped and the band felt like it had run its course. And, in any case, musically my head was in a very different place.

In the midnineties, I'd been getting heavily into the kind of industrial electronic music that was coming out of North America, such as Nine Inch Nails, Marilyn Manson, and Ministry. To me, much of it had the same primal urge and drive as metal. It was *heavy* music.

John Baxter hooked me up with a producer named Bob Marlette, who worked in both metal and electronica. He and I went into his home studio in Los Angeles and began knocking around ideas and doing some programming. It felt fresh, and exciting.

We needed a guitarist, so Bob drafted in John Lowery, a friend of his who had previously worked with Lita Ford, Paul Stanley, and Randy Castillo. John came in to work on the sessions and the three of us began to write music together.

It was instantly clear that the material we were producing would not fit Fight and I decided to step away from the band. Instead, John and I formed ourselves into a duo called Two (or, as we rather poncily preferred to style it, 2wo).

The electronic-driven songs we were laying down with Bob were like nothing I had ever done before, but *so what?* That was what I loved about them! I was totally into the project when we decided to take a two-week break from the studio.

I went to New Orleans, a city I have always loved, to hang out with an old friend, a fire chief named Chuck. We were driving around the city's Garden District when Chuck pointed out a building to me.

"That's Trent Reznor's studio," he told me.

Wow! I'd never met Trent, but Nine Inch Nails were my favorite of the whole new wave of techno-industrial-metal artists. The studio was an imposing former funeral home (well, *of course* it was!); I gazed at it, reverentially.

Chuck intercepted my gaze. "You should go in and say 'hi,'" he suggested.

"No!" I shook my head. I've never bought into all that schmoozing-with-the-stars crap. It can all feel false, and a bit daft. "I don't do stuff like that!"

"Well, you never know what might happen…" teased Chuck, as we drove on. We went for a coffee. An hour later, we were driving by the studio again. *Well, I suppose I WOULD love to meet Trent…*

"Pull over!" I told Chuck.

I knocked on the studio door. Which was not just any old door. After Trent had made Nine Inch Nails' album *The Downward Spiral* in the Hollywood mansion where the Charles Manson murders had taken place, he had bought the door as a souvenir and relocated it to his studio. So, I was knocking on poor Sharon Tate's door.

"Hey, Rob, what are *you* doing here?"

I didn't know the voice of the person in the house scrutinizing me on the security camera, but when he opened the door, he introduced himself as Dave Ogilvie, a musician and producer in the Canadian electronic group Skinny Puppy. *Cool band!*

"Um, I just wondered if Trent was in?" I said.

"No, but he'll be here in an hour!" Dave invited me in and showed me around the beautiful studio complex. We were sitting having a cup of tea and chatting an hour later when Trent bowled in.

"Oh my God, Rob Halford!" he said. "I'm a *massive* Priest fan!"

Well, this was going well! We talked, and I told him I was working on industrial-style material with Bob Marlette and John Lowery. "Wow, that sounds great!" said Trent. "Do you have any music?"

As you mention it, I just so happen to have a cassette here…

We played it, and Trent asked if he could keep the tape. A few days later, Dave Ogilvie called me. "Trent really loves this music," he said. "He wants to know if you'd like to collaborate on the album and he'll release it on his label?"

Well, what do you bloody think? I relocated to Dave's studio in Vancouver, and he got heavily involved in the production of the album. The way we worked was alien but fascinating. Dave had a team of four or five guys on computers creating quirky electronic sounds. He'd compile them, then come through and play them to me.

"Do you like this sound, Rob?"

"No, not really."

"How about *this* one?"

"Oh, yeah, that's fucking great!"

And that was how we created the electronic soundscapes for what became 2wo's *Voyeurs* album. Trent was executive producer, and he'd drop in every now and then to offer advice and feedback. I thought the whole process was fantastic.

While we were in the studio in Vancouver, Priest released their first album without me: *Jugulator*. I couldn't tell you what I thought of it because I never listened to it...and I still haven't.

It wasn't through spite, or anger. I had known they were making an album, and why *shouldn't* they get on with the band, and their lives? If I am honest, I think I probably thought that listening to a Judas Priest album without me on it would simply be too painful for me.

I was in a very different place from Priest at that point...and I looked it. My leathers were gone, replaced by fur coats and an alternative, even goth look, in which a goatee beard and eyeliner figured large. I looked as left field as *Voyeurs* sounded.

My 2wo image wasn't a false or calculated move. It was an extension of my personality in a new direction. I looked like an industrial-music Dr. Fu Manchu and I totally reveled in it. Like I said, I've always loved a good costume.

Voyeurs was coming out on Trent's Nothing imprint. It went through a major label, Interscope, and I had a meeting with that company's larger-than-life cofounder, Jimmy Iovine. I told him I'd like to make a controversial video for the lead single, "I Am a Pig."

In fact, I wanted to go a step further. "Why don't we make a porno video for it?" I suggested.

"Fucking awesome!" said Jimmy. "Let's do it! But who can direct it?"

"Well, as it happens," I said, "I know somebody…"

At this stage of my post-Pendleton infatuation with men in uniform, I had acquired a very extensive home collection of military-themed gay porn. Since Thomas had moved in with me, and come out of his shell a little, he'd shared my preoccupation.

In fact, Thomas had rocketed a long way out of his shell, and made a porno himself! He'd answered an advert on a military-themed gay porn website. They had accepted him gratefully—*An ex-Marine! You bet!*—and he'd shot the movie in San Diego.

It was quite a leap for a shy boy from Alabama! Thomas was nervous and self-conscious filming the scenes, and the director, a flamboyant drag queen and moviemaker named Chi Chi LaRue,* sat him down for a chat to try to help him to relax.

"Where do you live?" asked Chi Chi. "And do you have a partner?"

"I live in Phoenix," answered Thomas, "with Rob Halford, and…"

"*What?!*" Chi Chi said she was a huge Judas Priest fan who owned every album and had seen countless shows. We met up, she and I became firm friends…and now I couldn't think of anyone better to make a 2wo video.

A few days after I'd seen Jimmy Iovine, I was in a warehouse in Los Angeles with an army of porn stars. We shot a super-dramatic, high camp, erotic mini-movie, all pouts, licks, rippling torsos, and grinding. It was homoerotic, lesbo-erotic…it covered all bases!

Chi Chi made a great, arty pop video…although, oddly enough, Jimmy Iovine hated it. "*That's* not porn!" he told me angrily when he saw it.

"Well, we couldn't make a *real* porno, could we?" I asked.

"Yes!"

---

* Chi Chi was born a boy named Larry, but she dresses as, and sees herself as, a very glamorous female diva. So, I do the same.

"But then no one would play it, Jimmy!"

"Good! I *wanted* it to be banned!"

There's no pleasing some folk! "I Am a Pig" came out and was a minor hit on the Billboard mainstream rock chart. So, on February 25, 1998, I went to MTV in New York to talk about 2wo and promote the *Voyeurs* album.

It was an interview that was to change my life.

I didn't go along to MTV's new studios on Broadway, just off Times Square, with any particular agenda in mind. I certainly didn't intend to out myself to the world as a gay man. But, somehow, that was the way that it ended up working out.

I can't even remember the interviewer's name, but he asked me the kind of question I'd got so used to fielding over the last few years. It was all about the *rumors* and the *speculation* about my sexuality, and whether I would like to *set the record straight*, blah blah blah…

Normally, I would just blank the question, or say it was nothing to do with my music. But, this time, I didn't.

I opened my mouth… *and these words came out.*

"I think that most people know that I've been a gay man all of my life."

THUMP! The loud noise I heard behind me was a producer dropping her clipboard.

Well, I hadn't intended to make this speech, but now I'm doing it, let's go for it!

"It's only been in recent times it's been an issue I feel comfortable to address," I continued. "An issue that has been with me ever since I recognized my own sexuality."

I was sitting in front of the interviewer, and millions of TV viewers, in a fur coat and mascara, and with painted nails. I was talking slowly and looking preternaturally calm and happy in my own skin. And that was exactly how I felt.

"Maybe this [*the 2wo project*] has pushed me," I said. "Maybe this has made me say, 'What the hell? It's time to step out and to let people know what I'm about.'"

I smiled at the interviewer. "But didn't you know already?" I asked.

His eyes were like saucers as he realized that a world exclusive had just dropped into his lap. He stuttered something about "having heard rumors" and asked me if it would have been possible to come out in my Judas Priest days.

"No," I said. "I was constantly held back. I allowed myself to be intimidated…a lot of homophobia still exists in the music world."

We talked for another ten minutes or so. I advised fans to go back through their Priest albums to find the clues to my sexuality littered throughout the lyrics. And I struck a defiant tone as I hoped my coming out might help other gay people "in a society where they are still treated as second-class citizens."

"There are as many gay metal fans as there are gay fans of other types of music," I declared. "*We are everywhere!* That's the way it is."

It was all very chill and rational. It wasn't until I had finished the interview and got back to my hotel that it suddenly hit me:

Bloody hell! I've just outed myself on TV!

I had spent twenty-five years as a heavy metal singer hiding the truth about myself, living a lie…and I had brought it all to an end in a matter of seconds. *This was it. The end.* I no longer had to pretend, to conceal, to hide. I could finally be me.

I had confessed. And it felt fucking great. As I had said during the MTV interview: "This is a good feeling. I recommend it to everybody."

For *so* many years, I'd imagined that coming out would lead to an outpouring of disgust, end my career, and kill Judas Priest. Now… the exact opposite happened. I started to get letters from people all over the world; we had to open an office in Phoenix to deal with them.

People wrote thanking me for coming out and giving them hope and inspiration. "I've been hiding for so many years, and you've given me strength," they said. It opened my eyes to just how many gays were still going through the trauma of suppressing their sexual identity.

The great thing was knowing that…*I didn't have to hide anymore.* At a stroke, it killed the innuendo and the people talking behind my back. I'd occasionally heard comments in clubs: "Oh, look, the fag is here!"

Well, now I had an answer: "It's *Mr.* Fag to you!"

A tiny, tiny minority of religious fanatics wrote me letters saying they would never listen to my music again—and that I would burn in hell. But, do you know what? I didn't think I would miss those people too much!

Of course, there was another, fairly common reaction from friends, people who knew me well, and some fans:

"We've known for YEARS, you fucking idiot!"

Sue called me. She congratulated me, and said the family were all happy for me. It meant as much as any message in the world could possibly mean. Mom and Dad, my sister and brother: they'd known, but now they properly *knew.* At last!

I. Was. Out. The years of angst were over. It was like when I stopped drinking and drugging—the lies and pretense had gone. I had liberated myself from self-imprisonment and nothing could hurt me again.

I was gay, and I had told the world. *It was done.*

After I came out, I decided to do a big interview—and there was only one publication I wanted to do it with: *The Advocate,* the pioneering gay newspaper I had been so excited to get my hands on in San Francisco more than twenty years earlier.

"Had I considered coming out five years ago, it would have been very difficult," I told them. "But, right now, I'm experiencing the same emotions that my friends have told me they felt when they came out: this great clarity and this great peace."

And it was true. I had never felt stronger, or more at peace, in my life. It's a feeling that has lasted to this day.

Coming out as gay was the best thing that I had ever done… but it didn't mean 2wo would be a success. *Voyeurs* bombed. Techno-heads didn't get into it, and it was a step too far for Priest and metal fans. Career-wise, it had also been a step too far for me.

We played US club and festival dates to electronic audiences and dance music fans and got a mixed response. I felt out of my depth. And, in any case, by now I was desperate to get back to what I knew and loved.

I wanted to get back into metal.

2wo went to Europe. It was a disaster. We'd sold hardly any records there and, what was even worse, the football World Cup was on.

For a theater show in Switzerland, we sold *twelve* tickets, and our support was…a television, showing the World Cup. We had to laugh. Or we'd have cried.

We went back to the US with our tails between our legs, but we were set to return to Europe soon afterward to play a full-on heavy metal festival. We were sitting in a hotel in New York, about to leave for the airport, and I was very, very apprehensive.

I realized that if I went to a European metal gathering with 2wo, in my fur coat and painted nails, playing arty, left-field dance music… I'd no longer be Rob Halford, metal god, in those fans' eyes. It could kill my career stone-dead.

And I made a snap decision: *I'm not going.*

John Baxter, John Lowery…everyone in the tour party was clustered around me in the hotel, desperately trying to persuade me otherwise: "Rob, we've spent a lot of money! The gear is already on the way! We need to get to the airport!" I couldn't have cared less. When I've made my mind up, I'm the most stubborn bloke in the world.

I. Am. Not. Going!

They kept chipping away at me. I lost my rag. There was a TV remote control on a table beside me, and I picked it up and threw it, *hard*, at the wall. It embedded in the plaster and hung there, ten feet above the floor.

Is that fucking clear enough for you all?

We didn't get the plane to the European metal festival. We all packed up and went home. And that was the end of 2wo.

When I walked away from 2wo, I knew two things about my immediate musical future. I needed to go back to metal; and, more than anything, I needed to go back to Judas Priest.

I still didn't feel able to approach Priest directly. It was beyond me to pick up a phone and chat to Glenn, or Ken, or Ian: we were still very estranged from each other. I didn't know what to say, or how to say it. And, there was the little matter of them already having a singer!

So, I decided to talk to them in the language that all of us understood best: music. *Heavy metal.*

I knew Priest would have watched my solo career from afar. They'd have observed my diversion into thrash and speed metal with Fight. Christ only knows what they would have made of 2wo! I attempted to picture Ken's face watching the "I Am a Pig" video, and failed.

My next album was going to reestablish my identity as a metal god and be a message to Priest:

Here I am. Here is what I do. Here is what WE used to do. Could we do it again?

I was going back to metal, the place and the music where I could be the true me, and I wanted the world to know it. I wanted to make a full-on heavy metal record of the kind that I loved, and I wanted my new band's name to be my name: Halford.

John Baxter helped me to hold auditions and put the band together from musicians on the LA scene. I recruited two guitarists—*very Judas Priest!*—in Mike Chlasciak and Patrick Lachman, and we became three-quarters of the band's main songwriting team.

The fourth member was the album's producer. Roy Z had produced—and played guitar on—Bruce Dickinson's solo albums in the nineties. Bruce had quit Iron Maiden in 1993 but was now on the verge of rejoining the mega-band that had made him famous.

Which, I must admit, I found encouraging: *If he could do it, why couldn't I?*

When we started work at Sound City Studios in LA, I explained to Roy Z exactly what I wanted from the album. It should represent me as Judas Priest fans had known me, from *Rocka Rolla* right through to *Painkiller*. It should reinforce what I had always stood for.

Oh, and there was one more thing. The album would be called *Resurrection*. Because that was what it was going to be.

It would be a slow and careful process of rebuilding, and we didn't rush the sessions. We worked for weeks, months, writing songs and building up a strong, layered, kinetic heavy metal album. Every note had to be right. Every word had to be right. I was on a mission.

We didn't work every single day, but when we did work, we worked intensely. Roy had other projects on, so sometimes we'd take a week or even a month off. That didn't bother me at all. It was all coming together naturally and organically.

Through Roy, we got Bruce Dickinson to cowrite and sing on a track, "The One You Love to Hate." Bruce came up with the title and he, Roy, and I wrote the song on the fly in the studio. He was in and out in one day. Cool song, too.

During one of our downtimes from making the album, Thomas and I moved to San Diego. We'd grown fond of the city, and would drive or fly there for breaks to escape the extreme heat of Phoenix. Even though we were both sober, we'd hit the gay bars and clubs.

After all, we had a lot of catching up to do!

One day in '99, I was driving through San Diego on my own when I passed a construction site on the junction of two roads. They were building a ten-story apartment block but had hardly started. I loved the location as soon as I saw it.

I phoned Thomas and said, "I've found where we're going to live—except that it's not built yet!" When it went up, we were the first people to rent an apartment there. We were to live between there, my house in Phoenix, and Walsall for the next twenty years.

Thomas and I went to San Diego Pride in Balboa Park—*because I could fucking do that kind of thing, now that I was finally out!* We were walking around, soaking up the sun and ogling the talent when I happened to glance into a small side tent.

An old man was sitting there, on his own. He was in makeup, wearing a velvet jacket and a ruffled scarf, and was sitting behind a table with a few books. Nobody was paying him any heed.

It was Quentin Crisp.

My God! The second I saw Quentin, my mind flew back a quarter of a century to me, wide-eyed, watching *The Naked Civil Servant* on TV, my mind boggling at the very concept of a gay man being able to live his life so bravely and openly and flamboyantly.

I looked at Quentin Crisp now, in a changed world, sitting alone in the heart of a joyous, uproarious mass gay celebration, and I felt the same awe as I had felt then. I went into his tent.

"Quentin?" I asked.

He nodded.

"I'm Rob."

"Oh, hello!" he said, in that unique, singsong voice, still sounding as if he was talking through his nostrils. "How are you?"

"Very well! What a surprise! I never expected to see you here!"

"Oh, I do all the Gay Prides now," he drawled. "I like doing the Prides. They pay me money and they bring me here."

He was ninety years old, and it was an honor to meet such a gay icon. Quentin Crisp was to die before the year was out, but I bought his book that day and he signed it for me: "To Rob, from Quentin." I still treasure it.

The Halford *Resurrection* sessions continued in the new millennium, but a few weeks into the twenty-first century, I had a major celebration to attend. Thomas and I flew to England for a few days at the coach house as Mom and Dad celebrated their golden wedding.

We held a big bash for them at the Saddlers Club function room at Walsall Football Club. And, as well as raising a glass of Perrier to my parents' fiftieth anniversary, I had another interest in the night.

Because I knew that Ken would be there.

I'd hardly seen, or spoken to, anybody from Judas Priest in nearly ten years. I'd occasionally seen Ian, if I'd been around Sue's house and he had called in to pick up their son, Alex. That was always cool—but Ian and I had *always* been cool, ever since the Beechdale and the Dirty Duck.

Yet I'd had no contact at all with those squabbling twin guitar titans, Ken and Glenn—nor with Bill and Jayne, come to that. A deafening silence had reigned for far too long. So, seeing Ken was going to be a big deal.

It was…and it wasn't. We spotted each other in the bar, and nodded.

"All right, Rob?"

"Ar. You all right, Ken?"

And that was it. Two downbeat, deadpan Black Country blokes, who happened not to have met for nearly a decade, sat down, and had a good old natter. It was like we'd seen each other the day before. Nothing had changed.

We didn't talk about the elephant in the room, whether I might ever rejoin Priest—*of course we didn't!* We're Walsall blokes, and Walsall blokes tackle big questions by…pretending they don't exist! But our chat was easy, relaxed, and friendly. We parted on great terms.

That night, after Thomas and I had dropped Mom and Dad at their bungalow around the corner, I went to bed in the coach house with a warm glow. *Who knows? There might be a way back, after all!*

Back in the US, we finished off the *Resurrection* album. It was exactly the album I had wanted to make, and I was so proud of it. If *Painkiller* was Priest's ultimate album, *Resurrection* was equally definitive for me.

Everything about *Resurrection* screamed Judas Priest. That was its purpose. People say that it's the best Priest album that Priest never made, and while I don't particularly like that evaluation, I can see what they mean. It was me building my bridge back to the band.

The wrist merchants who had written me off during my 2wo adventure heralded it as the return to form that I had hoped it would be. They welcomed me home like a prodigal son. Magazine headlines were a sight for my sore eyes:

THE METAL GOD IS BACK!

Bruce Dickinson had rejoined Iron Maiden by now and invited us on their *Brave New World* Tour. Thomas came out on tour to help out and be my PA. I'd imported boyfriends on tours before, with very mixed results, but with Thomas it was tranquil, calm, and chill. It made my life on the road so much easier.

Halford joined Maiden in Canada in August, and we did five months playing the arenas and amphitheaters of North America and Europe. Our fourth date with them found me treading the stage of Madison Square Garden once again. The seats remained intact.

We went down great with the Maiden fans. Maiden and Priest had always had similar audiences, Bruce and I had been through a lot of the same things, and the good reception we got was like being welcomed back into the metal family. I felt like I was...*home*.

Iron Maiden's manager, Rod Smallwood, was looking after us well on the tour, and when we got to Europe, he fixed Halford up with a huge fuck-off double-decker tour bus with the *Resurrection* logo and "THE METAL GOD IS BACK!" down the outside. I played major arenas in England again, including Birmingham NEC. Unlike with Fight, I was throwing Priest songs into the mix, and belting out "The Hellion/Electric Eye" and "Breaking the Law" to a 10,000-people hometown crowd felt fantastic.

While Halford were in England, we also did a few club shows. Three weeks before Christmas, we played the Astoria in London. Ticket sales weren't great and we'd been downsized to their smaller room, which was a disappointment.

It was still a magical night. Bruce did a guest appearance and sang his part on "The One You Love to Hate," and Geoff Tate from Queensrÿche also joined us. I hadn't known either of them would be there, so it was fantastic.

There was talk of Bruce, Geoff, and I making a record and touring as "The Three Tremors." Then there was talk of Bruce and I doing it with Ronnie James Dio instead of Geoff. Rod Smallwood tried to organize it, but it came to nothing. It was a shame. It would've been fun.*

Halford's dates with Maiden rolled over into 2001 and stadium dates in South America, including a return trip to Rock in Rio.

---

* Oddly enough, there IS a Three Tremors group now, and it features Tim "Ripper" Owens. Funny, that!

I recalled from my trip with Priest that Rio's traffic was dreadful, and was grumbling about it to Rod Smallwood.

"It's a gridlock!" I moaned. "It'll take me hours to get to the show!"

"Take my helicopter, then," said Rod.

"What? Won't you need it?"

"No, I'm going there at the crack of dawn, when the traffic will be fine. You can have it."

Ace! The next day, I was taken to the helipad and got in behind the pilot. "We're waiting for two more passengers," he said. We sat there for five minutes, the rotors turning. Then the door opened and a guy climbed in. And he was Jimmy Page.

Whoa! I had never met Jimmy, even when we supported Zep in Oakland. But when I saw him, my mind didn't go back to then—it went back to lying on my bed on the Beechdale, having my mind blown by the stereophonic glory of "Whole Lotta Love."

"Hey, Rob," he said, as his girlfriend climbed in with him. "Thanks for letting us come with you!"

My head was on a swivel stick. I was lost for words. The journey was so short, and the chopper so loud, that we hardly got a chance to speak. We shook hands at the other end. "See you again!" he said.

Oh, I hope so! I thought.

I had a little downtime after the Maiden dates. Priest did another album, *Demolition*, which did worse than its predecessor. I didn't feel schadenfreude, because I love the band too much, but I did wonder: *Does that make it more likely they might have me back?*

And, once again, I couldn't bring myself to listen to it.

I felt in a way as though the Halford band had served its purpose in reestablishing me as a metal force, but in the absence of a call from Priest, we began gearing up to make the follow-up to *Resurrection*. Firstly, though, I got to indulge one of my old passions.

I've never shaken off—nor do I want to—the love of acting that took me to the Wolverhampton Grand. So, when Swedish director

Jonas Åkerlund approached me to play a cameo role in a movie, I jumped at the opportunity.

The movie, starring Mickey Rourke, was called *Spun* and was a black comedy-drama about amphetamine dealing, set in Oregon. Jonas said that he wanted me to play a porn-shop manager.

Ha! Talk about typecasting!

The film was to be shot within three weeks and I only had three short scenes, but I was looking forward to doing them. Which made it a disaster when I woke up on the morning of my first shoot as sick as a dog from food poisoning.

Well, I say woke up—I had hardly been to sleep. I'd been up nearly all night with stuff spurting out of both ends, and I felt horrendous. I asked Thomas to phone Jonas and say I couldn't do it and he'd have to postpone my scenes.

Jonas demanded to talk to me. "Rob! What's happening?"

"I'm dead, man," I said. "I've got the worst food poisoning ever. Can we delay it for a day or two?"

"No! We can't! I'm on set in Santa Monica now. Mickey is here in an hour. You'll have to come or I'll have to cut the scene—and it's a really important scene!"

Well, when he put it like that…

Jonas sent a limo for me, but it had to stop every fifteen minutes for me to shit and puke. When I got to the set, I collapsed into my trailer and did more of the same. Until there was a knock on the door.

It was Mickey Rourke, with a tiny dog under his arm.*

"Dude, I hear you're sick?" he said. "Come with me—I'll make you some chicken soup."

I followed Mickey Rourke to his trailer, and he made me some

---

* Mickey was inseparable from that dog. It was under his arm on set every second that he wasn't shooting.

bostin' chicken soup. It made me feel a lot better. He and I had a good gas over that poultry broth.

Jonas had hired a local porn shop for the day to shoot our scene, in which the script had me selling Mickey some porno mags and him throwing me against a wall.

"The funny thing is, I used to work in a porn shop," I told Mickey, thinking back to my two weekends filling in at the dirty-mags shop in Walsall.

"Really?" he said. "The really weird thing is, the porn store that Jonas has hired for our shoot—I used to work in that very same store!"

Wow! The crazy coincidences that life throws up! When we came to film our scene, I was getting flashbacks to those weekends in Walsall as I slid big-tits mags into a brown paper bag. Mickey riffed a lot of his lines—but what a craftsman! It was a great experience.

When Halford came to make our second album, *Crucible*, it was the Fight story all over again. Everybody wanted *Resurrection II*, but I didn't want to do that. There was some good stuff on the record, but it wasn't as intense as *Resurrection* and it didn't sell as well.

It did OK in Japan, where it went Top 10, and we toured there and across the US for six months at the start of 2003. I was safely back in the metal world now…but I still wasn't back where I wanted to be. Halford was good, but it didn't fill the hole in my soul.

So, I sat down and I finally wrote the letter that I'd been wanting to write for ages. The letter that I should probably have written years earlier. I wrote a letter pouring out my heart to Judas Priest.

I told them the truth: *I had never wanted to leave the band. It had all been a miscommunication that had got out of control. I had got my desire to do solo work out of my system. I had missed them as people, and missed being in Judas Priest, every day for the last twelve years. And we all made a lot more sense together, as a band, than we did apart.*

In summary: *I wanted to be back in Priest more than I could possibly begin to explain. Could we try again?*

I emailed the letter to Bill and Jayne to show to the band. I didn't hear anything for a couple of weeks. Then I got a phone call, and I heard a voice I hadn't heard for more than a decade.

I heard Bill Curbishley's voice.

"Hello, Rob," he said. "I think we should try to work something out."

20

The Queen and I

As he always is, Bill was to the point and straight-talking. He said the band had all read my letter, as had he, and it made a lot of sense to them. He suggested we all got together for a meeting, and asked me how soon I could get over to England.

If I had bloody wings, I'd get there right now!

I flew in within days. Before the band meeting, I thought it was important I saw Glenn. I'd chatted to Ken at my parents' party, and our family ties meant I'd occasionally seen Ian, but it was twelve years since I had last spoken to Glenn.

It was lovely to see Jayne Andrews again, and she drove me over to Glenn's house. Or, rather, mansion. It was a proper country pile by a river in Worcestershire: Glenn had even had a recording studio built next door.

He opened the door, and…all those years apart just vanished. Here was the guy I had been onstage with, traveled the world with, and written songs with for the best part of twenty years. All of the bad stuff fell away. We grinned and hugged each other.

As with Ken, it felt like I had seen Glenn yesterday. We had a brew and a good chinwag. Driving away with Jayne a couple of hours later, I finally felt sure: *This is going to happen.*

Bill arranged the meeting at a Holiday Inn in Swiss Cottage, London, the following week. I wasn't *nervous*, as such, I felt calm

…but for some reason, I wore my suit. Maybe it felt like a job interview. "You didn't have to wear *that*, Rob!" laughed Bill when he saw me.

There didn't seem to be any bad feelings. Nobody gave me a hard time. We just got down to it and focused on the business in hand. Apart, we had all been in reduced circumstances. Reunited, we could put Judas Priest back where the band belonged. The mood of the meeting was:

Thank Christ this is all over at last! Now, let's get on with it! Let's get back to work!

Bill gave a very matter-of-fact presentation. He told us where he thought we were at, gave some financial projections, and explained what he thought we should do next. He sketched out an action plan. And he had some very interesting information.

Sharon Osbourne had been in touch, asking Priest to be special guests on the upcoming American Ozzfest tour…but only if I were back in the band. It was an extremely timely offer. And it would be a very good way to pick up where we had left off.

When I left the meeting, I was back in Judas Priest…but I really *felt* I was back in the band a week later. We were to brush any cobwebs away and rehearse for the Ozzfest tour in the Old Smithy, a studio in Worcester owned by record producer Muff Winwood.

I turned up and saw all the familiar Priest guitars, and gear, and road crew. We plugged in, and the first song we played together in more than a decade was "Living After Midnight." *Whoa!* We all gelled and knitted together, as we always had, and it sounded amazing.

At last! What the fuck had taken us so long?

Ozzfest kicked off in Connecticut in July 2004 and was the heaviest lineup in the festival's history. As well as Black Sabbath and us, there were Slayer, Slipknot, Lamb of God, and Dimmu Borgir. Nearly all of those bands came up backstage and said they were big Priest fans, which was a nice boost.

The Queen and I

The tour was a perfect way for us to return. It let us reconnect with America and, after years of smaller crowds, it was great to be playing to 30,000 people a night and back in the spotlight.

One difference for me was that I started using a teleprompter. I had been sober, by now, for eighteen years, but that didn't mean the earlier years of booze and drugs hadn't wreaked some damage on my gray matter. I had begun forgetting some lyrics.

In Halford, I'd gotten Thomas to print out and laminate all the words to the songs, and I kept them in a ring binder on the drum riser. It wasn't an ideal system, but it was better than nothing.

Then I went to see Korn—a great band—and noticed Jonathan Davis squinting at a screen once or twice during the show. Afterward, talking to him backstage, I asked, "Were you using a teleprompter?"

"Yeah!" he said. "It's great! I've got so many Korn songs to remember. If I forget a few words, it's a safety net!" So, I embraced it as well. If it was good enough for Korn, it was good enough for me.

Six or seven weeks into the tour, we were staying in Philadelphia—a city I will *always* find poignant to return to—before an amphitheater show across the water in Camden, New Jersey. I was in my hotel room when my phone rang. "Hello?"

"Robbie? Hello, darling, this is Sharon Osbourne!"

Uh-oh! Mrs. O had never called me before! It must be serious.

Sharon said that Ozzy was having a hard time of it and his voice was getting a bit shot. Would I possibly be able to help him out at one of the Sabbath shows?

I was getting a distinct sense of déjà vu. My mind was racing, yet one thought dominated it: *You do not say "no" to Sharon Osbourne.*

"How many songs do you want me to do?" I asked her.

"The whole set."

Oh! "And when do you want me to do it?"

"Tonight."

Tonight?! I looked at my watch. It was now six o'clock, two hours before Priest's set. Sabbath were going on at nine. It gave me no time to prepare! There was no way I could do it…

You do not say "no" to Sharon Osbourne.

"Yeah, all right, then," I mumbled.

"Oh, Robbie, I love you!" Sharon dispatched a series of air kisses down the phone, promised to courier a VHS of one of the Sabbath shows from the tour to my hotel *straightaway,* and hung up. And I began getting incredibly nervous.

The courier showed up with the tape an hour later and I ran down to our tour bus, stuck it in the player in the back lounge, and sang along with Ozzy all the way to the venue. Our Priest set went fine…then Sharon collared me as we came offstage.

"Bill Ward is going to read a little note before Sabbath go on," she said, sweetly.

A note? What would it say?

Twenty minutes later, I was standing in the wings waiting to go back on. My heart was pounding. Tony Iommi stood next to me. We were in exactly the same situation as in Costa Mesa, twelve years earlier.

"All right, Rob?" he inquired, casually, as if he'd just bumped into me in the Bull Ring.

"All right, Tone."

Bill Ward made his way to the mic. The chant of "Biiiiiiiill!" from the crowd died down as soon as Sabbath's drummer began talking. "I've got a note from Ozzy," he said, and began to read:

"Hi, everybody, this is Ozzy! I'm really sorry I can't do the show tonight…"

Boooo! The crescendo of noise from the crowd drowned Bill out. He paused until they had quieted down, then continued:

"…but my good friend, Rob Halford, is going to help me out and sing tonight. So, big thanks to Rob, and see you next time!"

The Queen and I

There was a mix of boos and cheers. I looked at Tony and rolled my eyes. *God knows how this one is going to go!*

Some fans were *very* disappointed…including one guy right at the front. When we opened the set with "War Pigs," he did nothing but spit on me through the whole song. I was using Ozzy's teleprompter and, at the end of the song, a roadie had to run on to wipe the gob off it. *Nice!*

The gig got better from there (well, it could hardly have got any worse!). The crowd passed through the "Oh fuck, no Ozzy!" stage, and the "Bloody hell, not him from Judas Priest again!" stage, and then got behind me. I enjoyed it, and it went well, except that…I fucked up "Paranoid." I came in three bars too early. *Bloody hell!* If there's *one* Sabbath song you'd don't want to fuck up, it's "Paranoid"! But, apart from that, the set was virtually flawless.

Afterward, as I sat eating dinner with Thomas at the hotel, I felt like it had all been a dream.

After Ozzfest, it was time to go straight into a new album. Glenn and Ken had a well-meaning idea. "We know you spend most of your time in San Diego nowadays," they said. "So, we'll come to you for the first writing sessions."

This was…unorthodox. For years, Priest had kicked off the process at Glenn's house in Spain. This frequently riled Ken, for reasons I'd never quite understood. Glenn's place had a nice studio setup, and sunshine—*what was not to like?*

It was all to do with the friction between Ken and Glenn. When I had started talking to Bill about a Priest reunion, I'd allowed myself to hope things might be different between our guitar heroes. Well, no. They were exactly the same—or, if anything, worse.

I appreciated their offer to begin work in California, but it threw me into a tailspin. Thomas and I had a nice apartment, but we didn't have much in the way of recording gear. But I ran around and managed to throw together a mini-studio.

We were making our first album together in fourteen years, yet the great thing was that we still felt we had things to say and a lot more to achieve. *The fire was still there.* We fell straight back into a creative groove and our writing sessions were productive from the off.

We recorded the album back at the Old Smithy Recording Studios in Worcester—and I knew exactly who I wanted to produce the record. Luckily, the band were very amenable to my suggestion.

Priest had clearly paid attention to *Resurrection*, as I had hoped, and seen what a good job Roy Z had done on it. Working with Priest would be a dream come true for Roy, who knew every one of our albums inside out.

Now we were back, I wanted to write a song that traced the history of Judas Priest, and answered those US religious nutters who *still* believed that we were devil-worshipping heathens. I told the story of the band's origins in "Deal with the Devil":

> Forged in the Black Country, under blood-red skies
> We all had our dream to realize;
> Driving in that Transit, down to Holy Joe's

We called the album *Angel of Retribution* because I liked the idea of an angel of metal music, which we used on the sleeve, and the word "retribution," which to me said, "Priest are back—and we're on the attack!" Ken didn't like the title, but I held firm.

The *Retribution* tour was to last the whole of the next year and we transferred to Bray Studios near London to rehearse for it. I was very impressed to stumble across the *Teletubbies* costumes while we were there. I've always been partial to a bit of Tinky Winky.

Then I got some awful news. Pantera had recently split and Dimebag Darrell had formed a new band, Damageplan. They were a little bit of a metal supergroup: their singer, Patrick Lachman, had played guitar for me in Halford.

Damageplan were just starting a club show in Columbus, Ohio, when a deranged fan ran onstage with a pistol and shot Dimebag dead. He also killed the band's security man, a club employee, and a fan, before a cop took him out. ·

I had kept in touch with Dimebag and Patrick and, when I heard the news, I just felt sick. *To have a friend, and such a talented friend, murdered by a fucking psychopath!* I tried to imagine how they must have felt onstage when it happened. I couldn't do it. *What a tragedy. What a world.*

I don't think I was the only artist who got a little paranoid after the Damageplan killings. At the first couple of gigs on the *Retribution* tour, I felt twitchy onstage and almost afraid to stand still. But it passed. You can't live in fear.

The show must go on.

The tour was to last the whole of the next year. If we had had any doubts whether there was still an appetite for Priest, they were soon dispelled. As we kicked off in Scandinavia, *Angel of Retribution* went straight into the Billboard 200 at number thirteen—our highest-ever placing. It was significant, and such a boost for us. *Priest were back!*

I can't think of many things in my life that have been as important to me as Judas Priest's triumphant comeback after I returned to the band. But meeting the Queen comes close.

Ever since Her Majesty gave me a special wave in Walsall Arboretum in 1957, I have always been an arch royalist. I have no idea why, but I am. So, I couldn't believe it when Jayne Andrews phoned me with big news early in 2005.

The Queen was to host a reception in honor of British music and to recognize its contribution to Britain's culture and economy.

And she had requested the pleasure of the company of…one of Judas Priest.

The rest of the band never even stood a chance. *Go to Buckingham Palace? Are you fucking kidding me? Yes, yes, yes!* So, Jayne accepted on my behalf and I started mentally ticking off the days and working on my bowing and curtsying.

On the day of the reception Priest were right up in the extreme Arctic region of Finland, but that wasn't about to stop me. We had a day off on the tour, so Jim Silvia fixed me up a flight from the frozen North Pole to Heathrow.

As my taxi pulled through the gates of Buckingham Palace and into the inner perimeter, I couldn't believe I was there. *Wow!* Inside, I went up a huge, ornate staircase to be greeted at the top: "Welcome, Mr. Halford!" They gave me a name badge, so Her Maj would know who I was.

Once I got into the lavish party room, I knew a couple of people. I said hello to Roger Daltrey and had a bit of chitchat with Brian May. One of the lads from Status Quo was there. But, after that, I found myself sitting on my own.

The royal invitation had been strictly for one person—no plus-ones—and so I was all on my own. I looked around me at a room full of jazz musicians, classical musicians, impresarios, and…Cilla Black?!

Cilla was looking as lost and lonely as I was. *Cilla Black! What a legend!* I was drinking a glass of water, Cilla was sipping champagne, and I thought, *I should leave the woman alone. Give her some peace!*

Then, I had another thought: *Bollocks to that! I've been a Cilla Black fan all of my life! If I don't go and say "hello" now, I'll always regret it!* I made my way over to her.

"I'm sorry to intrude…" I began.

"That's all right, chuck," said Cilla, looking me up and down.

"I just want to say it's a thrill to meet you, and I love your music."

"Oh, thank you!" she said.

"Are you with anyone?" I asked, although she obviously wasn't.

"No," she replied. "I wasn't allowed to bring anyone. I suppose you wanted to bring your wife, or your girlfriend?"

"I don't have a wife or girlfriend, Cilla," I said. "I'm gay…"

Cilla Black was clearly one of life's natural fag hags. The second that I said that, she got up and gripped my arm. For the next two hours, we paraded around the room, arm in arm, and learned all there was to know about each other. We were inseparable!

We were having a whale of a time when, suddenly, the Queen appeared at the far end of the room. She is a tiny figure, hardly more than five feet tall, but she has such presence. How can I put it, exactly? She just…*radiates royalty*.

I'm a bit of a historian and, as I looked at her, being guided around the room by an equerry, the whole royal lineage passed through my mind, from the Tudors to the modern day. Cilla had met the Queen a bunch of times before, but I felt quite overcome.

So, I was standing with Cilla, drinking my water and trying to sneak a closer look at our monarch, when an equerry glided over. "Would you care to meet Her Majesty?" he murmured.

"Oh, that would be great!" I blurted out, before Cilla had a chance to say that she wasn't bothered as she'd already met her. "Thank you so much!"

A minute later, the Queen was standing in front of me. Receptions are one of the few times that she doesn't wear gloves, but she *was* holding a glass. Apparently, it's to stop people trying to shake her hand.

Well, it didn't stop *me*. Instinctively, without thinking, I stuck my hand out to her. Cilla gave me a poke in the ribs, as if to say, "No!"

The Queen regarded me, and gave my hand the slightest brush with the tips of her fingers. I didn't attempt a full-on bow, but I gave a very respectful nod.

"Thank you so much for coming," said the Queen. "Isn't it strange that we have no music playing, when it's a music event?"

"Yeah, that would've been nice!" I said, trying not to sound too yam-yam.

"I should have had a string quartet in the background," mused Her Majesty. "And what do you do?"

Before I could answer, Cilla chimed in: "He's in this band called Judas Priest! He's come all the way from Finland to be here!"

"Oh," said the Queen. "And what kind of music do you play?"

"Heavy metal, Your Majesty," I said.

The Queen gave me a slightly pained look. "Oh, heavy metal," she said. "Why does it have to be so *loud*?"

Whoa! The Queen just said the words "heavy metal"! Possibly for the first time in her life! But...how do I answer THAT question?

"It's so we can bang our heads, Your Majesty!" I told her. Cilla gave me another dig in the ribs.

The Queen smiled, *regally*. "It's been very nice to meet you," she pronounced. As she turned to leave, I instinctively stuck my hand out toward her again. And got yet another jab in the ribs from Cilla.

"You don't shake the Queen's hand!" she scolded me, as our monarch walked slowly away.

"Nobody told me!" I said. "I dunno anything about etiquette!"

"Oh, I can't take you *anywhere*!" sighed Cilla Black.

On my flight back to the Arctic Circle, I replayed the scene, and the encounter, in my head a million times. *Had it really just happened?* It was a day I will never forget. *The day I met the Queen.* And it had been even better than Walsall Arboretum.

The *Retribution* **tour** played to packed amphitheaters, pavilions, and arenas across Europe, Japan, and North America. Just as he had on the Halford tour, Thomas came along too. The band could see that he made me happy and, in no time, they loved him to bits.

The US leg of the tour ended in Phoenix, and Thomas and I had six weeks of downtime there. That included my fifty-fourth (*gulp!*) birthday, and that year I had got it into my head that I wanted my present from Thomas to be a ring.

Like a true metalhead, my fingers have always been festooned with skulls and dragons, so Thomas didn't want to get me yet another one of those. Instead, he bought me…a wedding ring. He put it on my finger in our kitchen, and I have never taken it off since.

The *Retribution* tour then picked up again in Latin America, which was quite an eye-opener. My sole previous experience of that part of the world were the two Rock in Rios. The rest of the band had toured South America with Tim Owens, so they knew better what to expect.

You get to be quite an anthropologist in this job. You observe the differences in people all over the world. They may be united by the same musical passion, but British, German, and Brazilian metalheads react to meeting Judas Priest in totally different ways.

South American fans are amazing. They have no inhibitions. They are powerful, emotional, and in your face from the second they see you. They live their whole lives like that. It couldn't be more different from my own low-key West Midlands stoicism… but I love it.

From there, our successful comeback tour swung back through the US and finished up that winter in Eastern Europe. We played a couple of great gigs in Russia, and then Bill Curbishley flew in to join us in the Estonian capital of Tallinn.

"I've got an idea for you," he proclaimed. "Let's talk. Over lunch."

Bill has always been a great ideas man, and so we were all ears to see what he was going to come up with. Over herrings and rye bread, he outlined an audacious plan.

"I've been thinking about where you might like to go next musically," he began, "and I wondered if it might be time for a concept album."

Ooh! Now THIS was interesting! Bill certainly had form in this area; as the longtime manager of the Who, he had helped to mastermind both their *Tommy* and *Quadrophenia* projects. *Tell us more!*

"I've got two possibilities," Bill continued. "The first is Rasputin…"

This was an interesting idea, but we had heard on the grapevine that Ozzy was already planning something along those lines (although it never came to fruition). So that ruled that out.

"…and the other one is Nostradamus."

Nostradamus! The second the name left Bill's lips, I thought it was a fantastic idea. What a brilliant, multilayered topic that was for a lyricist to wrestle with! I looked around the table and saw a lot of approving nods.

"We're on it!" I told Bill, emphatically.

As soon as the *Retribution* tour was done, I went home and buried myself in research about this legendary sixteenth-century French seer and prophesier. In books and online, I read about his lurid life and his predictions for history, society, and the end of the world.

Over the following weeks, I related his extraordinary life story and prognostications in song lyrics, and we booked the studio to turn it into an album. As with *Angel of Retribution*, we decided to make it at the Old Smithy in Worcester.

There was a good reason for this. The early members of Priest had all reached their midfifties by now. We were mostly in settled relationships, some of us had kids, and we didn't want to be fucking off to Ibiza or Nassau for weeks to drink, shag, and take drugs. That era had gone.

We were as serious about our music as ever, but now we treated making it like a task, a profession. We were disciplined and efficient.

We got up, clocked on every day, and got the job done. Just like they did in G. & R. Thomas Ltd.

We decided to produce *Nostradamus* ourselves. We had a vision for how we wanted the record to sound, and we'd coproduced enough albums by now to be confident in our ability to do it.

In my mind, *Nostradamus* wouldn't be just an album—it was going to be a *heavy metal opera*. On my drive from Walsall to the studio every lunchtime, I was playing *The Phantom of the Opera* and loads of movie soundtracks, such as John Williams's great compositions for *Star Wars, Superman, Raiders of the Lost Ark,* and *E.T.*

I loved Williams's string orchestrations and dramatic synthesizers and I knew that *Nostradamus* needed more than just metal guitars to tell its tale. We drafted in Don Airey, from Ozzy's band and Deep Purple, to play keyboards…and pulled our old *Turbo*-era synth guitars out of storage.

We knew some fans hadn't liked it when we'd dabbled with synths before, but this was a very different project and it needed them. We also saw on online message boards that some fans were rolling their eyes about *Nostradamus: What the bloody hell are they doing NOW?*

But we didn't care. We were on a mission.

Nostradamus took shape well in the studio as we went to town on tracks like "The Four Horsemen," "Pestilence and Plague," and "Death." I absolutely loved making it. It ended up as a double album and I am proud of every fucking word and note.

I'm no fool, and I know *Nostradamus* is the most divisive album in Priest's oeuvre, but I think it contains some of the most accomplished lyrics I have ever written. I also believe it's one of the greatest suites of music in metal history. *So there!* I stand behind it 100 percent.

When it came out, the response was all over the place. Some journalists said it was the greatest thing Priest had ever done.

Others compared us—yet again!—to Spinal Tap. Was this our *Jazz Odyssey*? No—strip away the frills and flamboyance, and *Nostradamus* is a strong, potent metal album.

It may have divided our fans, but the ones who liked it *loved* it, and it charted even higher in America than had *Angel of Retribution*. And I still think—here's a Nostradamus-like prediction for you!—that its day is yet to come.

It took twenty years for the Who's *Tommy* to become a Broadway musical. One day, I'd like Priest to tour *Nostradamus* as a stage show. It could be a classical symphony, or else we could give it to Cirque de Soleil to perform in Vegas. There's so much scope. It's all possible.

We toyed with the idea of doing a full-on theatrical production when we did the *Nostradamus* tour, but we ended up doing a conventional Priest set. In fact, we only put two tracks from the new album in the show. I think we bottled it.

It was the start of a very long stint on the road. We played a load of European festivals, then it was on to the aircraft hangars of America. These dates segued into the *Metal Masters* tour, which also featured Heaven & Hell, Motörhead, and Testament.

We picked up the *Nostradamus* tour in Australia, South Korea, Japan, and Mexico. Then—deep breath!—it was time to hit South America once more.

It didn't disappoint. In Colombia's capital of Bogotá, the city was in virtual lockdown because of a spate of killings linked to gangs and drug wars. The grounds of our very enclosed hotel were patrolled 24/7 by security guys with fully automatic weapons.

We were playing a 12,000-capacity arena. The driver taking us there got completely lost and drove us into a park nearby, where thousands of Priest fans were congregating pre-gig. *Panic!* Jim Silvia was yelling at him, but the guy didn't speak a lick of English.

"What's going on, Jim?" I asked him, rattled.

"I dunno!" our Noo Yawk tour manager barked. "I'm trying to fucking tell him to turn around! We need someone who speaks Colombian!"

The fans saw us, pounced on the van, and began rocking it from side to side and screaming, "Priest! Priest! Priest!" It was really scary. The driver finally realized his mistake and fast-reversed out of the park. We made it to the safety of the venue…

Except it wasn't remotely safe. When we got onstage, the kids were so psyched and the crowd so wild that it was total anarchy. It would only take one thing to tip them over the edge. I kept thinking about Dimebag.

Some undercover US Drug Enforcement Administration guys fighting the drug trade in Colombia had warned Jim Silvia before the show that it might kick off, and Jim had planned accordingly. At the end, when we ran offstage, Jim directed us into… *a tank.*

It was a full-on military armored vehicle, and we all cowered inside on low metal benches as our getaway tank trundled away from the venue with hyperventilating fans hanging on to it and banging on the outside. It took us back to our fortified hotel and its machine gun–wielding guards.

Just another day in the life…

The tour rolled on, and on. Christmas came and went, and the early part of 2009 saw us touring the UK and Europe on an outing we gave the somewhat bizarre heading *Priest Feast*. I'm sure it made sense at the time.

When we got a three-month break at the end of March, the rest of the band headed home for some much-needed rest and recreation. I didn't. In springtime, as the crocuses poked their heads through the soil, I made…a Christmas album.

John Baxter was still managing my solo career, and while I knew that I would never again do anything that took me away from Priest,

I still hankered after the occasional side project. I reformed Halford and we recorded *Halford 3: Winter Songs*.

This album raised a few eyebrows. Hymns and carols are not the most obvious material for a heavy metal maniac to cover. I'm certain *nobody* had ever expected to hear me trill "We Three Kings" or "O Come, All Ye Faithful." But, for me, that was the point.

Ever since I was a kid, I have always loved Christmas. I have such fond memories of special things like carol singers coming to our door on the Beechdale (not to mention selection boxes!). There was also a spiritual angle to me making that record.

Am I a Christian? What I would say is that Christianity fits me like my stage clothes, and gives me unbreakable faith. There's a lot about it that I like. And when bigots allege that Priest are a devil-worshipping band, I often fuck with their heads and say, "Oh, no! I'm a gay heavy metal Christian!"

I've also learned over the years that, particularly in America, there are metalheads who are totally into our music while leading faith-based lives. And I figured if a record like *Winter Songs* could help those people, so much the better.

I wrote a couple of Christmas songs myself and looked for others that had never been covered by rock or metal bands. I told Roy Z, who produced it, that I wanted the album to be nuanced and sensitive, and not just a raucous punky thrash. And I think it worked.

We released the album on a label called Metal God Records that John Baxter and I had set up. Essentially, we were self-releasing it. Its sales were thus fairly unspectacular, but I hadn't done it to make money. I'd done it because I wanted to.

At the same time, I trademarked the phrase "Metal God." I had found myself being called that ever since we'd recorded the "Metal Gods" track on *British Steel*, and I'd grown used to it and become quite proprietorial about the phrase.

I'd never taken it remotely seriously. *Nobody* from the Black Country is ever going to keep a straight face while claiming to be a Metal God! But I didn't want any companies to be able to describe their goods or products as "metal gods" *if they weren't heavy metal.*

Trademarking the term prevented that. So, now it was finally official! I was the only Metal God! Bow down and worship! (*If you want to, that is. I'm not really fussed either way.*)

By summer of 2009, we were back on the road in the US to play *British Steel* in full for its thirtieth anniversary. It had been a game-changing album for Priest so I understood the logic behind celebrating it…but the timing was all wrong. It was a tour too far.

By the time we set out on this two-month American jaunt, we had already been on the road for more than a year. We were all getting physically and mentally frazzled and badly in need of a break. I love touring, but it can wear you down.

My sixtieth birthday was only two years away and Thomas and I had a private running joke between us that it was time I retired. One day, we extended the joke to Scott.

Thomas and I were sitting eating in an airport kiosk when our young drummer wandered over to join us. "Well, this is the last tour for me, Scott!" I said, as he sat down.

Scott's eyes jumped out of his head: *"What?"*

"Yeah! I'm just over it all!" I deadpanned.

Scott went off and anxiously told Ken and Glenn about my comment, and later Glenn collared me and took me to one side for a chat. "Are you seriously thinking of retiring, Rob?"

"Not exactly," I told him. "But I don't know how much longer I can keep this up."

Many a true word spoken in jest! From being a harmless in-joke between Thomas and me, the concept of retirement soon came to dominate the tour. It became a regular topic of conversation as we slogged our way across the vastness of America.

A few of us were struggling. Glenn was not holding up well

on this outing. He looked exhausted and even his usually immaculate guitar performances were suffering slightly. He seemed to be finding playing the gigs more challenging than usual.

Glenn's occasional errors would predictably irritate the crap out of Ken, who started surmising that his mistakes were down to him drinking too much onstage. *If only it were that simple.* Further down the line, we were to learn that Glenn had far more to cope with.

It all came to a head in a heart-to-heart before a show in Florida toward the end of the tour. What was the future of the band? *Did we even have one?*

Our chat was inconclusive, but we knew something had to change. Glenn was frustrated that his playing seemed to be going downhill, although he didn't mention it, and nor did we. Ken was pissed off with Glenn, our management, the tour…*how long have you got?*

We weren't all on the same page. Ian wanted to carry on, as did Scott. I made it clear I'd be up for making future Priest albums, or playing one-off shows every now and then. We weren't saying we were definitely going to retire, but we'd had enough of mega-tours.

Out of the meeting came the idea that we would just do one final huge outing of that kind, in a year or so, and call it *Epitaph*. And if Judas Priest *were* to end then…well, that would be not a bad way to go.

We played a few dates in Japan and then, post-tour, told Bill and Jayne of our plan. They understood, and didn't try to talk us out of it—especially as we were leaving the door open to future records and shorter tours. It was all very polite, rational, and reasonable.

The rest of Priest then scattered to put their feet up and do a whole load of fuck all for the next year. It might have made sense for me to do the same, but for some reason I went into full-on workaholic—or should I say masochistic?—mode and decided to make another new Halford album. I got the band together again, and wrote the songs for *Halford IV: Made of Metal* in double-quick time, and we recorded it in California with Roy Z.

I took some time out from making the record for a couple of very important events. That March, Thomas and I went back to Walsall for my mom and dad's diamond wedding anniversary party in a town center hotel.

Sixty years! And it felt like yesterday that I was at their golden bash. Had it really been ten years since I had met Ken there and begun the reconciliation process that had got me back into Priest? *Where had the fucking time gone?*

Time is a cruel mistress and my parents weren't doing so well. Mom had recently been diagnosed with Parkinson's disease, which she nicknamed Parky after TV chat host Michael Parkinson. "Parky's off again!" she'd quip, as her hand began trembling.

Her medication largely controlled it, but Dad was having a hard time of it. He had had a few falls in the bungalow, and not long after their celebration, got hospitalized after a bad one. When he came out, he went into a nursing home. It was horrible for all of us.

Speaking of mortality…I also went to Ronnie James Dio's funeral. I'd met Ronnie a lot over the years and he was a hero of mine. I knew he was ill, but when I woke up in San Diego to texts saying he had died from cancer, *I blarted like a bab.*

There were hundreds of fans outside the memorial in the Hollywood Hills, and I saw Tony and Geezer from Sabbath and a load of other rock and metal mates there. It was a beautiful day, full of love for Ronnie. I still blast out his music today before I go onstage. He inspires me.*

Halford IV: Made of Metal turned out well and I was pleased with it, but the sales on our own Metal God label were fairly limited— tiny, compared with Priest. We took the album out on tour, firstly

---

* Just a few months ago, Ronnie's widow, Wendy, gave me one of his collection of dragon statues, and a ring that he used to sport onstage. I wear it with pride.

for a few US club shows, then a couple of dates in Japan, and then on the road with Ozzy for six weeks in America and Canada, leading up to Christmas 2010. The shows were great…and I didn't even have to fill in for Ozzy once!

Meanwhile, Jayne announced Priest's farewell (well, maybe…) *Epitaph* tour to kick off in June 2011. This major outing was to take up the best part of a year, and in October, while I was out on the road supporting Ozzy, the rest of the band had a meeting to confirm the details.

Ken didn't turn up, and when Jayne phoned him, he claimed he had forgotten about it. It was out of character but, well, *these things happen*. Ken apologized, and no one thought anything more about it. Jayne set up another date for the end of November. The plan was to meet at Glenn's for her to finalize the details with Ken, Ian, and Glenn before she had to go to the States.

Then, a couple of days before they were due to meet, Kenneth "K. K." Downing emailed us to inform us that he had quit the band.

21

The April Fool that wasn't

Ken's resignation email came totally out of the blue. It was a fucking thunderbolt. None of us had remotely seen this one coming and it completely knocked us sideways. *What?!*

Ken had been moaning and griping about things a lot on the last tour, but we hadn't thought that much of it. *That was what he did*: what he had always done. We had no idea that his dissatisfaction was intense enough to make him quit the band.

There was no way we could postpone the *Epitaph* tour. The venues, the flights, and the hotels had all been booked, and it would have cost us an absolute fortune. Whether it was intentional or not, Mr. K. K. had dropped us deep in the shit.

Glenn, Ian, Scott, and Jayne reached out to Ken to see if they could change his mind, but I never thought it was likely. It seemed pretty made up to me. We had no choice but to launch a frantic, race-against-time search for a replacement guitarist.

Ken had asked Jayne if we could wait until the eve of the tour to announce his departure, so we tried to go along with this as we sought out alternative musicians during early 2011. We were looking for somebody up-and-coming with some touring under their belt.

Somebody recommended Pete Friesen, who had played with Alice Cooper and Bruce Dickinson. Pete sounded great, although he was Canadian and my preference was for a Brit. After Scott, I didn't want to dilute our identity as a British heavy metal band any further.

Jayne got in touch with Pete, who said that he was flattered, but he thought he was too much of a bluesy guitarist to fit into a full-on heavy metal band like us. However, he did suggest that we tried a guy named Richie Faulkner.

Jayne sent Richie an email saying she managed Judas Priest and would like to speak to him. He didn't reply and Jayne sent three or four more before giving up on emailing and phoning him instead. He picked up.

Richie confessed he had been deleting the emails—by this time it was April (just two months before the tour was due to start!)— as he had assumed somebody had been doing a belated April Fool's wind-up! When he realized it wasn't, he was super-keen to meet up.

Richie got a train from London to Worcester and Jayne picked him up at the station and drove him to Glenn's country pile. He gazed around wide-eyed as he shook our hands. "It's a bit *Lord of the Rings* round 'ere, innit?" he commented.

He was right but, as soon as he'd said it, he looked like he wished he hadn't. He was probably a bit nervous. We laughed and agreed, and it broke the ice, but the first thing we noticed was how *Lahndan* his accent was. We might be needing a Cockney–yam-yam translator!

Richie was thirty and came with a good pedigree. He'd been in a few bands, including playing with Lauren Harris, Steve Harris from Iron Maiden's daughter, and had supported Maiden with her. So, he knew his way around a studio, and all about life on the road. A good start!

"Well, do you fancy having a knock?" asked Glenn.

Richie had brought a guitar with him, so he and Glenn vanished to the studio next door and I waited in the house. Glenn reappeared about fifteen minutes later for a chat with me. "What do you think?" he asked.

"He seems a cool guy," I said. "He's not an arse-licker, and he's saying all the right things about metal and about Priest…"

We were still discussing Richie ten minutes later as we wended our way across Glenn's gravel path to the studio. Then we stopped. *Dead*. From the window above, we could hear him jamming, riffing, and noodling like a virtuoso. We grinned at each other.

Bloody hell, listen to that!

Richie was still wailing away when we walked into the studio, but he stopped when he saw us. "No, no, carry on, mate!" we said. He was a fantastic player and we could already imagine how good he'd sound in Priest.

We had our man. Our search was over.

Having kept Ken's departure under wraps for months, Jayne put out a press release in late April to say that he had left and Richie had joined, and we set about teaching our newbie our back catalog. Luckily, he was a very quick learner. He knew most of the songs already and if he didn't, he nailed them instantly, every time. He was a dream.

While I was in the Midlands, I also spent as much time as I could with my parents. It was not an easy time for either of them…or for me.

Sue and Nigel had warned me that Dad was going downhill fast, but when I went to visit him in his care home, I was shocked. He was spending nearly all day in bed and he looked like a skeleton. He was fading to dust before my eyes.

Getting old, and the passage of time, is such a bitch, and it was heartrending to see my strong, hale dad, who had always been there for me throughout my life, dwindling like that. He could hardly breathe—but he still knew me, and who I was.

I leaned in, and spoke to him gently. "This is no good for you,

Dad," I said. "If you want to go, *go*. Don't hang around for us. We love you and we understand." His eyes told me that he understood, too.

Mom was also struggling. Her Parkinson's was worsening and she wasn't visiting Dad in the home. Her sister, Iris, had died in the same place a few years earlier and she found it too upsetting to return. But mostly, she couldn't bear seeing Dad as diminished as he was.

Anybody who has ailing parents but lives far away from them will know the pain and guilt I went through each time I left them. I was so grateful, as were they, to Sue, who saw Dad every day and was virtually a full-time carer for Mom. She was a wonder woman.

Back with Priest, it was just as well that Richie was a guitar wizard, as his first appearance with us was mad. We guested on *American Idol* in LA doing "Living After Midnight" with one of the contestants, James Durbin. So, Richie's debut was playing live in front of 20 million US TV viewers.

No pressure, then!

We kicked off the *Epitaph* tour with a warm-up theater date in the Netherlands, then headlined the Sweden Rock Festival to 50,000 Scandi metalheads. Richie coped with it all as if he'd been doing such things all his life. It was fantastic to watch.

When we got down to the *Epitaph* tour proper, we had an unusual structure to the evenings—and all because of a new artist who had aroused my gay-metal-pop-tart side (that's never too hard to do!).

I was blown away by Lady Gaga as soon as she appeared on the pop scene. She looked fantastic, and I loved her crazy costumes and the fact she wrote her own songs…and, most of all, I adored her voice. For me, it *always* comes down to the voice.

I was smitten, and started reading everything I could about Gaga…and was amazed to learn that she had once been a teenage metalhead, and one of her favorite bands was Priest! Through Jayne, I sent her a message: "If you ever want to come to a show, just say!"

"Thanks, I will!" the message came back.

I also read about Gaga's best friend, Lady Starlight, who had just DJ'd on Gaga's *Monster Ball* tour and who sometimes opened up for rock and metal bands or DJ'd at their after-show parties. A light-bulb came on—*Ting!*—over my head: *Why not take her out with Priest?*

So, every night we had one support band—from a selection including Motörhead, Thin Lizzy, Whitesnake, and Saxon—and then Starlight's DJ set. Our fans loved it as she played metal classics, flashed devil's horns, and went crazy behind her decks. She fucking rocked it.

It became clear to Priest early on the *Epitaph* jaunt that…*this would not be our final tour*. Thoughts of retirement went right out of the window. Richie's playing, enthusiasm, and dynamism had given the band a whole new lease on life.

Our new boy was giving me a real run for my money as he zig-zagged and bombed across the stage, and the formerly brooding, fractious atmosphere in the band was replaced by a new positivity. I couldn't escape one, exciting thought:

Fucking hell! Look at the potential we have now!

It wasn't the end for Judas Priest. It was a new beginning.

Richie was riffing like a demon, as was Glenn most of the time… but he had the odd night he wasn't quite on it. Glenn is still better when he's slightly off the pace than most guitarists are at their peak. But he's a perfectionist, so those errors bothered him.

They didn't bother us. *We all make mistakes, mate!* And in any case, Richie was such a colossus he could cover any occasional lapse. It was odd, but it was no big deal.

As the tour wound on, I got matey with Lady Starlight. One day, she gave me a brilliant proposition from her pal, Lady Gaga. We were to headline the High Voltage festival in Victoria Park, Hackney, when Gaga would also be in London. Could she do a guest spot with us?

Yes fucking please! Her people spoke to our people, and we arranged that, when I rode my Harley onstage for "Hell Bent for Leather," Lady Gaga would be sitting on the back of the bike! It was exciting, and I had a job keeping my gob shut and not ruining the surprise.

Sadly, a few days before the show, Gaga emailed to say she had to go back to the States to film a video, and wouldn't be able to do it. *Shit!* She sounded as disappointed as I was.

There was a new sunniness in the air in Priest, but conflict had still not been completely removed from my professional life. There was some tension between Bill and Jayne and John Baxter, who continued managing my solo career.

I should probably have knocked it all on the head when I went back to Priest. I had hung on to a faint hope that I might be able to run a successful solo career alongside the band. Now, it obviously wasn't going to be…and I didn't mind. I was fine with that.

But I felt loyalty to John. We went back a long way, so, whenever disputes arose between him and our management, I just tried to keep my head down and smooth things over. I did a lot of compromising, and I hoped things would get better…until I finally had to accept that they never would.

Our record label made a mistake with our accounting. They paid some royalty money that should have gone to Ken and Glenn into my account. It was no big deal. We noticed it, and Jayne sorted it out. End of story.

Or…it should have been. John got wind of what had happened, got the wrong end of the stick, and flew into a rage. While Priest were on tour in Spain, he went on my personal website, robhalford .com, and wrote a load of awful things about Priest.

It was mortifying. We had to put out a band statement apologizing to the fans for it.

The April Fool that wasn't

There has recently been some nonsense and propaganda posted on the Internet including on Rob's website, regarding the band and management. (Rob currently is not controlling his website and absolutely does not agree with the comments.) We refuse to get drawn into any public arguments—it is below us and will be dealt with legally.

And I realized...*I can't do this any longer.*

Priest were in a new era with Richie, and these distracting squabbles were a toxic throwback. I took a deep breath...and asked my lawyer to write to John ending our management agreement.

And, as soon as I did it, I felt an enormous sense of relief. Although it wasn't the end of it. A few weeks later, I got the news that John was suing me for fraud, breach of contract, and "intentional interference with contractual negotiations"...for the sum of around $50 million. It was a very unexpected and deeply unwelcome shock. Even so, we pressed on with the tour, and I tried to put it to the back of my mind. If you *can* put a $50 million lawsuit to the back of your mind.

We journeyed down the long and winding *Epitaph* road, through South America, the US, Canada, and Southeast Asia. Then we returned to Europe...and when we got to Russia, and St. Petersburg, the mayor of that beautiful city gave me a pre-gig warning.

The mayor had heard that I was gay, and announced that I would not be allowed to make any reference to homosexuality (which was still viewed as a "mental illness" in Russia as late as 1999) when I was onstage. If I did, he said, I would be arrested.

I was aghast, and wondered at first if I should make a stand. *Should I go on and wrap myself in the rainbow flag? Wear a discreet gay-rights badge? Dig out my old Tom of Finland T-shirt, the one that I had been wearing when I met Andy Warhol?*

I did none of those things. First, because it would have impacted on the band, and it was nothing to do with them. Secondly, because it *just isn't me.* Like I said, I've never been an activist—I've always left that side of things to people who are better qualified than me. So far, anyway.

But mainly, I realized that *I didn't have to do anything.* Just being there, out, defiant, and proud and fronting an arena-filling heavy metal band in Russia was message enough: *Here I am. This is me. Deal with it!*

As I told a magazine at the time, I didn't need to go on waving a rainbow banner. I *am* the rainbow flag of metal. So, we simply played our normal Priest set in St. Petersburg. And it was a great gig.

From Russia, we wended our way through Scandinavia, Germany—which went wild for us, as it has done since 1975!— and Austria. And we had got as far as the Czech Republic, on May 8, 2012, when my dad finally passed away.

We were due to go onstage in Pardubice when Sue called me from his care home. She was sitting by Dad's bed with his sister, my Aunty Pat. "They say he's going to pop off at any minute, Rob," she said. "Do you want to say goodbye to him?"

"Yes."

Sue put the phone to Dad's ear. I told him the same thing I'd said when I'd last seen him in Walsall: "Dad, don't hang around. You've had a wonderful life. Just go, now. We'll see you again."

Dad was too weak to say anything back. But I like to think that he understood. Because he always did.

I hung up. We went onstage. When we came off, Thomas told me that Sue had phoned again and Dad had gone. I phoned Sue and we chatted. We were sad, as anybody is when they lose a loved parent, but both of us knew it had been a merciful release. *It was his time.*

Ten days later, I flew home from San Sebastián, Spain, for the funeral. The trip was a right mess—I had to sprint through Barcelona airport and only just made my connecting flight to Manchester, and then had to get a taxi from there to Walsall. I didn't need *that* on the day I was burying Dad.

The service was moving. Mom was in a wheelchair now. She hadn't seen Dad since he went into the care home a year earlier, and now he was coming into the church in a coffin. The pallbearers stopped as they went by her and she put a shaky hand on it for a few seconds.

There he lay. The bloke she had spent more than sixty years of her life with, and raised three kids with. And now he was at rest.

I already knew I didn't like giving wedding speeches...now, I found the same was true for funeral eulogies. I chickened out of speaking at Dad's funeral. Nigel spoke for us three kids instead. Afterward, I regretted that I hadn't done it, and wished I'd been braver.

I went to the wake...then flew straight to Belgium to rejoin the tour. Priest did a cool thing: they paid for a teensy private Honda jet to fly me to Antwerp. We played an arena that very night. Having a gig to focus on took my mind off the grief.

For a while, anyway.

I was back in England three days later to round off the *Epitaph* tour at Hammersmith Apollo (although, to be honest, it will always be the Odeon to me!). The stage door is down the side of the venue, and fans always congregate there before shows.

We arrived a bit late, so I had my head down as Jim Silvia led us through the throng, as I knew I didn't have time to stop and chat. For once, I ignored the hands reaching out to me, the selfie requests... and the voice I could hear saying, "Hey! Hey, Rob!"

We got inside, Jim closed the door behind us, and Thomas grinned at me. "You do know you just blew off Jimmy Page, right?" he asked.

"*What?!*"

"Jimmy Page! He's right by the door and he said 'hi'!"

"Silvia! Open that bloody door again!"

Jimmy was still standing outside and I beckoned him in. I started to gabble an apology to one of my all-time heroes. I think I went a bit yam-yam.

"Jimmy, I'm so bloody sorry, mate! I didn't see you! First of all, I meet you in a helicopter and I can't talk to you, and then *this* happens! And I'm the biggest Zep fan ever! Bloody hell!"

Jimmy gave me a broad grin, and said, "Don't worry about it!"

A thought struck me: "What were you *doing* out there, anyway?"

"Ah, just talking to the fans!" He smiled. What a lovely, grounded bloke.

As we toured the globe, my thoughts often turned to Walsall. My mom was in no state to live alone in the bungalow, and nor did she want to. Sue came to the rescue and moved her into an assisted-living flat...and she loved it. We knew she was in good hands there.

Back in the US, John Baxter's legal action against me was grinding on and my lawyer, David Steinberg, recommended John and I try to reach an agreement to avoid having to go to court. But it was not to be. We tried, but an agreement was beyond us.

So, John and I went before a litigation judge and reached a settlement. I'm not legally at liberty to go into the details here, and nor would I want to, but I was happy with it, and it brought an end to a turbulent chapter in my life.

I was extremely glad to see the back of it. Now, it was time to move on.

Now that the *Epitaph* tour with Richie had revitalized Priest, we knew there was no way we wouldn't be doing another album. We agreed to begin producing the record that would become *Redeemer of Souls* in mid-2013 in Glenn's studio, with Glenn producing.

Richie took the place of Ken in the songwriting triumvirate. After the *Epitaph* tour, he was firmly embedded in the band, and he brought a lot of new ideas and energy to the material. It worked from the off.

For the title track—and the album sleeve image—I envisaged an avenging figure, along the lines of Mel Gibson in *Mad Max*, redeeming souls for heavy metal:

> On the skyline, the stranger draws near,
> Feel the heat, and he's shaking with fear

On the production, Glenn did a brilliant job with Mike Exeter, a metal producer and engineer who had done a lot of work with Tony Iommi and Sabbath. But, on the other side of the studio glass, Glenn's puzzling problems continued.

He was still the powerhouse guitarist and fount of titanic riffs he had been ever since he joined Priest from the Flying Hat Band. But he had to do a few retakes and felt that something just wasn't right. He decided to get looked at.

Jayne Andrews took him down to London to be examined in Harley Street. And a few days later, just as we were wrapping up work on *Redeemer of Souls*, a somber Glenn had grim news to share with us.

"It's like this, lads," he said. "I've got Parkinson's disease."

22

The fire and power of heavy metal

Glenn's news hit us like a punch in the gut. *Parkinson's!* I was all too well acquainted with this pernicious disease through watching Mom's battles with "Parky." As I immediately pictured the way her hand and arm sometimes violently shook, I had one terrible thought: *Poor Glenn! There is no way he is going to be able to carry on playing guitar if he has got that!*

The specialist had told Glenn that he had probably been living with the condition for as long as five years. He'd been carrying it ever since *Nostradamus*. At once, everything fell into place. *That* was why he had struggled at times, on tour. It made everything he had achieved in that period seem heroic, almost miraculous.

Glenn was clearly knocked back by the news, as anybody would be, but he was taking it with a kind of phlegmatic resolve. *It was what it was.* At least now he understood the symptoms he had been having, and could begin taking the medication to fight them.

Glenn understood that there was no way he could know the state he would be in three years, or five years, down the line, but for now, he felt strong enough to carry on in Priest. He was just going to *get on with it*, and keep going until he couldn't keep going anymore.

The way Glenn Tipton took the news of his illness was totally heavy metal. I wouldn't have expected anything less.

Once we had finished work on the album, I flew back with

332

Thomas to spend the summer in Phoenix and San Diego before our tour kicked off that autumn. And while I was in California, I finally got to meet my new favorite gay-metal-pop-tart crush.

Lady Starlight phoned me up to tell me that Lady Gaga was bringing her *artRAVE: the ARTPOP ball* tour to the Viejas Arena in San Diego. "You should come and see it with me!" she said. "But I won't tell Gaga that you're coming, because she'll lose her mind!"

I somehow found it unlikely that Gaga would go bonkers over *my* presence at the gig, but I was totally up for seeing her show, so I went down and met Starlight after her DJ support set. She kept me out of Gaga's way and took me into the photo pit for the show.

We stood next to one of Gaga's long stage ramps, and a few minutes into her set, she came dancing along it with her backing dancers. She glanced down, saw Starlight, saw me standing next to her...and fell to her knees.

Huh? I saw her dancers exchange puzzled glances: *What the hell is she doing?* And right above me, and in front of 12,000 screaming pop fans, Lady Gaga was bowing down to me, and doing that *Wayne's-World*-meeting-Aerosmith "we are not worthy" thing.

Blimey! You wouldn't call THAT keeping a "Poker Face"!

Gaga was mouthing to me: "Thank you so much for coming!" After the show, when Starlight introduced me to her backstage, Gaga could not have been more generous in her praise for Priest. She said she truly hoped she and I could do something together in the future.

We haven't done so far. But I really hope we do.

Redeemer of Souls came out that July. The reviewers largely liked it, although a few of them had to qualify their approval by saying they were relieved it was more straightforward, and less of a concept album, than *Nostradamus*. But, well, that's wrist merchants for you!

We've always valued the opinions of the people who put their hands in their pockets to buy the records the most, and that verdict was a definite thumbs-up. It went into the Top 20 in Britain, and went into the Billboard 200 at number six—our highest US chart placing ever.

It was a major delight, and a relief, because obviously we were very aware that *Redeemer of Souls* was appearing after the *Epitaph* tour had given the world the impression that Priest were as good as over as a band. It could easily have tanked. It was great that it didn't.

When Priest got together to rehearse for the *Redeemer of Souls* tour, it was good to see Glenn in fighting form. His medication was doing its job and, apart from the odd hand tremor, there was little sign of the Parkinson's. He was as up for it and raring to go as the rest of us.

It was to be a long outing, covering around fourteen months, and the guys were a little uncertain when I told them who I wanted to take out as our support act: "Are you *sure* about this, Rob?" But I was.

I'd followed the career of Steel Panther since they started out on the Sunset Strip fifteen years earlier. They were essentially a spoof of hair metal acts like Mötley Crüe and Poison, and it worked like a dream because they had fantastic tunes and they absolutely *rocked*.

As I've always said, Judas Priest take our music seriously but not ourselves, and I howled at Steel Panther and their songs like "Asian Hooker" and "Fat Girl (Thar She Blows)." Their bassist, Lexxi Foxx, had a full-length mirror onstage to preen himself in front of. How he has escaped legal action from Nikki Sixx is beyond me!*

I also had a personal link to Panther, as my old guitarist from Fight, Russ Parrish, had reinvented himself as their flaxen-haired, spandex-clad guitarist, Satchel! Russ had always been a smart, quick-witted lad who loved a joke, so that made absolute sense.

Some rock fans hate anything that pokes fun at the genre—like those metalheads who Glenn and I had seen storming out of *This Is Spinal Tap*—so there was a little initial antipathy toward them. But Panther are so full-on and talented that they won over every crowd.

* Well, actually, it isn't: Nikki has a good sense of humor, too.

The tour coincided with the thirtieth anniversary of *Defenders of the Faith*, a hugely important album for Priest, and we brought a couple of its songs, which we'd hardly played live in years, out of cold storage. It was great to get to grips with "Love Bites" and "Jawbreaker" again.

We were a tight unit as we rolled around our usual ports of call: the US, Canada, Australia, Japan. We did a load of dates in South America, including the Monsters of Rock festival, with Ozzy and Motörhead.

After the last date of the tour, in Santiago in Chile, I was mooching around the airport late at night, waiting for our flight to LA, when I saw Lemmy sitting on his own. Normally, if Lemmy was on his own, he didn't like to be bothered, but I went over and joined him.

"All right, Lem?"

"All right, Rob."

We had a bit of a chat but Lemmy seemed quiet and subdued by his usual lively standards. For some reason, I took his hand, and we sat like that in silence for a few minutes. Then, I said, "Hey, Lem, let's do a selfie!"

He gave me the Lemmy Stare, and I braced myself to be told, "Fuck off, Rob!" But instead, he smiled and said, "Oh, go on, then." I took a snap of us together. It was the last time I was to see him. Before the end of the year, Lemmy was dead.

I spoke at his funeral in Hollywood. "Whenever I was in the presence of Lord Lemmy, I always felt a bit overwhelmed," I said. "Admiration, mainly. Here is a man that lived the rock 'n' roll life on his own terms. A true rock 'n' roll maverick!"

And you can say *that* again.

At the end of 2015, Priest were back in England for dates including a nostalgic return to Wolverhampton Civic Hall. It gave me the chance to have a couple of days at the coach house and catch up with Mom.

She was doing OK. That bastard Parky was kicking her arse as hard as he could, but she had grown used to life in a wheelchair and was making the best of things. *Again: getting on with it.* She'd been in her assisted-living flat for five years, had made friends, and liked it there.

Sadly, it wasn't to last. The Parkinson's reduced her ability to swallow and the next spring she spent a short spell in the hospital. They assessed her as needing full-time care, so when she came out, she had to go into a care home.

Mom hated it there and her decline was quick. Within six weeks she was back in the hospital, then got pneumonia, which she was too weak to fight. By then, she just wanted to go and be reunited with Dad, and she died on July 29, 2016, at the grand old age of eighty-nine.

Mom's funeral was in the same church as Dad's, and I'm glad to say I had learned my lesson from how empty I'd felt after chickening out of speaking at Dad's service. This time around, I managed to locate my inner resolve and said a few words to bid farewell to Mom.

I said simple things, and I meant them: that she had always been a kind, loving, and gentle mom (well, except at the wrestling!) and had supported us kids in everything we wanted to do. And I recalled her mantra that I'd heard so many times as a kid:

"Are you happy, Rob? Because if you're happy, *I'm* happy."

Saying it again, it sounded as beautiful as it always had sixty years earlier.

Since Priest had gotten back together, we'd made three killer albums. I was very proud of *Angel of Retribution*, *Nostradamus*, and *Redeemer of Souls* in different ways. But I didn't think that any of them had captured the *essence* of Priest in the way that *Painkiller* had the first time around.

When we came to make our next record, in 2017, that was exactly what we decided to do. We wanted to channel the classic elements of Priest from albums like *British Steel* and *Screaming for Vengeance*, and as far back as *Sad Wings of Destiny*, but to do so with a modern twist.

To do that, we knew we needed a producer who knew the Judas Priest sound inside out…so we went back to Tom Allom.

Tom had remained part of the Priest family, and had worked on various live and compilation albums for us over the years. He was now in semi-retirement, but couldn't have been keener to answer our call to get the old gang back together.

We knew Tom was crucial to the project but, at the same time, we didn't want to make a retro or old-fashioned album. We wanted a modern, contemporary interpretation of Priest…which brought us into contact with Andy Sneap.

Or, rather, Andy brought himself into contact with us. He was a thirty-eight-year-old metal guitarist, engineer, and producer who had previously worked with Exodus, Obituary, Testament, Trivium, Megadeth, and Dimmu Borgir, and he sought us out.

Andy wrote to Glenn saying he would love to produce Priest if there was ever any opportunity. His timing was very good. When we met up with him, we liked him, and what he was saying, and decided to take a chance on him by pairing him up with Tom.

There was no guarantee they would hit it off or work well together, but we all got on like a house on fire from day one. There was an immediate camaraderie that made us feel like a strong, unstoppable team—a *metal* team.

We all convened at Glenn's studio and got down to work. *Hard work.* And, far from being a respecter of our august reputations, our new boy, Andy, soon earned himself a well-deserved nickname— Andy "Do It Again!" Sneap.

I've always been assiduous about recording my vocals, and strained to give them my very best shot every time. After all, once they're down on vinyl (oops, showing my age!), they are captured for posterity to be heard by millions of people across the globe.

So, I've never been a slacker in the studio, but Andy took musical perfectionism to a whole new level. I'd turn in a vocal performance that I thought was spot-on, and our no-nonsense young Derbyshire producer would rapidly disabuse me of that notion.

"Can you do it again, Rob?" he'd ask me when I'd finished.

"What? I thought I just nailed it!"

"No. Do it again!"

I could have gotten testy and pulled rank—*"Hang on! I'm the fucking Metal God!"*—but the truth was that I appreciated being pushed like that. I wanted direction, and discipline, and Andy coaxed me to turn in the best performance I could...*then that little bit more.*

"Can you do it again, Rob?"

"How many times have I got to bloody do this?!"

"Until you get it *right.*"

It was exactly what I needed. Like anybody, my voice has changed over the years, and with age, but I took inspiration from the fact that some of Pavarotti's best vocal performances came when he was in his midsixties. And if he could do it, so could I!

I wanted my lyrics to capture the essence, the *soul* of Judas Priest as definitively as the music, and I strove hard to communicate the raw, fundamental fire and power of heavy metal. So that was what we called the album: *Firepower.* The title track said it all:

> With weapons drawn, we claim the future
> Invincible through every storm,
> Bring in the foe to be defeated
> To pulverize from dusk till dawn

I wrote "No Surrender" about Glenn, the bravest bloke I know, willing to face down a debilitating neurological disorder to play the music that he loves, and to push himself to the very limits of his capabilities for the cause of heavy metal:

> Living my life, ain't no pretender
> Ready to fight, with no surrender

When I presented the band with those lyrics in the studio, I didn't say to Glenn that the song was about him...but I didn't need to. He just *knew*.

Glenn's courage making *Firepower* was limitless, and he was as strong creatively as ever. We succeeded in our audacious aim of making the definitive album for the later incarnation of Judas Priest. I think it's up there with any album in our canon—and maybe even above all of them.

Even so, when we reconvened at the Old Smithy to rehearse for the album tour early in 2018, it was clear Glenn was struggling. Despite the medication, his Parkinson's was really taking hold, and some days playing even basic riffs and chords was proving taxing for him.

It was heartbreaking to watch one of the greatest metal guitarists in history, who had always played with such ease and fluency, laboring so badly. He tried using lighter strings, and anything else he could think of, but his body was thwarting him.

One day was particularly difficult. He'd managed to get to the end of some songs, but there had been others he just couldn't do. Then I noticed him sitting in the control room on his own. I put my head in to see if he was OK.

"All right, Glenn?"

He shook his head. "I need to speak to you about something."

"What?"

"I can't do it."

"You can't do what?"

"I can't do this tour," confessed Glenn. "It's too much."

As soon as Glenn said it, it was a massive weight off my mind—

and, I knew for sure, off his. I walked over to him. "Give me a hug," I said.

He tried to stand up. He couldn't. So, I bent down and hugged him.

"I'm so happy for you," I said.

"What do you mean?"

"Because only *you* could make this decision," I told him, and I meant it. There was no way that the rest of the band could have told Glenn he wasn't up to the tour. He had to reach the conclusion himself.

"So, what do you want to do?" I asked him.

"If you and the rest of the guys are happy with it," he said, "I'm going to see if Andy Sneap will do my parts."

"Brilliant!" I replied. Andy was a very accomplished metal guitarist who had been in a few bands along the way and, of course, he knew the *Firepower* songs inside out. We were not in an ideal situation…but he was clearly the ideal solution.

I went in search of Andy, said, "Glenn wants a word with you," and left the two of them to it. Andy was thrilled and excited by the idea—*he'd dreamed of producing Priest; now he was going to join the band!*—but, most of all, he just wanted to help Glenn out.

As we all did.

We were incredibly proud of *Firepower*, and when it was released, in March 2018, it was clear our fans shared our high opinion of it. It went to number five in both the UK and America—our highest chart position ever in both countries.

Those two markets are very important, but the metal family—and the Priest family—covers the globe, and they loved *Firepower* everywhere. To our delight, it hit number one in Sweden; number two in Germany, Finland, and Austria; and reached the Top 5 in Canada, Norway, and Switzerland.

It was *such* a fillip for us. It justified our faith in the album, but also it felt amazing, so far into our career, to still be setting new records and reaching new landmarks. We were still climbing, higher and higher. And long may it continue.

Taking on Glenn's guitar role was a big step-up for Andy, but he took it in his stride, just as Richie had. When we kicked off the *Firepower* tour in Pennsylvania, he showed no sign of nerves and slotted into the band so well, you'd have thought he had been there for years.

It was a different Priest lineup from the one our fans had grown to love over the years, but it rocked just as hard and true. Richie and Andy fired out such pulverizing metal riffs that we sounded as strong as we ever had, and we got incredible receptions every night.

Glenn came out on the road, and joined us onstage as and when he felt up to it. Every night that he walked out to strap on a guitar and do "Breaking the Law" or "Living After Midnight," the crowd would lose their minds. Their roar would take the roof off.

They'd have cheered even harder if they knew exactly what Glenn was going through to be there. I would always give him a hug when he came onstage…and I would feel his entire body vibrating with the Parkinson's. *He is a man of steel.*

We did a sweep of European festivals in the summer, and when we got back to the States in August, Deep Purple joined us for a month. It was fantastic. They were a band I had always idolized, but now, as well as heroes, they felt like kindred spirits.

Purple had been through the ringer in so many of the same ways as us, from addiction issues and band fallouts to lineup changes, yet, just like us, the *integrity* of the band and the music remained intact. We had been living the same lifestyle, in studios and on the road, forever.

Ian Gillan sounded as colossal as always. I stood at the side of the stage each night, tingling to see him at close quarters—*Ian fucking Gillan!*—singing "Highway Star." He took my breath away. Just as he always has.

The Purple dates gave us a chance to catch up with Roger Glover. It was brilliant to see him again, more than forty years after he'd produced *Sin After Sin*—and, with a smile on his lips and a twinkle in his eyes, he returned to an old topic like a dog with a bone.

"You still haven't paid me for that album, Rob!" he told me.

"Roger, mate," I said, "I don't know a thing about it. Speak to bloody Arnakata!"

It was a very long tour and we used a host of support acts. Purple had moved on and been replaced by fellow rock veterans Uriah Heep when we reached Illinois in May 2019. It was here that I had a rush of blood to the head—or, rather, the foot.

In some ways, gigs are just the same as they were when we started out…and, in other ways, they have changed. One big difference is some fans now like to spend the entire show holding their phones in the air, trying to capture the experience.

Well, it's up to them. I always prefer it if they get into the music, and the moment, like we do, but they have bought their tickets and they can basically do whatever they want. But that doesn't apply if they bring that intrusive technology into my space.

We played the Rosemont Theatre in Rosemont, just north of Chicago. It's a lovely little venue, but they don't put up barricades to make a photo pit, so the front-row fans are actually leaning right on the edge of the stage, two or three feet behind the monitors.

At our Rosemont show, there was a guy literally propped up on my monitor, with his phone trained square on my face with a bright light on that showed it was recording. It was an irritating distraction, but I tried to ignore it. Mostly, it was easy, as I had my eyes shut.

I sing with my eyes closed a lot. Without sounding too poncy here, I hope, it helps me to go to a different place. Even though I'm onstage in front of people, it's a very private, personal experience for me. Singing is what I do: *what I am.*

The fire and power of heavy metal

Closing my eyes helps me to express myself and give the very best performance I can…but when I opened them in Rosemont, during "Judas Rising," that guy was still there, his phone up in my face, its flashlight twinkling. *Fucking hell!* I saw red.

Without pausing my vocal, I took two steps forward and booted the phone out of the bloke's hand. It wasn't a bad kick, if I say so myself. It arced through the air and vanished into the crowd twenty feet behind him. I watched it go. *Goal!*

Me being me, I instantly had two simultaneous thoughts fighting for space in my head:

1) I'm really glad that I did that!

2) Oh, shit! Why did you do that? That wasn't very nice, you dickhead!

The poor guy looked like a deer in headlights. I kept an eye on him, and saw his phone get passed back to him. He put it straight in his pocket. After the next song, I glanced at him again, and he was holding out a hand for shaking.

"I'm so sorry!" he shouted. He *looked* it, as well. I shook his hand and gave him the devil horns because my red mist had cleared, it was all over and I bore him no ill will. Plus, to be honest, I felt a little bit silly.

In the old days, that would have been that, but—ironically!—a fan had captured a video of me booting the phone on their own phone and, of course, put it on YouTube as soon as they got home. For the next day or two, my indiscretion was quite the internet talking point.

I'd say the feeling was divided almost exactly fifty-fifty between:

1) Yay! Go, Rob! People who film gigs on phones are bastards!

2) Halford, you fucking wanker! How dare you treat your fans like that!

If I am truthful, I agreed with both sides. In the end, I put out a press statement to clarify the band's position. I think it is fair to say that my tongue was wedged very firmly in my cheek.

The facts are we love our fans, and you can film us all you want
and watch our shows on your phone rather than in the flesh.

However, if you physically interfere with the Metal God's performance, you now know what will happen!

Even after forty-five years on the road, we can still explore new frontiers. In December 2018, we took *Firepower* to Indonesia. As a boy, that was an impossibly exotic name on a map, a land that might as well have been on a distant planet: *I'll never gew there!*

Well, *here I was*, still on my lifelong mission to convert the world to heavy metal. I knew the authorities there had unsavory attitudes toward gay people but, well, *so what? I wasn't scared anymore*. My attitude in Jakarta was the same as it had been in St. Petersburg: *I'm here, mate! I'm out and proud. This is me. Deal with it!*

After those Asian dates, it was back to Walsall for Christmas, and after Priest wrapped up the *Firepower* tour in the summer of 2019, the festive season was on my mind again. For no other reason than that I wanted to, I made another Christmas album.

I got a band together and I did a follow-up to *Winter Songs*, ten years earlier. This time, on *Celestial*, I wrapped my metal tonsils around "God Rest Ye Merry Gentlemen," "Away in a Manger," "Deck the Halls," and even "Good King Wenceslas."

I credited it to "Rob Halford with Family and Friends," which was exactly what it was. My brother, Nigel, is a drummer in a local Walsall band, so he played drums. My nephew, Alex—Ian and Sue's lad—was on bass. Sue even jingled a few sleigh bells.

I sang Priest songs rather than Christmas carols in mid-December at my Phoenix neighbor Alice Cooper's annual *Christmas Pudding* charity concert at the local Celebrity Theatre. Alice's original band were there, as were Joe Bonamassa…and Johnny Depp.

Johnny Depp! Johnny plays guitar, along with Joe Perry, in Alice's supergroup, Hollywood Vampires, and I hoped to get to meet him because I think he's a great actor. He was in the dressing room next to mine with a big entourage and loud music pumping out.

We all did a meet and greet before the show, and then I became a fanboy and collared him on the way back to the dressing rooms.

"Johnny, I'm a big admirer of yours!" I began. "I'm Rob from Judas Priest, and…"

"I know who you are, man!" he interrupted. "I've been a Priest fan all of my life!"

Oh! Well, THAT surprised me! "Can I pop into your room and have a chat a little later?" I asked him.

"Any time at all! It would be an honor!"

I went back to my dressing room and then, shortly afterward, headed next door to see Johnny. His entourage had all vanished, and he was sitting on his own, apart from his assistant. "Come in, come in!" he beamed.

Johnny could not have been more friendly and charming, and we talked for an hour or so. And then, out of the blue, he said, "Hey, Rob! Do you remember the Treehouse days?"

What?! From nowhere, my mind raced back to the notorious all-night Fort Lauderdale club where I'd cavorted until dawn, night after night, as we mixed *Screaming for Vengeance*, yowling Priest songs in Yul Vazquez's covers band and drinking myself crazy on champagne from Gigi's shoes.

"Fucking hell, Johnny! How do you know about *that*?" I asked.

"Because I used to come down to watch you."

"To watch *me*?!"

"Yeah! I had heard that you used to go down and jam on Priest songs, so I'd go down in case you turned up." He laughed. "You always did!"

I was lost for words. "But…I don't remember you?" I said.

"You wouldn't. I was just a long-haired skinny punk back then, in a band that was going nowhere. But I remember *you*."

Bloody hell! I was absolutely gobsmacked. You think that life can't do anything to surprise you anymore…and then it pulls a fast one like that. What is it that people say? *You couldn't make it up.*

I ended 2019 on a real high. Priest had a potent and powerful new incarnation, we had a new album and a major anniversary to work on the next year, Thomas and I had never been happier in Phoenix, and life was looking very good. I had a lot to look forward to.

And then 2020 dawned, and the world ended.

Epilogue

Screaming my tits off forever

Honestly, you get to near the end of the seventh decade of your life, you think that you have seen everything that the world can possibly throw at you—and then a global pandemic comes along!

Well, if I have learned anything in my life so far, it's that you never know what is going to be around the next corner…

At the beginning of 2020, Thomas and I went to Walsall for a couple of months. It was a trip I had been looking forward to because, as well as catching up with friends and family, we had a whole load of exciting new Priest projects to begin and plan.

We started work on a new album at Glenn's studio. Having been so pleased with *Firepower*, we decided to keep the production dream team together, with Tom Allom still in place and Andy Sneap now doubling up on guitar alongside telling me to "Do it again!"

Glenn has come to accept that he is probably in semi-retirement as a live performer with Priest, but is still just as involved in writing songs as ever. In these early sessions, we came up with some brilliant new material. The next album will be a killer.

We also began planning our fiftieth anniversary tour—an outing to celebrate a half century of Judas Priest, a band that started out with a guy called Al Atkins singing when I was still a spotty little oik selling flared trousers and kipper ties in Harry Fenton's.

It's a tour about how long Priest have survived, and so I want to celebrate where—and *what*—we came from. I want to go back to our roots and create a live set that looks like an old Walsall heavy metal factory. I want to create Judas Priest Metalworks.

I want to take G. & R. Thomas Ltd. on the road.

Nearly sixty years on, I can still picture those G. & R. Thomas workers, or rather their silhouettes, tipping molten metal out of giant furnace cauldrons to make pig iron. I can still remember gasping for breath as I ran over the cut. Those images, those men, those factories *made* us, and I want to acknowledge their formative influence.

"Can we have molten metal pouring out on the stage?" I asked one of our production guys at the first planning meeting.

"Not *exactly*, Rob," he replied, possibly a little nervously. "Maybe we can try to do something with colored water?"

Well, it's still a work in progress…

I want our golden jubilee tour to reference Priest's West Midlands heritage as strongly as possible. I've had a few brainwaves so far…and I like to think that foremost among them is the enormous inflatable bull.

Birmingham is the heart of the West Midlands and, for centuries, the foremost symbol of the city has been the Bull Ring. Back in medieval days it was used for bull-baiting, then it became a meat and grocery market, before transforming into the magnificent state-of-the-art shopping center that it is today.

So, I want to celebrate the Bull Ring with a giant—and I mean totally *humongous*—inflatable bull that towers over the stage. Our crew will come on before the show, in Judas Priest Metalworks overalls, pushing out a crate. The crowd will think, *Eh? What's this?*

And when the moment comes…*the bull will emerge*. It will inflate in just ten seconds and it will blow everybody's minds. It will be so awe-inspiring that everybody in the arena will snatch their phones out* to film it and run home to put it on YouTube and Facebook afterward.

G. & R. Thomas Ltd., the Bull Ring...what can be truer to our roots, and origins as a band, than that? And I'm sure that a few wrist merchants will sneer at the giant bull, and compare us to Spinal Tap and their Stonehenge, but do you know what? *I don't fuckin' care—* because it's going to be brilliant.

After the anniversary tour, we were hoping to stay out on the road with another great Birmingham institution—Ozzy. Just twenty-eight years after his first farewell tour, Ozzy is doing *No More Tours II* to bid farewell to his live career.

That has had to be postponed once already because, unfortunately, Ozzy is the latest figure in my life to fall victim to that utter bastard, Parkinson's disease. I know he and Glenn have had a few heart-to-hearts about it. Ozzy is getting treatment and he swears he'll beat it to do the tour. I'm sure he will.

Sharon asked us on the tour, and says we can bring our Judas Priest Metalworks and inflatable bull with us. Knowing the wily Mrs. O, she may well have calculated that she'll also have a ready-made standby in the unhappy event of Ozzy having a minor health lapse.

But that couldn't happen *again—could it?!*

Our planning for all three of these events had been coming along nicely when Thomas and I flew back to Phoenix in March. And then the repercussions of something terrible that happened in a food market in Wuhan, China, swept across the globe and the world closed down.

I've never known anything in my life like the coronavirus pandemic. *Nobody ever has.* It's been horrific each day to scroll down the news websites, or watch TV bulletins, and hear about tens of

---

* There will be far too many for me to run around kicking them out of their hands!

thousands of people dying all across the world. You feel shocked…
and helpless.

Bunkered down at home, emerging to see streets deserted apart
from a few panic-stricken people in blue face masks scurrying back
to their own boltholes, has reminded me of the apocalyptic sci-fi
books I used to consume. It feels like living in a terrifying Asimov
novel.

It feels strange, and overwhelming, and mostly I've been consumed with admiration and gratitude for the doctors, nurses,
ambulance drivers, and police out there on the front line, fighting
against this invisible foe. I applaud them. For me, they are humanity
at its very best.

In fact, the COVID-19 pandemic has been a direct, deadly
reminder that there are things in this world that are even *more*
important than heavy metal. *Things that are actual matters of life and
death.*

It's meant that all of Priest's grand plans have been postponed
or are up in the air, of course. The fiftieth anniversary tour has been
postponed to 2021, and the same may well happen to the Ozzy
dates. The new album will happen when it happens. No matter.
They will all be worth waiting for.

And while I've been on lockdown, with nothing to do except
walk around the house and wash my hands twenty times a day, it's
given me a lot of time to think about my life.

I think you'll probably agree that a lot of things have happened
to me, and many of them now have a hazy, dreamlike quality. When
I look back on handcuffing myself to Andy Warhol, or playing Live
Aid, or nattering to the Queen about string quartets and headbanging, I can find myself wondering…

*Did all that really happen? Did I imagine it? Have I been living in a
bizarre, unlikely movie?*

I could not have written *Confess* if I were not sober. I could not have
faced my past, and my demons, in the way I have. I've been sober for

more than thirty-four years, yet I never take my sobriety for granted. It's the same as it has always been—you take one day at a time.

The most important thing for me, every single day of my life, is to get through the day without a drink. I've still never been to an AA meeting but, when I left rehab, over a third of century ago, my sponsor, Ardith, gave me a book of meditations.

That book has been around the world with me. It contains a meditation for each day of the year, so I have lain in bed, last thing at night, and read each one thirty-four times now, and counting. If I don't read my daily meditation, I can't go to sleep. It's that simple.

The main thing that sobriety brought into my life was *honesty*. It put an end to the lies and pretense that went with drink and drugs. And the other event that let me start being totally honest with myself was coming out as gay.

When you live life in the closet, when you *live a lie*, you are so pent-up and repressed every single day of your existence that, when you finally emerge, you have an explosion of openness and candidness. You don't want to hold anything back. *You want to confess.*

I often ask myself why I took so long to come out, and why, even when I finally took that giant step, it was by mistake, in an MTV interview! And yet, writing this book, I've come to realize *it had to happen like that*. It was destined. I wasn't ready to do it any earlier.

Throughout my life, especially in my youth, gay people have had to deal with homophobia and prejudice, in the papers, on TV, and all around us in everyday life. We've had to live with feeling as if we are pariahs to people at school, at work…*even in our own families.*

Well, it has all given us so much strength. We have endured daily horrors and struggles, just trying to be accepted. So, you go through all that, and when you come out the other side, nothing can hurt you anymore. *Sticks and stones…*

If I were twenty-one now, and starting out in a band, I'd come out as gay from day one. The world is a different, and better, place than it was back in the early seventies. Mr. Humphries, bless him, has minced off. Gay men are no longer figures of fun, to be ridiculed… or bashed.

Prejudice and ignorance aren't dead. I still get the occasional message informing me that all faggots should die. Sad bigots still try to bully me on social media. But I'm happy to say they simply don't bother me anymore. They're what the "delete" button is for!

Contentment eluded me for so long. Now I *am* content, and happy, it's not just down to my sobriety, and being out. It's about having spent twenty-five years with a partner that I am incredibly close to and interwoven with. If we're lucky, we all meet "The One," and, for me, Thomas is The One.

We are together every day. We're near to inseparable. Thomas comes out on all the Priest tours with me—in fact, I don't think I could do them without him, nowadays. He is my rock, and totally indispensable.

When we're in Phoenix, I rarely go to bed before three because of my insomnia. So, we sleep in until noon, then drive to our nearest strip mall to grab some lunch. In the afternoon, we might take a dip in our pool. We do very little. We like it that way.

Maybe Priest fans assume that I take my Ferrari out for a spin each morning, meet Lady Gaga to drink champagne, then go parachute jumping. *Dream on!* When Priest are off the road, that's not how Thomas and I live. We're pretty…boring.

On tour, we're surrounded by so many people every day and night. It's nonstop. So, when we're back in Phoenix, we're happy to watch Netflix every evening…and hit the casino once or twice a month for an hour of penny slots. That's all we need.

We're equally low-key in Walsall. Thomas loves coming to Walsall with me: we can walk places, rather than having to drive everywhere as we do in America. We see my family, we hang out together…and, every evening, we do what we call our "night walks."

We stroll a little circuit of the streets around the coach house that I've lived in for the last forty years. Our route takes us past the end of the tiny cul-de-sac where my parents finally let me buy them a bungalow. I'll never forget how happy they were there.

For the longest time, after my parents died, I couldn't walk down that street and look at their old house. It was too poignant. The road felt too full of memories. *Mom and Dad: gone. Our old life: taken away.* I would find myself blinking back tears.

I *can* walk down that cul-de-sac OK, now. But I usually don't.

I am going to be seventy next year, and one thing I have learned is that I want to be in Priest for as long as I possibly can. I made the mistake of walking out of the band once, and I am never going to do it again. They'll need a shepherd's crook to drag me off the side of the stage.

I want to be screaming my tits off forever!

Singing is my mental release, my purpose, my meaning. I only feel truly, fully alive when I am onstage and singing with Judas Priest. The joy that I feel when I do it is extraordinary. Nothing else comes close. I want to be still yowling fucking "Painkiller" when I'm eighty!

Glenn is in his seventies now and he always calls our fans "the kids"—even if a lot of them are now in their fifties and sixties themselves! I think that's a very sweet, and true, way of looking at things. Because, whatever age you may be, when you go to a heavy metal gig, you're a teenager again.

By now, like a lot of veteran bands, Judas Priest are a time machine. We can play songs from the seventies, or eighties, or nineties, and transport you straight back to that era. *Hey, it's 1978 again! Yay! It's 1985!* We're a family, with kids…and families have great memories.

I'm still as in love with heavy metal as I ever was. Every day, I sit on my iPad and I scour metal websites for new artists and music.

There are thriving metal scenes in places you would not *believe*, like South Africa and even Iran! I want Priest to play all of them.

These days, when I go to bed every night, after I have read my book of meditations, I say my prayers. I say the Lord's Prayer, and I say the Serenity Prayer, and then I pray for all the people in my life: for Thomas, for my family, for our fans, for everybody. I believe *emphatically* in the power of prayer.

I don't particularly know who I'm praying *to*, but I know somebody, or something, is listening. There is more to life than our time on this planet. There is definitely life after death. I learned *that* lesson the night I met a Jamaican woman called Pearl in a nightclub in New York City.

I am not scared of death. Not in the slightest. It could come at any minute—I might crack my head on the side of my swimming pool tomorrow. I might fall off my bike onstage again, on our anniversary tour! Life can be taken away in a second, *just like that*.

Let me get this straight: I'm not saying *bring it on!* I love my life far too much to want it to end! But I am ready. Sometimes, I wonder what my funeral should be like. I reckon I'd like a coffin covered in leather and studs, with a big metal guard, and people weeping.

Lots of weeping, and camp grief. I love camp grief!

Where will I be laid to rest? I've thought of trying to get a plot near to Ronnie James Dio, up in the Hollywood Hills…but I think I'd rather be buried in Walsall. It's where I came from, and it's where I should end. And I think I would rather like a statue.

Maybe my statue could stand in the town center, where the public toilets used to be where I went cottaging (*surely* that deserves at least a blue plaque?!). But I think I'd like it to be outside St. Matthew's Church, at the top of the hill that overlooks Walsall.

Oh, and, at night, I would like my statue to have some dry ice and a few lasers, *please*. That doesn't seem too much to ask.

I keep returning to Walsall, where I began, but Walsall has changed for good. Panicking schoolchildren no longer think, *I'm suf-*

focating! That dark, dour Black Country home of heavy industry, the town of G. & R. Thomas Ltd. and pig iron, has gone, never to return.

A few years ago, I did a day trip with Thomas, Sue, and her daughter, Saskia, who was then about ten, to the Black Country Living Museum in Dudley. It's a superb open-air history lesson, a lovingly reconstructed village that preserves the industrial and mining heritage of the area.

We were walking around the cobbled streets, and peering in the old forge and factory windows, and at the barges on the cut, when Saskia came up to me and held something out.

"Uncle Rob," she said. "What's this?"

I peered down. She was holding a lump of coal.

"It's coal, Saskia," I told her.

"Coal? What's coal?"

I couldn't believe my ears. "Saskia, you are winding me up!" I said.

"No, I'm not! What's coal?"

So, I explained to my little niece what coal was, and what we used to do with it, and I told her about the soot-black coalman who used to walk down our Beechdale entry every week with a sack of it. "Wow!" she said. And she wrapped it neatly, in a tissue, to show her friends at school.

Heavy metal will never die… but the landscape that gave birth to it has perished. Still, I keep coming back to Walsall, and you know what? Every time I return, I like nothing more than heading down to my local chippy for fish, chips, mushy peas, and a pickled egg.

Because I do like a nice pickled egg.

I always said that I would never write my memoir: it just seemed too intimidating a task. But I am so glad that I have. I am glad that I have gone through my extraordinary past, that I've looked deep and hard at my life… and that I've got all of this stuff off my chest.

Because, sometimes, it does your soul a power of good to *Confess.*

Metal Blessings

I couldn't have confessed without the love, help, and encouragement of so many, and to name everyone would be biblical. These are the wonderful ones in the front pews:

Thomas, Mom, Dad, Sue, Nigel, Alex, Sass, Jo, Issy, Harper, Ollie, and Liz.

The extended Halford family and blessed loves that have passed.

Jayne, Bill, Glenn, Ian, Scott, Richie, Ken, Tom, and Jim Silvia.

My fans, my fellow musicians in bands, my friends in the music industry and the media, particularly Scott Carter from EPIC NY, Mark Neuman, Chip, and Ian Gittins, "The Confessor."

My close friends: Pagoda, Jeff, Patsy, Jim, Hillbilly, Jaymz, Jarvis, Shane, Rem, Richard, and Kevin.

The entire congregation, who all have a place in the heart of the life of the Metal God.

Song Credits

Page 67 "Run of the Mill" by Tipton/Halford/Downing courtesy of Gull Songs

Page 67 "Dying to Meet You" by Tipton/Halford/Downing courtesy of Gull Songs

Page 89 "Sinner" by Tipton/Halford courtesy of Sony/ATV Music Publishing

Page 89 "Raw Deal" by Tipton/Halford courtesy of Sony/ATV Music Publishing

Page 90 "Here Come the Tears" by Tipton/Halford courtesy of Sony/ATV Music Publishing

Page 99 "Beyond the Realms of Death" by Halford/Binks courtesy of Sony/ATV Music Publishing and Universal Music Publishing

Page 111 "Take on the World" by Tipton/Halford courtesy of Sony/ATV Music Publishing

Page 128 "Breaking the Law" by Tipton/Halford/Downing courtesy of Sony/ATV Music Publishing and Round Hill Songs II (ASCAP), MFN

Page 150 "Screaming for Vengeance" by Tipton/Halford/Downing courtesy of Sony/ATV Music Publishing and Round Hill Songs II (ASCAP), MFN

Page 150 "Jawbreaker" by Tipton/Halford/Downing courtesy of Sony/ATV Music Publishing and Round Hill Songs II (ASCAP), MFN

Page 166 "Eat Me Alive" by Tipton/Halford/Downing courtesy of

Song Credits

Sony/ATV Music Publishing and Round Hill Songs II (ASCAP), MFN

Page 180 "Turbo Lover" by Tipton/Halford/Downing courtesy of Sony/ATV Music Publishing and Round Hill Songs II (ASCAP), MFN

Page 185 "Parental Guidance" by Tipton/Halford/Downing courtesy of Sony/ATV Music Publishing and Round Hill Songs II (ASCAP), MFN

Page 237 "Painkiller" by Tipton/Halford/Downing courtesy of Sony/ATV Music Publishing and Round Hill Songs II (ASCAP), MFN

Page 306 "Deal with the Devil" by Tipton/Halford/Downing/Ramirez courtesy of Sony/ATV Music Publishing and Round Hill Songs II (ASCAP), MFN

Page 331 "Redeemer of Souls" by Tipton/Halford/Faulkner courtesy of Sony/ATV Music Publishing

Page 338 "Firepower" by Tipton/Halford/Faulkner courtesy of Sony/ATV Music Publishing

Page 339 "No Surrender" by Tipton/Halford/Faulkner courtesy of Sony/ATV Music Publishing

Picture Credits

Except where indicated, all photos courtesy of Sue Halford.

Page 9: top: Chris Walter/WireImage/Getty Images; bottom: Richard McCaffrey/Michael Ochs Archive/Getty Images

Page 10: main: Fin Costello/Redferns/Getty Images; inset: Michael Ochs Archive/Getty Images

Page 11: top and inset: Koh Hasebe/Shinko Music/Getty Images; bottom: Fin Costello/Redferns/Getty Images

Page 12: top: Chris Walter/WireImage/Getty Images; bottom left: Dave Hogan/Getty Images; bottom right: Amy Sancetta/AP/Shutterstock

Page 13: top: Annamaria DiSanto/IconicPix; inset: author's personal collection; bottom: Bettmann/Getty Images

Page 14: top left: author's personal collection; top right: Andre Csillag/Shutterstock; middle: © John Eder; bottom: author's personal collection

Page 15: top: Tim Mosenfelder/Getty Images; bottom left and right: author's personal collection

Page 16: © Travis Shinn